In loving memory of Hayley May.

Gone too soon, when your adventures were only beginning.

Part 1

Kicks, Hicks and Dixie Chicks

I

"As Mulligan awoke one morning from uneasy dreams he found himself transformed in his bed into a gigantic insect"

–*Franz Kafka.*

Kind of.

There's possibly nothing more exciting than that feeling of anticipation you have when your next adventure is coming up, and in the case of the seasoned traveller that usually means that the next big trip is all organised and you're just waiting for the date to finally arrive. You then live that adventure, and are the hero in the book of your life with stories unfolding, and characters appearing. If you're travelling not because you are running from something you know – which isn't a bad thing – but rather you are running towards something you don't, then you will eventually return home with the latest volume of your escapades bursting to be told. And tell them you do! Those funny stories are living memories, and as with all memories, they get better as the story is told over and over again. One of the wonderful things about great memories is that, in the case of getting out on the road, they remind you to get up off your arse and do it again. Mainly because there reaches a point where you have told the same tales to the same people just enough times that you see a slight grimace on their face as the old favourite stories come out.

Luckily, one of the other things that happens after you arrive back from a journey is that even as you are still thinking about the exciting shenanigans that you have had, the amazing things you have seen, and the people you have met, you are also planning out your next adventure. You look at maps. your ears prick up when someone mentions a country you haven't been to. You find yourself daydreaming at work.

The fact is, I had realised a long time ago, was that I was living two stories simultaneously. Every time I got off a plane, or train, or coach, at the end of a journey, two things happened. In one story, I worked, played Punk or other music as a DJ in venues, dabbled with youth politics, and went to pubs and clubs way too often. It was the old work hard, play hard effect, and I hardly seemed to sleep. The Shenanigans, like the craic, were mighty, and life was fine. But in the other story, I stepped off that plane, or boat, or bus, and had already embarked on the soil of my next adventure on the road. And as I arrived, the shenanigans from the first story closed down for a while, like a folder on a computer, and my travelling folder opened up where it had left off.

I'd explored this line of thought before, somewhere on the road, and had come to the conclusion it was some leftover survival trait from ancient humanity as it explored the world. Clearly at some point, humans headed off into the unknown, till they eventually spread all over the globe, a remarkable achievement. And not just our Homosapien ancestors either. In 1930, Olof Stapleton wrote one of my favourite sci fi novels, Last and First Men, a kind of future history that explores humanity evolving from us, the first men, through to the eighteenth men way out on Neptune. I love the book, but we are not the first men. We are maybe the third or fourth, or even another number depending on which fossil evidence turns up from time to time. But even the last men before us, Homo Erectus – (and the child in me always giggles at that) – expanded out of Africa, and had sown the seeds of yet other men, other humans that were to greet our ancestors as they left the Rift Valley and expanded their world.

Oddly, none of either, or indeed any other possible species, ever knew that they had left Africa. They had no more idea they were in Africa than a Dolphin knows which sea it is swimming in. They just knew they needed to keep moving, for reasons we can mainly only speculate on, like food, or shelter. Or maybe we were a species born to explore and expand. And those skills that were needed to travel in those ancient days needed to be at the fore when they were on the move, mainly to recognise or predict danger. Memories of a comfortable cave were put in a certain folder to be opened up when the journey could end. If it ended.

I'm guessing that right from the start there were different levels of enthusiasm for this. There were no doubt innovators, some hardy men and women who, on predicting the good life was coming to an end in an established settlement, would push out till they found new pastures for their groups.

"Look," they'd say. "The berries here are not the same as blood, but like the sky. And there are animals to hunt like the others, but a different shape. But the berries and animals taste good. And here, see, we can shelter in those caves. They are higher up, and will give better protection from these large growling predators that are here instead of the long maned roaring predators on the plains we have left behind. This is ideal, we shall collect the others who will be joyous in our find, now that the water runs low back there. This stream is bountiful."

They'd have returned back, maybe even after losing some of their numbers, and after much moaning and whining and pointing out of problems, the others would have followed them, still complaining through their parched throats till they arrived at the new land.

"What's this?" they'd cry. "Berries like the sky? I like the blood berries. And what's that funny shaped prey animal? I bet it tastes like chicken. I don't like chicken. And that's a bit of a climb up to the caves isn't it? Weren't there any lower ones? Those giant growling things can't be that dangerous, can they? I hate climbing. I'm not a monkey. Well, not any more….."

9

But bit by bit, grumble by grumble, our various ancestors spread out and even got it on with other humans they found, once basic speciesism had gotten out of the way and retained that instinct to travel that is still in us. And if you're lucky – and I mean very lucky – you can live in a part of the world where travel is a leisure activity, and not a means to escape war or famine. And there are still those types who head out to the unknown, the way the explorers and adventurers do that so capture our imagination in films and books. Or the hippies and backpackers who find wonderful rarely visited places for a while until they are eventually followed by the general tourist en masse. The ones that come and moan that the food is different, and hope not to mix with the people already there, except maybe the owner of a bar they like, if not the beer in it.

After the last of my adventures, I had arrived back from Africa broke, and a bit of time left before I started back work at the Post Office. The African Expedition had originally been planned to take a lot longer, but the war in Algeria cut two months off that, as we travelled East to West, rather than North to south. I was about to go and ask if I could start back early, as the time I had booked off was unpaid, but then two things happened.

One, I bumped into a good friend from the punk scene, Mr. Rib, who was now working as a long distance lorry driver.

"You could come over to the continent with me," he suggested. "Sure, it's just in the lorry, but better than sitting at home." He was right, it was. He was heading out on one of his trips the next week, so I stayed at my Mothers till it was time to go, in the meantime hearing that a couple of other friends also had some plans which I could join in on.

The other thing was that when my Gran passed on, there was a little bit of money left, including some to my Mother. As mothers do, she promptly lent me some of it when I mentioned that I was not happy being back and wanted to go back out on the road. I don't suppose I ever paid it back, well, till later years, which is a story yet to come.

In my other parallel story, I got off the plane from Egypt, from which during my last shenanigan I had decided to cycle through a desert on a rickety old bicycle in the blistering heat to the Valley of the Kings. Valley of the Eejits, more like it, for doing that. But as usual I survived, as I had in the past survived being shot at in France or being trapped in a toilet by a lion on the Serengeti and embarked, in this parallel, not at the airport but in a car park where Mr. Rib pulled up in his lorry, and told me to jump in.

II

Well, it was good to catch up. It would be fair to say that Mr. Rib was a good old friend, and that we'd been through a fair few scrapes together. We'd met back in the early punk days, when myself and another old travelling companion, Brody, had shared a rather run down flat in one of the rougher districts in town. People had came and went all the time, some we kept in touch with, others we did not. Mr. Ribs had come up from London and stayed for a while. For the life of me I have no idea exactly how he came to be in the flat in the first place, but we'd become good friends, even though a lot of us lost contact over the years as we all moved in different directions.

There was, of course, a very good chance that we met through a girl somehow, or at least that's how he came to be at the flat, possibly after a gig. After any punk gig in the city there would be a gaggle of punks, or skinheads, or hippies, or anyone really, staying overnight, or even longer in some cases. Punk had been a great blender in its day. Though we did not realise at the time, it was the first "youth culture" – and how I hate that expression – where the lads and the girls were completely equal. Before, there had been Teds, or Mods, or Rockers, and the expression referred to the boys on the whole. There were great girl singers and bands within punk that were there not just to be a pretty face, but because they wanted to sing or play. It was also colour blind, though tended to be seen as a white working class movement.

11

Well, it was seen as working class, but there was a bigger middle class art school and fashionista following at first than was given credit, till new trends would come along for them to develop.

There was never a problem with it being mainly white. At the time, the working class black kids were producing fantastic reggae and there were a certain amount of crossover gigs, and appreciation for each other's music that led quite soon to a music called Two-Tone, a Ska/ Punk crossover that caught the world's imagination and is still going strong today. And it was born in Coventry, no less, my hometown, as kids of all colours and sexes blended their working class music together and made rock against racism. It was quite the feat, but oddly it seemed bigger in retrospect. At the time it was just some really fun, crazy days, with a shit hot soundtrack going on in the background.

But however it was, friendships were made that were to last a lifetime, and maybe even involve climbing into an old mates lorry, armed with a sleeping bag and some toiletries, and heading off to the French border. It was no problem being in the cab. Mr. Rib had his document for the lorry, so onto the ferry we drove, and before I'd even finished a pint onboard, we were in Calais.

Well, this was a better start than my last arrival in France, when myself, Brody, and my ex-wife to be had been shot at when we got caught up in a local gang dispute. We skirted around Paris, though for the first time I saw the Eiffel Tower, albeit from quite the distance. We spent our time on the road discussing all sorts of odd stuff.

"Do you believe in omens?" I asked him, going down a French B-road at one point.

"Oh Yes. I certainly do. Why do you ask?"

"Because of him."

I pointed at a guy I saw on the side of the road up ahead. He wasn't wearing a robe as such, but had on a long mac with the hood up and was carrying an old fashioned scythe over his shoulder. Nothing like the sight of a Grim Reaper prepared for the rain to make you think that it was going to be one of those kinds of trips!

Sleeping was a bit tricky. Mr. Rib had the bunk in the back of the cab of course, but I had to spread out over the two seats in the front. As a result, the middle of my back was kind of hanging down between them , giving me a bit of an ache for the first hour after waking up. But hell, I'd slept in worse in the past. And not even always when I was on the road, to be fair.

The Swiss border was coming up on us, and we were talking about kids. My ex-wife had conceived my oldest son in Amsterdam, we'd got married, had the lad, then it all went wrong. The details of which are, as is always the case, complicated, but seem to reside in the other story folder that was shut whilst out on adventures. However, the fact that my ex, Eva, was Swiss, and had returned to and raised our kid there made it a tricky topic to avoid. And why shouldn't it be? I was a little reflective at first, but then we began to make a few jokes about it, till in the end mischief called. We waited till we got over the border, and I bought a postcard at a service station with a nice picture of the Alps on it. I think all Swiss postcards probably have pictures of the alps on them. I simply wrote, "Hi honey, I'm home", and posted it. I think I remembered the address of her parents' house correctly, but I'll never know for sure. If it didn't get to her then at least some lovely Swiss folk in her town would have had a nice picture of the Alps to look at, which would save all that looking out of the window nonsense.

I have to say that the Alps were quite beautiful. Though I'd visited Eva's parents' house once after my son was born, we hadn't really had a chance to see the country. Well, I didn't, she obviously had. So going through the mountains in the lorry was quite a nice experience. There are times on a journey when it is time to shut up and just enjoy the view as it passes by. Trains, especially, are great for this. I learned to love train travel. The slower the train the better. You can have a beer, or a coffee, sit back, then just take it all in. And although in a lorry, with Mr. Rib driving, I got the chance to do that here. And on a couple of occasions, he threw caution to the wind, as he always had, and pulled up at some beautiful lakes and we just went plunging in. It was great, though sitting in damp underpants afterwards had brought it down slightly.

13

His trip involved a number of drops and pick-ups, mainly of fresh produce. So we'd dropped off his original cargo of vegetables in France, then picked up peaches to take to Switzerland. So I did get to help him load and unload, and was happy to find out that a good few of the places we visited had showers and changing facilities for lorry drivers and their mates. After the peach drop over the Swiss border, we headed to Zurich to collect the next product, which I was really hoping, but not really believing would be Cuckoo clocks. This was because when we had been on good terms, me and Eva joked a lot about Swiss Cuckoo Clocks, as her Father apparently collected them. I told her about the one my Granny Strong had, that always fascinated me. It had the little cuckoo in the top, but was also a weather house, with a little man and woman who came out in turns, depending on the weather. Or at least, that was the theory, but it always seemed to be the bloke with the umbrella that was out. I guess when these things were made, it wasn't in a country where it pisses down with rain most of the time.

The odd thing about the Brits is that we never really got the hang of the weather. Celt or Saxon, at some point our ancestors travelled over here, possibly in search of blue berries, but more likely fertile ground. And this ground was fertile because of a hell of a lot of rain. Yet that ancient racial memory of far warmer climates still seems to be stuck with us. So year in, year out, we reach autumn and look back and say,

"Well, that wasn't much of a summer, was it? Bloody pissed down at least once or twice a week."

And it would be true. Possibly the descendants of the first Brits originally enthused about the ability to grow unlimited turnips and cabbages, and solid oak to build houses, but got tired of the others that came after them moaning about the weather all the time, so they eventually pretended to become criminals so that they would be sent to Australia and leave the whinging Poms behind. The plan seemed to work, and no one really questioned the logic of sending the villains over to a lovely hot country when there were plenty of horrific leaky Victorian jails that never really worried about overcrowding. I guess by this time they had given up going back for the others and wrote that concept off as a bad idea.

It wasn't cuckoo clocks, sadly enough, but a large consignment of some kind of pharmaceuticals we were picking up that were going into Germany. I happened to mention to Mr. Rib that I was loving the trip, but would not be adding any of my embroidered patches to my little box, until we reached Italy. During my early shenanigans, I'd picked up the sort of country emblem patches that you can put on Backpacks or sleeves, or whatever you fancy. They were becoming a sort of diary, where I'd look at one and a flood of happy memories would come back about that country. If I passed through a country a second time, I would get one from the city I was in, if it was a major one. I decided on this trip that motorway stops and laybys did not count.

"Actually," Mr. Rib suggested, "I think you can add Germany."

I pointed out that I had been to Germany already. In fact, me and Brody had actually planted a homemade flag on the top of a little hill and declared it ours, a fact that the Germans had completely overlooked ever since.

"That was West Germany then, though. We have now just entered Unified Germany, so technically it's another place."

Now this was, I considered, a very subjective point. When is a country not a country. He was right, of course. In November of 1989 the East Germans had pulled down the infamous Berlin Wall, followed in 1990 by Germany becoming unified once again into the country it was before the end of WW2, where the Allies had divided it up into control zones, and the Russians had put communist government into the East.

In fact, this Europe I was in now had changed since the times I had hitched around just a decade or so ago. The Schengen zone meant the old borders had gone. Back then we had to get visa stamps at every crossing, but now travel was much more freely done, which was great. Germany had unified. When I had travelled through Russia, I had been in the Soviet Union, which now no longer existed. At the same time, Yugoslavia had broken up, returning power to the various republics that had made it up,

15

and only in the last year had Czechoslovakia split into two new countries, The Czech Republic and Slovakia.

This was quite an insight into the way the world works. Empires come, Empires go. But in today's high speed world, this can happen a lot quicker. For context, the Romans occupied Britain for around 400 years. Generation after generation grew up and died never knowing anything but being a part of Rome. There were a few revolutions which came to nothing, but in the end the Romans left as Rome itself was increasingly under siege, and they needed the soldiers back, many of whom would have been born on these shores. But Rome had occupied Britain, not England, and the population had been celts. The English came after they left, in the Anglo-Saxon wave of immigration, and established 7 different countries, the Heptarchy, which lasted another 400 years, though with the kingdoms fluctuating regularly, meaning generations grew up and died in say, the Kingdom of Mercia, without ever knowing any different either. Though maybe a little worried about the state of the roads. The roads would have been a major problem in the long period between the Romans and the Tarmacers. There are those that would argue that the Tarmacers aren't necessarily the greatest of road builders either.

However, eventually the various Kingdoms became All-England. Then that became part of the United Kingdom. No one ever included the Isle of Man though, which to this day has its own parliament, the oldest in Europe. I guess that even in the Dark Ages, the Gentry understood the need for a good tax haven.

Try talking about the history of the British Isles to a random group of people in a pub today, and you'll get as many answers about it as there are people, with at least half of them thinking that the Great in Great Britain doesn't mean 'larger', but unfeasibly means 'Bloody fantastic.' (Lesser Britain, or the smaller land of the Britons to the Romans, is now roughly the region known as Brittany in France, and to be fair is a really nice place to have a holiday. The Celts there apparently retained much nicer cooking skills. Try the Crepes and Galettes, they are to die for, and you can wash it down with a lovely drop of cider too! Anyway, in this hypothetical talk in a pub about the Island history, there would be much arguing about who shit on who the most, someone wouldn't give a F*** because they had an Irish Granny, and the people at the next table would overhear and start singing Rule Britannia.

Of course, all these historical shenanigans were in the past, we have learned nothing, and eventually once the communication and record keeping skills reach a point where generations can grow up and die in a world where we can both live in the moment, and understand the past, some complete idiots will burn the books and pull down the statues so that they can feel awfully noble and self-righteous, and sod the generations to come. It happens all the time in history, and has never ended well.

None of this, mind you, deterred from the fact that Mr. Rib and Myself were now in Germany, and I found I was worrying not so much about Germanic history, but rather if I could buy a new patch or not. I decided in the end not to, unless we actually went into old East Germany, which would not happen till I visited Berlin some years later.

All worries of what patch to get or not get were forgotten, however, when we pulled out of the next services we had stopped at. After a decent breakfast, we cheerfully got back in the lorry, went to drive out of the lorry park, and spotted two absolutely gorgeous Swedish girls, as revealed by a flag on one of their backpacks. Their thumbs were out, and they smiled at us as we drove up. Mr. Rib looked forlornly at the girls and gave an apologetic sorry motion to them, clearly emphasising that he had no room in the cab.

"Wow," I said," I never thought of that. I bet that's a real perk of this job, eh?"

He looked at me and laughed.

"You know what? You know fucking what? That's the first time that has ever happened! I have fantasised about that happening for friggin' years! And the first time two hot girls need a lift, your ugly carcass is stuck in the cab!!"

"You want me to get out?"

"Would you?"

"No…"

We laughed about it. However, I noted that he never asked me to come with him again. Fair play. At some point we dropped the pharmaceuticals, and picked up a load of toilet roll for Italy. Now there was a swap, I thought. Hell, if Brody or any of his new crowd since we all left the old flat knew that you could swap drugs for toilet paper, shares in Andrex would be going through the roof. Hell, they wouldn't have needed that puppy to advertise it unless it was sitting up and begging for spare change in a doorway somewhere.

Italy was the last port of call, where we picked up a full load of tomatoes to come back to the UK. All in all, it had been a nice trip. It was weird to think that only weeks earlier I had been out in Africa on an overland truck, seeing wonderful places, experiencing a different world, and interacting with amazing animals, including sitting with Gorillas. Yet this much shorter journey was still an adventure, still exploring the unknown, and again seeing and experiencing yet new things.

It was also nice to catch up with a good old mate. Mr. Rib had always been a guy who would get things done. He'd followed his nose around the world a fair bit himself, and would do anyone a favour. We reminisced during one conversation about the time I had told him that I really fancied his girlfriend's sister, who I'd met in London with them once. Two days later, he turned up on my doorstep with the said girl just after midnight, who had recently broken up with someone and he suggested to her about staying up in Coventry to get away from it all. She came in, with some luggage but he couldn't stay, and headed straight back to London. This in itself was awkward enough, but hey, what a hell of a guy to do that. Now that's a mate!

Somewhat unsurprisingly, my own girlfriend who was stopping over at my flat that same night never really saw it that way.

III.

Next up was a trip to Bruges, a charming little town in Belgium. Or rather, a city that seems like a charming little town. Even though it has a population of around 117,000, and covers 54 sq miles, it just comes across as a beautiful little place, full of canals and impressive old style buildings. These canals, in fact, are the reason that it is known as the Venice of the North. This is a somewhat overused term, mind you, as anywhere with canals tends to get called The Venice of the North by someone or other and my guess would be it's by the type of people who write tourist guides. In fact, Both St. Petersburg and Amsterdam are also known as the Venice of the North as well. Even Birmingham, Coventry's bigger and somewhat more annoying neighbour likes to point out that at 35 miles of canal, they have 9 more miles than Venice. Well that's great, except that if you tried to sit romantically on a gondolier drifting down the Grand Union with a cornetto ice cream, the odds are that someone would throw paint or something at you from a bridge.

Most seasoned travellers would agree that the last people you should let recommend a town or city to you should be a tour guide writer. Especially in regard to places to eat. They also will happily steal stories from neighbouring towns when they find they cannot come up with enough quaint crap to write. At some point in its tourist guide history, Coventry tried to market itself as "The City in Shakespeare Country". Seriously? Not only did that really piss off the good people of Stratford-upon-Avon, a lovely little place, but annoyed the crap out of Coventrians who had never once thought of William Shakespeare as being connected in the city in any way at all. In fact, since at that time we had ceased to be in Warwickshire and had become part of the West Midlands, along with our bigger and somewhat more annoying neighbour, we were not even in the same county that young Bill had ponced around in, wearing tights and writing worthy plays with a feather.

Actually, I understand that they used swan feathers back then. If you ever visit Stratford-upon-Avon, you will see a fine population of swans swimming graciously along the river, and waddling

19

considerably less graciously through the lovely parks. I like to think that these are descendants of the very swans that an eager Shakespeare had ran up behind and plucked a few feathers out of their arse while they weren't looking. Now this was a missed opportunity for the guide and marketing writers. If it was me, I'd organise an event where people could run around Stratford pulling feathers out of swans backsides, and seeing who could come up with the best short story. Though I imagine that the animal cruelty people would jump all over that one, so maybe some kind of robot swans could be knocked up. Plus, instead of snow globes with Anne Hathaway's cottage, you could have an annoyed looking swan with a bare backside.

So all in all, Bruges was in fact nothing like Venice, but nevertheless I headed off there on the suggestion of a friend from the Post Office where I worked in between adventures, my good old mate Lucky Andy.

It had been Lucky Andy's idea to go. He'd been a good few times before, and assured me it was one of his favourite places to visit.

"Very civilised place to drink," he enthused. "There is a bar called the 'T Brugs Beertje', or Bruges little bear, where they do 300 beers. 300!! Can you imagine? "

It was fair to say that Lucky Andy was a true beer connoisseur. This was way back before craft beers and microbreweries were to take off in the UK, and people drank either lager or bitter, with very little to distinguish between the various brands. It was a tragic period of British drinking, but there were always the Real Ale guys who would travel for miles for a half pint of flat piss with a quirky name, such as Squirrels Stool, or Badgers Hard-on. Lucky Andy was one of these. Him and his best friend Gaz were inseparable in their quest for hand drawn beverages, to the point that they were referred to as Gandy on their beer excursions. There was no depressingly quiet tavern full of old geezers that they would not visit, once they heard that a pint of Black Death or Rabid Rabbit had been tapped and poured off.

However, on this occasion, Gaz had come down with a shocking cold as a result of the pair of them toppling into a Birmingham

Canal after one too many Devils Penis's, and had left Lucky Andy with a spare coach ticket. He'd asked a few people who shared a passion for unusual and delicious ales and beers but it was too short notice. That left me, who he considered to be some kind of heathen Lager drinker, which apparently is a lot worse than homophobia, or racism, or murdering a spouse in the eyes of the fine bearded folk from CAMRA., or to give it it's full name, the Campaign for Real Ale. This noble institution set about keeping small breweries alive and financially viable, which they decided to do by demanding a 10% discount on each measly half pint they would drink after sampling a couple of good sized swigs from every tap in a pub. But though my lagering was a terrible concept to him, and as we had been drinking together for years, he swallowed his pride and asked me along.

There is no right or wrong way to travel. Backpacking, Overlanding, Hitching, Flying, Sailing, Euro railing.....It's a long list, and a journey will have many crossovers. Included on this list, though probably near the bottom, is "Reg Potters Coach trips." Every city probably has the equivalent, basically some bloke who got kicked off driving local buses and bought a couple of old second hand coaches to set himself up, once his licence was good again. As time had gone by, Reg had expanded to quite the fleet, but I suspect that the one we boarded may well have been the original old banger that he started up with.

We were lucky to get on really. The part of Coventry Bus station where you caught these kinds of coaches was somewhat primitive back then. You left the main bus station through a badly lit and dodgy looking underpass and found yourself in a kind of building site with a port-a-loo where unmarked coaches pulled in. Truth be told, it's not much different now, except they have taken the port-a-loo away as part of Coventry Council's ongoing mission to create the only city that you can't have a piss in unless you know a couple of the secret ones that are marginally worse than a Rock Bar Toilet. So I was half way down the coach that arrived looking for a seat, when a kindly old feller pointed out that this was the coach for the Ramblers association on its way to the Malvern Hills. I had noticed it was mainly full of people in waterproofs and sporting beards and big boots, but in all honesty I thought that they were just CAMRA members off to drink fine Belgium beers. You'd have thought the driver might have mentioned it when I showed him my ticket to Bruges, but maybe he thought I was just sharing non-snow globe related souvenirs. So off the bus I got, which was a shame as they seemed a friendly bunch. They even waved goodbye at us as they drove off. Mind you, as the driver had no idea that they weren't going to Bruges, lord only knows where he took them. Possibly to this day, a lost group of anoraked Ramblers are still walking their way home, cold, tired, hungry, but still able to give a cheery wave and a hallo to a passer-by going the other way.

We finally got the correct bus, to discover that we were the only two people below 90. Any plans of meeting girls on the trip seemed doomed, though I guess there is many a good tune played on an old fiddle. In any case, when I'd brought this up, Lucky Andy had looked at me in horror and explained that we were going to look at a lovely city, and drink fantastic ales brewed by monks from their own holy piss, and that we weren't likely to be coming across women. He had a point, outside of CAMRA WAGS, establishments that sell a range of real ales and choice beers tend to be mainly full of men. In fact, you will find more straight women frequenting gay bars for a fun night out than there will be in real ale pubs on any given night.

I'd like to say how the exhaust pipe fell off, and the wheel buckled, and how we got towed to Bruges, but alas, the coach for all its basicness, including having no toilet, arrived safely and deposited us at the hotel that was part of the price. It was pretty basic, as you'd expect, but that is all you need. I've always preferred backpackers hostels myself, not just because of the price – which is essential if you are travelling the world – but the company. Why stay in a hotel room if you are travelling alone, where you leave a bar and turn on a TV set in a language you don't understand? This of course is subjective. I know people who detest the hostels, even if they have never stayed in them.

I was all for getting out and about straight away, but Lucky Andy was feeling a bit sick by the time we got there, and needed a lie down.

22

"How long are you going to be, do you think?"

"No idea. I usually get sick when I've been travelling a while. I'll catch you up somehow."

I find it hard now to remember, but for most of my life there had been no mobile phones. So unless you knew where you were going, catching up in a strange town was not always that easy. With this in mind, I decided to go and get a drink in the hotel bar where I found a number of other people from the coach in a similar situation. Though we'd all come with Belgium beers in mind, we found ourselves sat drinking indeterminable lager while we waited for our queasy friends to recover enough to come downstairs. They were actually a nice bunch of people to be fair. One old guy was telling me how he takes a Reg Potter trip every month to somewhere or other since he retired. Cool, I said, you must have a few funny stories.

"Not really," he said. "I usually spend the coach trip waiting for toilet stop to toilet stop and the hotels are not very good. I don't really like foreign food either."

"Oh. But I guess you enjoy the sight-seeing then? There are some lovely places to see."

"No, my legs aren't very good these days, and by the time I get off the coach, they kind of seize up a bit and don't really get better till it's time to go. It usually takes me a week at home before I'm recovered."

"But you still keep coming?"

"Oh yes. I love these Reg Potter trips."

I had a couple of drinks and then wandered up and down the street we were on, looking in souvenir shops. I had promised a friend I would buy a thimble for his wife, who apparently collected thimbles from around the world.

"But wouldn't it be better if she only got them from countries that she had been to?" I'd asked quite reasonably, but this seemed to annoy him.

"Well, of course not. We don't go abroad. In fact, we don't go on holiday at all. She won't leave the dog, you see."

23

"But there are plenty of places where you can take a dog on holiday nowadays. Especially if you like walking and things like that."

"Not her dog, we can't."

"Why, is it vicious?"

"No, it's buried in the back garden."

I forgot to buy her a thimble in the end.

By the time I got back, Lucky Andy had come down to the bar and was sitting with the others from the coach whose numbers were getting bigger as the sicklier folk drifted downstairs after a nap.

"Feeling better? I was nearly going to have a nap myself, but thought I'd leave you in the room till you recovered. A good kip sorted it then?"

"I haven't really slept that much. I kept vomiting. It's all up now though."

"Yes," a bearded fellow at the table said, " I was vomiting too. Just once though."

"Twice, me," added a little skinny woman at the next table who had been listening. "I've got some Milk of Magnesia tablets if anyone wants any though?"

A couple of people took her up on the offer, and another feller pulled out a packet of indigestion tablets just in case anyone might suffer from reflux. My last couple of adventures had included backpacking around Asia, and staving off Malaria in Africa. It was occurring to me that this was a whole different kind of trip, with a new set of problems that I had never really encountered before.

After about half an hour of everyone around me chatting about the best tablets for gout, various types of creams and balms for dry skin and why GP's waiting lists are too long, I decided I'd had enough and suggested to Lucky Andy that we went and got something to eat, then head to this Bruges Bear bar. He was reluctant to be torn away, as they had just moved on to joint problems, but he came anyway and we got pasta somewhere then hit this bar of some fame.

Well, if you like your beers, this was indeed the place to be. Andy hadn't been wrong, there were over 300 to choose from. And every one of them came in a unique glass. It was already quite late when we got there, but we enjoyed a couple of super strong dark beers, and nattered happily to a few of the other customers, mainly about the joy of beers.

"You see," Lucky Andy explained as we wandered through the charming little streets back to the hotel when the bar closed, "You don't always have to go out and get twatted to enjoy beer. This is a much more civilised way to drink. Go on, admit it, you enjoyed it, didn't you?"

To be honest, I had never thought I wouldn't, but he seemed eager to make a point of some kind, so I agreed wholeheartedly."

"In fact," I replied, "I'm looking forward to a longer night there tomorrow to sample more of those beers. Delicious."

We found a place that sold chips in a cone near the hotel and ate them before retiring. I enjoyed mine, and was pleased to see a healthy dollop of Mayonnaise on them so as to make me feel quite European, but Lucky Andy was sick in the night again.

A bit of sight-seeing the next day, during which we spotted one of those walking tours about to leave the square and joined it at the last minute. It was by the 4th or 5th chocolate shop we stopped at that I realised that we had actually joined a specific chocolate tour, and was going to see very little else. Still, by the end of it, I was extremely knowledgeable about Belgium chocolate, of which I did not really retain any information through life at all.

We had a bit of dinner in the hotel later on, which was Ok, but we were joined by the old boy who took the monthly trips. He hadn't left the hotel yet and was quite interested in the tour we had ended up on.

"Oh, that sounds very educational. I wish my legs were better, I'd have enjoyed a trip like that. Did you get to sample the chocolates?"

"Yes, most of the places gave you a piece."

"Oh, lovely. It's supposed to be really nice, the chocolate here. And in Switzerland. They make lovely chocolate there, too. I was on a trip to Switzerland last year, and managed to get on a chocolate tour."

"Did you buy chocolate there?"

"Oh no. I don't really like chocolate."

It was time soon enough to head back out to Bruges Bear, so a quick shower and shave and off we pottered.

"Hi again," Lucky Andy greeted the bartender. "It's just us again."

The barman looked at us with no sign of recognition whatsoever and handed us a couple of beer menus. We chose a couple of lighter beers to start, and sat back comfortably set for an evening of exploring exciting new tastes, and pleasant conversation with any of Andy's fellow connoisseurs that were to pass through and put up with him quoting the name of soccer teams to them, as he had long decided that football was an international language which you only needed to say the name of a team and you would be both engaging with, and delighting kindred soccer fans. Being a person who never really cared much for any sports, this went somewhat over my head, plus I couldn't fail to notice that the other people never quoted teams back, they just looked at us like we were a pair of idiots.

The evening drifted pleasantly by, and I found myself getting much drunker on much less beer than I normally would, and somewhere along the way my personal volume levels raised a bit till I found myself holding an imaginary microphone and Djing the music in the background, before interviewing people about where they come from. There were Germans, Dutch, French and of course Belgians, and most of the people in the bar began joining in the fun. This included a young American lad who really took to the interviews and began trying to snatch the imaginary microphone from my hand. I kept pulling it back, which seemed to annoy him, so he'd lean in to get closer to it. It was at a point where he was bent double over a table trying to talk into it that I dropped my hands down and said,

"It's not a real microphone, y'know."

Finding himself in the strange position of being bent over with his head in front of my crutch, and with a bar full of people laughing at him seemed to change his mood a little, and he went into some kind of rant about Americans in Europe being here to help. Now, I am actually a huge fan of Americans. I have friends there, I have enjoyed travelling there, and found most of the people I ever met over there to be friendly and helpful, and I even like American tourists, who generally seem to annoy people for some reason. But in the light of having many strong beers and also having an audience, I smelt mischief, and pointed out a few flaws in the American character that I think I'd seen on a comedy show or something. He bit.

Pretty soon he'd forgot about the imaginary microphone and was arguing with the bar in general about how we'd all be fucked without America. I'm not sure everybody picked up what he said, but as he got louder and more animated everybody was laughing more till he had had enough and stomped out of the door. Not for long though, as he'd clearly got part of the way down the street and remembered something, so came back, stuck his head round the door and called in.

"And another thing," he hollered, "Let me tell you that if the US hadn't stepped in during world war 2 and saved your asses, none of you guys would be sitting here now. You'd all be drinking German beer, and speaking German."

The Germans in there just shrugged.

"Well, that's just typical of Americans though," I answered calmly. " We were having a bit of a domestic squabble, and you guys had to come in all heavy handed."

"Domestic squabble? Domestic squabble? It was World War two, for fucks sake, and we saved the day."

"Well, thanks and everything, but well, it's all fine at the moment. We're all Europeans now, aren't we, lads?"

I said this, turning to the other customers and raising a glass. The rest of the guys in the bar raised their glasses and gave a rousing cheer. The poor lad seemed utterly speechless and just left, swearing.

"You had to, didn't you?" Lucky Andy said. "Now can we just have a drink?"

Amusement over, and the bar having been suitably entertained, we had a few more beers, ironically German, and left as the bar closed with friendly waves from everyone, including a highly amused barman.

Well, back home tomorrow," Andy mused as we wandered through the streets. "And that was quite fun tonight. It's still a more civilised way of drinking, don't you think. A nice pleasant change. Though I agreed with him, something else had caught my eye. Though the street was deserted, there seemed to be a well-lit establishment ahead, where I could hear the sound of awful pop music and the sound of laughter. Female laughter. Young female laughter.

I was right. Bang on the corner was a quite trendy looking bar, not only still open, but looking like it was just filling up.

"Bullseye! " I announced happily. "C'mon, we can get a few more drinks."

"Oh no," Lucky Andy groaned, "It looks terrible. It's probably horrible beer, and it's full of kids all dancing and whatever. We might as well head back to the hotel and get some rest before the coach back tomorrow."

"Bollocks. I've indulged in your civilised drinking, now one drink in a place with a bit of life won't kill us."

"Ok. But just one drink, then back, yes?"

We didn't have just one drink. We got talking to a couple of young local lads who offered to buy us a drink as they thought we were a bit lost. So naturally, it would have been rude not to buy them one back, and so on. Andy was right about the beer though, there only seemed to be one drink, a cheap fizzy lager which was as much like everything he hates about beer as was humanly possible to get. But the lads were pretty cool, and gave us a bit of a younger insight into the city, and how they intended to move to Brussels soon. We had a good few beers until it looked like closing time was looming.

"How are you guys getting back to your hotel?" one of them asked.

"Just walking. It's a nice night."

"Just wait here by the door. I'll get my car, it's only round the corner."

So we stood in the doorway for what seemed longer than it would have taken us to walk, when we heard a loud roaring and the lads turned up in a pretty nifty open top sports car.

"C'mon, get in," They called, revving up the engine. We did, and the lads proceeded to take us on a very fast, very loud tour of the city. I have to give it to the kid driving, he sure knew how to get down the narrow little streets. At some points we must have had only about a foot or so, if that, on each side of the car from the walls of the old buildings. I imagine these would be very quaint and interesting buildings to look at, but to be honest they were a bit of a blur as we went past.

Finally, we arrived back at the hotel, said our farewells, and retired to the room. It seemed like no time at all till we were back on the coach, heading our way to the port for the ferry and nursing one of those hangovers that comes from cheap beer. There are, I learned years ago, a number of different types of hangovers, and the cheap fizzy beer one is the worst. Luckily, we were offered lots of headache tablets by our fellow Reg Potter companions, and caught a bit of kip on the way back, though a drink on the ferry was much appreciated. We arrived back in Coventry bus station and said our farewells to the other good folk that we had met.

"Well," said the old boy with the bad legs who hadn't left the hotel. "I thoroughly enjoyed that trip. Hope to see you again, lads. There's one going to Amsterdam next month if you're interested in canals and canal history and that."

I'd had a history with Amsterdam. I'm not sure canal history had been part of it.

I think I can safely say it was a nice little trip. Why, I'd got to share with Lucky Andy his civilised drinking experiences, and he'd got to throw up in a really fast car.

IV.

Next up was a venture out to the Canary islands with a good old friend of mine, who had the unlikely name of shovel. This was originally a name given to him by a mutual friend of ours, Ferret, whom I'd travelled up and down the East Coast of the USA a few years earlier. The name referred to the way the front of his then rockabilly haircut had looked, and though the haircut had long gone, the nickname just kind of stuck. But he was a good lad, and had suggested that we took our mountain bikes out to Tenerife.

This we did. We'd both got pretty good bikes that were lightweight and broke right down. The weight came within the luggage allowance weight for the plane, so that's what we put in the hold, and took just a couple of small bags on board with some shorts, tee-shirts and the all-important toiletries. You can get by in a new place without most things, but always – always – make sure you have a decent toothbrush and toothpaste. It's a kind of quality of life thing.

We hadn't actually booked any accommodation, which luckily did not end up biting us in the ass. Arriving at the airport, we assembled our bikes and headed down to Los Cristianos which was only about an hour's cycle from the South Airport. Or would have been if I hadn't managed to have two punctures along the way. This struck me as being a bit worrying, but turned out to be a small thorn from the first puncture I had missed. Confident in my newly patched tyres, we arrived on the edge of the town, and stopped by the first bar we came to.

Like many of the pubs and bars we were to come across, it was owned by an English feller. We got chatting to him, and when we explained that we were cycling round the island he told us to look out for a certain symbol that meant Pension, which is a type of small guesthouse. He also told us that if we got stuck later, we could come back to the bar and sleep on the couches. We did think about that, but ended up getting a pretty good room in the town which was a surprise due to the amount of holiday makers there.

There was a big difference in these kinds of trips I was making with Shovel, or Lucky Andy, or even Mr Rib, and the adventures I had had previously. My earlier shenanigans had seen me as a young punk rocker hitching across Europe being turned away from bars, grocery shops, even towns! Even as I toned down the clothes somewhat when I went out to the Soviet Union, and college in Israel, the hostility and general assumptions were there. After that, folk in the smaller towns in the states or Australia would be sceptical of the much thinning remains of my mohawk, or bleach, or whichever nod to my punkness I was still sporting. Backpacking across Asia and Overlanding around Africa hadn't been too bad, as travellers tended to gather in certain places and anything goes amongst them.

So, now wearing kind of sporty t-shirts and shorts – Though I have to say, not the lycra shorts beloved of many cyclists which I find completely offensive to my poor eyes – and by this time just having short cropped hair, meant that not only were we not turned away from bars, but even had offers to sleep in them. And as we stopped off in the small villages around the island, I was very aware that had me and my original punky companions knocked on the door of the pensions and asked for a room, most of those doors would have been slammed in our faces. I say most. Not everyone I came across over the punk years was as judgemental as each other; In fact, some openly welcomed us into their circles. And these folk were some of the most interesting kinds of people you could meet, usually with hilarious or fascinating stories to tell about their lives or jobs or friends. Which was great, because it's always about the story.

So here I was, looking sporty, yet exactly the same bloke, though a little older, than the punk kid who first began travelling many years ago and got shot at on the first night on French soil. Well, if that hadn't set the pace for the adventures and shenanigans to come, nothing would have. But due to a change of clothes, the world was now open to me, and having a bloody good bike meant there was an island to explore.

On securing some digs that let us lock our bikes up out back, we freshened up and headed off to Playa De La Americanos, which we knew to be a bit of a party area. Sure enough, even arriving early, we found the bars already full of mainly Brits getting drunk nice and early. We sat in one bar at first that had a whole bunch of Scottish lads standing under a Scottish flag that was hanging up, singing Scottish songs and generally shouting out the word Scotland every so often, always to a rousing cheer. The waiter brought us over a couple of bottles of beer and we mentioned this to him.

"I take it that a Scots guy owns this bar then?"

"No, no. It is a local owner."

"Oh sorry. I just saw the Scottish flag and presumed."

"No," he laughed, "That is the Tenerife Flag. A white cross on a blue background. It is the same as Scotland."

"Really?"

"It's to do with San Andres, the same guy as Scotland's saint. But every night, groups of Scottish people sing songs under it because they think they are in a Scottish pub, and tip us well when they leave. Who are we to argue?"

We wandered round a few bars over the night, watching the holiday-makers getting swiftly drunker and drunker, till later in the evening the familiar British city centre sounds of crying girls, fighting boys, unisex vomiting and police sirens began to make us feel just like being at home again. If I'm honest, much as I love drinking beer and partying, I never really got the attraction of this kind of drunken revelry that the Brits are famous for. I would be lying if I said I had never ended up in a similar condition to so many we saw there, but it was usually by accident rather than by planning. We did find one little rock bar on the edge, complete with unmatching furniture, solitary rock guy in XXXl t-shirt with a Deep Purple logo, and piss coloured toilets. But in all honesty it was dull as hell, so we went back to the party bars. Hell, we might even meet some women, we thought.

We didn't meet any women. At the start of the night we had saw many groups of quite hot girls arriving in the bars all dressed up for the night, giggling and ordering nice cocktails, but by later on most of them were nearly crawling on all fours, urinating in shop doorways and snogging equally pissed blokes with beer stains all over their no longer pristine shirts. I guess the few years I had on them had changed my perspective on who I wanted to end up waking up with. That, plus the fact none of them took a blind bit of notice of the pair of us anyway.

We had booked two nights in the pension, but both agreed once we got back that probably one night out down there had been enough. I'm not knocking it, everyone seemed pretty happy – apart from the crying people – but I could go out any Saturday night at home and see the same thing. Though minus the good weather!!

So the next morning we forfeited the next night's room money and headed North. It was, to be fair, very scenic. We'd stop at every little village for a cup of tea in a café, or maybe a beer in a bar. This we did for the best part of a week, taking little side roads and exploring. Tenerife, we were told, had once been full of trees, almost completely a forest. However, the Spanish had used it as one of their main sources of timber for their fleets, and as they had been there since the 15th century, had pretty much deforested vast areas, including what was needed for agricultural land as the population grew. However, this meant many pretty villages with friendly locals, especially when we tried to talk a bit of Spanish. This was appreciated, even though the smaller villages have their own kind of Canarian Spanish. It didn't matter, we weren't very good at it anyway.

In fact, armed with a phrase book, I made a point of trying to make sure I could at least order one whole meal in Spanish at least once. So in one of the small villages, I said to Shovel one night that I think I'd cracked it. Out we went, into a nice restaurant, and I ordered both our meals and some beers in Spanish, then felt quite proud of myself. Or at least I did till the waiter answered me in Spanish and was clearly trying to clarify something that I had said. I had no idea what he was asking, and just sat looking dumb. Luckily, he picked up that I had no idea how to actually speak Spanish, then talked to me in fluent English. For a traveller, who was even married to a Swiss German girl once, my lack of language skills are indeed an embarrassment. I have to acknowledge that in general, Brits are not very good when it comes to other languages. We are, quite frankly, lazy. We just assume, or hope rather, that everyone else can, or should, speak English, which luckily enough for us, a fair amount of less lazy people can. Or rather, they speak American, which is close enough to get us by. I can see why it does annoy some people, who are aware of our assumption that they should speak our language, and the annoyed look that some tourists from all English speaking nations give them when they can't. And yet, just picking up a few basic words, such as please, Thank you, Yes, No, Excuse Me, etc, can change the tone of a conversation by showing that you are at least trying. Though as I learned in that bar, don't try too hard, because if they speak back, your cover is blown and you're buggered!

So after a number of pleasant evenings in charming villages, cycling out to see things recommended to us that were mainly interesting rocks – including a group of rocks we had seen the day before, which the people that recommended them seemingly had two different names for – we reached Puerto De La Cruz, a small city in the North of the island. This was, it turned out another hotspot for tourists, but this time it seemed it was were the Spanish themselves went on holiday, often in the summer when the temperatures on the mainland could get extremely hot. The difference was remarkable in regards to the type of tourists. The first night we went out, it was around midnight before the bars began to fill up, after people had been out to eat. This is about the time people back at Playa De Las Americanos where heaving up their guts before searching for chips or kebabs. The music seemed to be more local, with Spanish and Latin tunes filling the dancefloors, and a generally more relaxed air about the place. We liked it here.

In fact, it seems tourism on Tenerife owes much to this city, from its origins as a small fishing village in the 15th century which grew as European trade increased, to a point before mass tourism hit the islands where many of the privileged elite were drawn by the tranquillity, and interests in botany and climatology. Though not as tranquil now, it was certainly much more preferable and peaceful than the drunken shenanigans we had left in the south.

So, after a good week of visiting places of interest, and resisting the urge to buy snow globes, we woke up early on the last morning for a bracing cycle to the airport back in the south. We were looking forward to this, and had left in what we thought was plenty of time, patting ourselves on the back at what great cyclists we were, and what a great way to see the island it had been. The last bit was true, but not so much our cycling ability. We realised about half way there that we were either slower cyclists than we thought, or had seriously misjudged the length of the route, and we were not going to catch the plane. Luckily, we flagged down a bus, who let us put our bikes in the luggage hold, and eventually we arrived in ample time, sharing the plane with Brits looking a lot less fresh than when we flew over. We never patted ourselves on the back about our cycling abilities again.

V

Tenerife had been a great place to cycle around, and confirmed my belief that I was not especially interested in what would be regarded as the normal "holiday" locations. In fact, in all my years of travelling, I had never really considered any of my shenanigans to be a holiday as such. They tended to become adventures and that was just the way I liked it. So cycling in the Canary Islands was the first time I thought of it as a holiday. And this was swiftly followed by another one, when Lucky Andy, seemingly not too traumatised by events in Bruges, suggested we go to mainland Spain on a package deal.

Package deal. Those words actually made me feel uncomfortable, like I was cheating on my travels. The only other two words that scare me more are All-Inclusive, an expression that actually sends a shiver down my spine. However, I had long learned that any experience of travelling is better than not travelling at all, so Lucky Andy, myself, and another lad, John, from the Post Office depot where we worked headed off to the Costa Del sol.

An international tourist destination since the 50's, the name Costa Del Sol was a name that the Spanish had come up with as mainly a marketing device, and refers to an area of about 800km2 that takes in a lot of the towns by the south coast. I had never booked a package deal before and left it all to Lucky Andy. As a result, I have no idea of the name of the resort we stayed at. It looked like just how I had always imagined these places, with chalets and swimming pools and a couple of bars. I can't say it was actually unpleasant, but I couldn't really seem to get into this sitting by a pool thing. However, in no time at all I learnt that all was not lost. I discovered excursions.

Lucky Andy had indeed done us proud when it came to a chalet, by getting a last minute deal. In fact, we didn't really know where we were going until the last moment. Coincidentally, at the airport we met one of the ladies who worked in the canteen at work, also heading out on her holidays with her husband. They had booked well in advance, and it turned out we were all on the same resort. It also turned out that they had paid a hell of a lot more than us, and found themselves in a chalet by a motorway, both of which facts seemed to annoy them greatly. A very bubbly young girl greeted us all on our arrival and presented us with a drink, some advice on something or other, and assured us that she was there for any of our needs. We promptly decided that we probably had no needs she could attend to, and never saw her after that.

We did pop into whatever nearby town on a couple of evenings, but they were not the kind of bars that held much attraction to any of us. There was a bar in the middle of the camp that Andy decided that we liked, though I'm pretty sure that Me and John preferred the other one. Lucky Andy was determined that we should like this place, even though there seemed to be no consistency in prices, and the first time we ordered a meal there, his came out frozen in the middle.

Two trips out made it all worthwhile though. One was to the nearby Caves of Nerja. Visiting places such as Ayers Rock, Australia, and the church of the Nativity in Bethlehem amongst others, I had discovered that there is something very special about going into ancient places. Something that connects you to the place not just in location but in time. I'm sure wiser men than me could describe this feeling in a scientific way that makes absolute sense, but in all honesty nobody likes a smart-arse. And so it was that I felt that feeling as soon as we entered the caves.

According to the guides, the caves had only been discovered in the late 1950's by a group of 5 lads out hunting for bats. They went through a fissure in an existing well, found a looming gallery where they stumbled across some human remains and so scarpered. Now, I would personally think that if they found human remains in there that they hadn't actually discovered it at all, but in fact only re-discovered it, but who am I to argue with guide book writers. In any case, proper exploration revealed that there has been a human presence in these caves for maybe 30,000 years. And not only modern humans either. Evidence points to some of the cave paintings possibly being neanderthal in origin. This of course also pushes the claim of being discovered in the 1950's even further back in the plausibility stakes. Not only were these 5 lads not the original discoverers, they were not even the same species of human that found the caves in the first place. With that being said, the Spanish once discovered a whole continent full of people with sprawling civilizations and managed to claim finders keepers whilst not really considering that the ancient ancestors of the millions of people living there may of actually discovered it once themselves, so I guess a cave system is small beer compared to that.

I like caves. I enjoy going into the earth. Not just caves, I've explored old mines and get the same feeling of excitement. However, caves are older. Much, much older. They are truly ancient places, and you can feel that. And I felt it as I entered these caves and followed the well-lit route designated for us to walk through. It is truly remarkable to think that generations of ancient peoples, both ourselves and other types of humans, managed to live and thrive in these networks, apart from probably the odd scrap with cave bears who also like such places and in all fairness had probably been living in them for far longer. But due to their inability to evolve an opposable thumb, their superior size and strength meant they were shooed out the hard way. That'll teach them.

But what grasped me the most was a cabinet near the end of the trip with the skeleton of what they believe to be a young woman.

37

Most people had a look, read the card and carried on looking at other interesting artefacts, but I found myself strangely drawn to her. It was one of those moments that the connection over time I had felt before arose, and I found I could almost see her as she was.

To Be honest, It is clearly the fact that we have seen so many images, films, and reconstructions of such things that enables us to form such a clear image. I do not think, exactly, that I am looking through time, or at least not in the conventional sci-fi sense of looking anyway. But mixing that bit of knowledge with a strong imagination, and then adding the feeling of awe and mysticism that these places allow you to feel, you will connect if you want to. So I looked at her, felt her presence and wondered why we feel it OK to put the remains of a member of a people that we know probably buried their dead into a glass case and put her on show. I hope to hell I don't die in a cave and get found aeons from now. Or if I am, I hope I am at least wearing clean underwear, which will be all the more likely if I didn't meet my fate at the hands of a pissed off cave bear who was glad that people now used their highly developed opposable thumbs to tap on phones instead of spears.

Another pretty good trip we decided to take was out to Gibraltar. I particularly liked the idea of this as it meant crossing a border, giving me that feeling of excitement I get whenever I do such a thing. So off we headed, merrily crossing back into British territory, albeit a much disputed one. First thing was to buy a decent meal, as the breakfast Lucky Andy had bought in his favourite bar on camp had been somewhat inedible. Mine and Johns had been OK, but hey, never turn down a meal. Food taken care of, we effectively wandered around the rock, generally looking at things, getting excited over shops with the same name as back home, and stopping off for the odd drink.

Everywhere we went was effectively buzzing with tourists, who make up a fair portion of the local economy. Gibraltar has had a turbulent history of occupiers, from the Vandals to the Visigoths, from the Moors to the Spanish and finally ceded to Britain in 1713 under the Treaty of Utrecht, in a bid to get Britain out of an alliance with the Dutch in one of the many wars and campaigns that Europe generally was having at any given point. Since then, various Spanish monarchs have tried unsuccessfully to negotiate it back again, even though the Gibraltarians have never really wanted that. This has pissed the Spanish off somewhat, who feel the British have unfairly occupied territory they consider rightfully theirs, especially due to its massive importance as a tactical place to be at the opening of the Mediterranean sea routes, which is the reason Britain tends to want to hang on to it. This history goes back a long, long way, as there is evidence of Neanderthal man being there maybe 50,000 years ago, till being displaced by our ancestors who started as they meant to go on around 42,000 years ago.

In fact, the Neanderthal evidence found on Gibraltar at this time suggests that it may be that The Rock was one of the last strongholds of the species. It may be that the last of these people died out through possible starvation due to being out hunted in the very place that Lucky Andy wolfed down a hearty breakfast this very day. We'll never know. What we do know is that their whole species had evolved from a common ancestor to ourselves, which had migrated from Africa before we had evolved into Homosapien, no doubt following the hunting, the scavenging, the gathering of fruit and other edible roots, pushing their boundaries to the limit whilst they explored, and risked death to make sure that they survived, until one day they didn't. The other thing we know for sure was that the equally highly evolved hominid that is Lucky Andy was still going to insist that we went back to a horrible meal in the bar he had decided was our favourite.

Another thing I enjoyed about The Rock was the famous Barbary Apes. Now, these I really did want to see, as I have always had a passion concerning Primates. Not long before my current shenanigans I had crossed Africa, which involved sitting amongst Gorillas, even being chased by one, and wrestling a backpack from a baboon that didn't give up the fight easily. These were going to be a much less worrying creature to see. It's common knowledge, I think, that they are not apes at all, but in fact Europe's only species of monkey. A Macaque in fact. The mistaken name of ape was due to the fact that they have no tail, the major visual difference between Monkeys and Apes. Plus, at only about 2 feet long, they are not in the same size league. Similar to other monkey species they had long discovered that Humans can be a source of food, and can be seen fairly close up as they sit and wait for people to give them tasty snacks. And no doubt pretty bad stuff that is probably no good to monkeys, and makes them fat and unhealthy. A similar relationship, then, to fast food operators and other humans.

A good few of these critters that we saw seemed to have no real fear of people. This is probably quite justified, and most people seeing them like to coo and aww and take photos. They are quite lucky in this respect that so far there has not been a Spanish monarch who takes things way too literally, as there is a legend that while the monkeys live on the Rock, the British will have control. I have no idea where such an idea would come from, unless someone somehow had a notion that the Barbary apes would form some kind of monkey army in the case of invasion and stay loyal to the crown. I'd like to think that this was started by a pissed off Aztec descendant who got drunk in a bar one night and was able to tell a great tale. And why not, the Mayans had managed to once convince a whole generation that the world was going to end because they had run out of dates. And for all we know, they might have just meant that they'd used up their allowance on some ancient fore-runner to Tinder. It would just take some Eejit in power to believe that if they got rid of the monkeys then the British might leave and the fate of these adorable fruit stealing furballs would be sealed. Luckily for them, that level of Eejit tends to be confined to British politics so they are quite safe so far.

Though a ground based monkey, they can climb when they want to, and it was one of these that had clambered up the side of a small building that we were passing that managed to shit right on top of Lucky Andy's head and shoulders. Monkey shit is usually pretty solid to be honest, but I'm guessing this one had been feeding on some unhealthy human food as it left quite the splash. And to be honest, until we found a public toilet where our shit covered friend could clean up, he smelt rather like human poop as well, which I'm pretty sure seemed to linger even when we'd got most of the crap off.

"I guess this happens a lot to visitors" I mentioned to a couple of locals that were watching us wipe him down.

"No, not really. In fact, I've never seen it ever happen before. Did it throw its shit?"

"No, we don't think so, it was on a small roof and seemed to shit over the top."

"I thought it might have thrown it. They do that to each other when they think their rival is a threat to the females."

Actually, looking at Lucky Andy, he did look a bit like a macaque, especially since his unfortunate insistence of trying to grow a beard, and he certainly didn't have a tail, so maybe the monkey did throw it at him. Either way, even after a shower and change of clothes back at the resort, he still seemed to smell of shit as he ate a plate of cold lasagne and chips in the bar he insisted we preferred.

That was to be the last of these merry little jaunts out. After overlanding across Africa, I'd figured I could do the same kind of thing through South America, and then China. It was time to start putting some serious money to one side. I was back working full time on the post, and Djing in a couple of clubs in the city, so this was doable. I knew from my experience in Africa that being with the same amount of people for that long 24/7 could cause serious problems, so figured that the best thing to do would be to do a short overland, not much longer than six to eight weeks, then head off alone backpacking, as I'd have a bit of a good handle on the continent by then.

As far as I was concerned, the world was there for the taking. I'd enjoyed the few short breaks with friends, because any and all travelling is an adventure, and every new way of doing it adds to your experiences, but in my heart I knew I needed to be away longer and further afield. I was restless. But even as I began to put the pennies to one side for the shenanigans to come, I got a message from my old friend Jake from New York, who I had visited with Brodie and Ferret a few years ago when we had travelled up and down the East coast of the States. For reasons unknown, he was now calling himself Neil, and when I asked him about this, he simply said who'd want to be called Jake. Well, guys called Jake, I guess, but who was I to argue.

"Hey Rich, how's it going? I've moved over to Portland, Oregan now, and got my own place. If you're ever over the states again, just give me a holler."

Hmm. The states, eh?

VI

It was time to start working hard and putting some cash together. I took every bit of overtime at the Post Office, and picked up a fair bit of DJ work. It was '95, the summer of Britpop. The UK was enjoying a feel-good attitude, though there were stirrings of unemployment rising again. However, there was still a ceasefire in Northern Ireland between the IRA and the Loyalists, and things felt altogether not too bad. There's nothing like a bit of feel-good factor to get people back into the pubs and clubs, and so getting the work was easy. I was sometimes playing in clubs till 2am, grabbing a nap, and back in the depot for 4.30am.

And partying. I was equally enjoying the fuzzy feeling of enjoying new music and soaking up the fun atmosphere. Though in all fairness, if I am being honest, I have always kind of thought that life was pretty good anyway. Outside of my travelling shenanigans, plenty was always happening, I had a great bunch of friends, and never really saw the point of moaning too much. I had become increasingly involved in Trade Union work, and had been elected a rep for the North Division. The Post Office was not a bad place to work, but there is always room for improvement, and the fear of privatisation was hanging over everyone's head. I think that is the crux of the matter; If you feel something is wrong, or that things need improving, the best thing you can do is try to find a way to push for the changes you can see are needed. In my case it was the union work, which came quite naturally after my background of chairing the Coventry Youth Council in earlier years, which had been the reason I had gotten out to Israel and Russia, but also that punk attitude, that anti-establishment, do-it-yourself, fuck authority attitude was still very much alive in me. Combined with my family background from Belfast, where the Catholic minority had been forced to fight back against the government for generations, I was never really afraid of a good scrap.

Somehow, and with incredibly little sleep, I managed to fit all this in. I probably never saw more than 4 hours of sleep a day, sometimes in a couple of 2 hour naps. Every so often, it would catch me up. Usually a Monday. I would get back from work, and go to bed for an hour, and just not wake up. Or I'd hear my alarm, recognise the feeling, and go back to sleep till the morning. This seemed to work really well for me, and I'd continue my Every Letter a Mile, Every Letter a Mile philosophy on getting ready for my next shenanigans.

And of course, the time eventually came when I had put aside enough cash to head off, and dutifully went and asked management for a period of unpaid leave, as I had in the past, so I could head out.

However, management had changed. Gradually over my time at Royal Mail I watched the rather worrying trait of the new style management creeping in, as it had in many companies across the country, and probably the world. When I was first there, a lot of the first line managers had started out as postmen, or sorters. Many went up the ladder like this. Even the Postmaster General in the UK had begun as a sorter. I can recall incidents where someone, myself included, would go in to work in the morning, be called to one side by the line manager who would tell you that a letter had been left in the frame when you went out on second post, possibly in error, and that he had drove round to the address on his way home and posted it, but warned you to make sure you keep a vigilant eye out for such errors. These guys, usually old boys, looked after their divisions and were very loyal to Royal Mail as an employer, and the service it provided.

Over time, this became less common, and the graduate managers began entering the business. Straight out of University where they had worked in a pizza place, or behind a bar, or wherever, got a degree and applied for all sorts of jobs till they ended up at the Post Office. And of course, they had lots of bright ideas that saw the beginning of Royal Mail's decline. I remember being called in as a rep for someone who had indeed accidentally left a letter in his sorting frame, and was being disciplined for it. Now, often this happened because after the postie had left the depot, someone had found that letter in amongst their own mail, after being mis-sorted, and dropped it on the correct frame, but too late. That had happened in this instance, so the discipline (What a word, eh? What, no whips?) didn't happen. However, what was revealing was the fact that the said letter was produced at the disciplinary meeting in a sealed, clear bag, with "EVIDENCE" written on it. This was two weeks after the event. Never mind that someone was waiting for that letter. It could have been anything. Appointment, results, job offer, news someone died. But there it was in a bag, meaning that someone in management knowingly delayed that letter so that they could discipline someone who accidentally missed it. And that probably summed up the new style of running a massive public service more than any other incident I saw.

So, in keeping with the new way of doing things, my request was turned down, as why the hell would some grunt from the shop floor need to go travelling when there was work to be done. Though the young manager who informed me of the decision did cheerfully tell me about his gap year when he went across the Andes.

So it was, a little reluctantly , time to depart from the Post Office. It was either stay there, and enjoy a week long break every so often, or continue my shenanigans around the world. So one Saturday morning, I did my last post round, posted my last letter, and packed my bag to head off to the States.

Not, of course, without a good seeing off by the lads. Off we headed into town, caring very little that Blur had beaten Oasis in the so-called Battle of Britpop by securing the number one spot after a much publicised standoff, and somehow I ended up taking home a rather attractive French barmaid from one of the pubs we got aptly drunk in. The next morning, my friend John, the guy who had travelled to Spain with Lucky Andy and myself, came round to give me a lift to Birmingham airport, and oddly the girl decided to come along as well. In fact, she insisted we got breakfast at the airport, never a cheap option, ordered an incredible amount of food, ate only the toast, and then reminded me she had no money. And could she talk. She did not shut up for the whole journey out to BXM, and the last I saw of her she was chewing John's ear off as he found he had to give her a lift home. Only while she nibbled the toast from her mighty big and expensive plate did Me and John get a chance to chat.

"So, Lucky Andy went out to Belgium again last week," he began.

"Bruges again?"

"Yep. He got arrested."

"Andy did? He's never done a wrong thing in his life! What for?"

"Jaywalking. He crossed the road when the traffic lights were still on green when a copper was standing there, and found out it was illegal. He tried to explain that he didn't know, as it wasn't illegal back home, but the copper told him he wasn't in the UK now. I think he then tried to speak about football teams or something to the copper, who thought he was taking the piss. They let him go in the end."

That really made my day.

It was quite a flight, firstly flying into Chicago O'Hare airport, then changing to Seattle. This is where Neil had arranged to pick me up, in a couple of phone conversations we had had prior to my heading out. However, there was no sign of him, and no reply when I rang his number. This was, of course, the days when people still used mainly landlines. I wandered around the airport till I found some advertisement boards where I spotted one for a hotel charging $32 per night. It struck me that a night or two in Seattle couldn't do any harm, so figured I'd catch a cab down to this hotel, and eventually get a bus to Portland. I was cheerfully heading off to the taxis when I heard my name being called, and there was Neil and another feller, looking rushed.

The other guy was a friend of Neils called Treeve, and apparently the pair of them had been enjoying a day in Seattle but somehow misplaced the car. They'd been relying on another friend that they had been with to get them back to it, but he'd disappeared. After much step retracing, they eventually found the car, and here they were, good as gold, to pick yours truly up. I hadn't got the heart to say that actually I would have quite liked to have stayed in Seattle for the night.

We stopped off at a place to eat on the way, which was more than welcome, and caught up a bit on our respective news since we last met up in New York. Neil told me an interesting tale about a guy he had met in Coventry.

"Remember that guy from that huge band who lived next door to you for a while?"

I did. Punk bands, like most bands, tend to have a high turnover of people, and this guy had played with one of the bigger bands from the newer anarcho-punk genre for a while years previously, when Neil had been staying in Coventry. One of my best friends then was a punk girl called Jenny, and we'd ended up with neighbouring flats in a tower block in the inner city area of Hillfields. These two apartments had been the site of many a crazy party, as a balcony joined the two flats up, and we'd clear my furniture into one room in her flat after a gig, set up a sound system, and bought beer in to sell. We had even put our own gigs on together, along with another good friend, under the name of Total Noise Promotions. The after parties were crazy, with the bands coming back to the flats, along with half the punters from the gig. The noise must have been tremendous, especially as we lived on the 13th floor, but the flats in Hillfields had long been the home of many Jamaican sound systems and blues parties, so generally any neighbours that couldn't sleep just came to the party. It was after one of these gigs that she began dating one of the lads from the band, who eventually moved in with her, till she got pregnant and they moved on.

"Yep, I remember him. What about him?"

"Well", Neil asked, "What happened with him and Jenny?"

"Bit of a long story. Basically, they got married, had a kid, then it all went wrong. I'd lost contact with them by then, but I gather that he came home from a tour one night, and the place was cleared out. She'd packed up, lock, stock and barrel, and left the city."

"So did she come over here?"

"That was the rumour. She had an Uncle in the States, and the word was that she came to stay with him. However, it later came out that she'd never left the UK after all, but moved up north to a friend's house and didn't tell anyone."

"Fuck. That explains it then. I bumped into him doing road crew work for some band when I was back in New York and went over to him to see if he remembered me. He told me he'd left the band, and was doing crew work up and down the East coast instead."

"Really? Did he say why he left the band?"

"That's the thing. I asked him the very same question of course, and he just muttered that he was looking for his wife."

Boy, had he got that wrong. I'm guessing that he never found Jenny, but I hope at least he got a bloody good snow globe to take home.

I have to give Neil his due, he'd got a pretty good apartment in Portland. I didn't know much about the city myself, but it had, it turned out, a reputation as a pretty cool place to be, hence Neil moving out there. And a bloody good call, I have to say. The area he lived in was comfortably suburban enough to be a generally nice, safe and pleasant place to live, but was only a bus ride from the City centre, which I was to find to have a completely unique vibe from the American cities I had stayed in before. In later years, it would be described as very Hipster, but at this point the term hadn't been invented yet, so it would have to stay with just being 'cool', even if that was a description of places I never really cared for much.

Perhaps the origins of hipster began here? If nothing else, there was a definite difference in the beer from what I had previously drank in the US. Budweiser is a good example. I hadn't realised on my first trip to New York that the Bud was considerably weaker than the Bud back home. I have often wondered did this catch out unsuspecting Americans visiting the UK, who after a few bottles of what was still regarded in Britain as a fairly tame session beer, found they were perhaps a bit tipsier than they would be back home. No real problem, unless you were driving I suppose. But here in Portland, rather than the predictable lager type beers, they had Microbrewery beer, and this was something I had never come across before.

We had microbreweries back home, but often as not they were an annex of a real ale pub that brewed small amounts of cask ale, usually just bitter. Here was the American version of Microbreweries, which were huge big places that produced hundreds of gallons of a variety of dark and light beers in kegs, and distributed them around Portland, Seattle, and no doubt other appreciative cities and towns. And, boy, were they good beers! In fact, the first day Neil took me into the town to show me around, we stopped off in a bar where I had my first supping of these delightful new tastes, and suitably impressed, persuaded Neil that we should try some more in other similar establishments. His original intention had been to introduce me to some friends of his, but it took very little persuasion apparently, and we began exploring Portland bar by bar. Needless to say, we eventually got back to his apartment pretty late, and slept deeply till the afternoon. At this point, Neil wasn't working a day job as such, but was playing in a band, Banner of Hope, which took him out and about.

At some point we headed back into town ,and finally got to find Neils friends at the little store they owned in the West Burnside area. Neil introduced them as Connie and Frank, and I think he may have said he'd known one of them from New York. However, they had a pretty interesting little punk shop, with a whole range of clothes, jewellery and cosmetics catering to a fairly young punk/goth/skater clientele in the city. In fact, during my time in Portland, I was to head there and hang out a few times, as they were nice people and seemed quite interested in the fact I was from Coventry. This was mainly due to the popularity of ska music on the punk scene, which they knew had its origins in a couple of the bands from the town, mainly the Specials and the

48

selector, but also the fact that they led to the whole two tone thing of which their shop was pretty stacked. That black and white square logo stuff can be seen everywhere, and sometimes it's easy to forget that it started in a small recording studio near my parent's house. Fun fact about the specials was that their EP that hit the number one spot in the UK, Too Much Too Young, was only the second live recording to do that in British chart history. Though the A side was recorded live in London, the B side was a live medley of skinhead anthems recorded in our home town. The first live recording that hit the number one spot was My Ding-A-Ling by Chuck Berry. This is only really interesting because though one of the absolute legends of American music, that particular song was recorded live at the Lancaster Polytechnic, now the Coventry University, seven years earlier, in 1972. I have no idea who had a number one with the third live recording, if anyone, but that's not a bad track record for a city that over the years suffers from a lack of big venues for bands to play live in.

Actually, it looked like well before the two tone thing, 1972 was somewhat of a peak year for Coventry connected music. There, beating the giants that were Bowie, or T-rex, The Jackson Five or The Osmonds, there came from our fair city a David to these goliaths. They were a band called Lieutenant Pigeon, with their somewhat bizarre tune, Mouldy old Dough. Just for one week in September, sandwiched between The Drifters and The Sweet, they hit the top spot with a song that was basically a kind of bloke-in-pub bashing out a honkey-tonk piano riff while a couple of blokes growled its only lyric, "Mouldy Old Dough." The piano was played by the singer's Mum, the adorable but somewhat elderly Hilda Woodward, who I'd like to think also supplied sandwiches and tea during the recording intervals.

Sadly, Frank, Connie and assorted characters that I met passing through the fantastically named Another State of Mind shop displayed no interest in these musical anomalies, but were keen to ask how many of the Specials I had met. Coventry isn't a big town, and it was probably all of them at some point or other, as they were still known to frequent the local pubs. Well, some of them more than others. Though no big deal at home, this apparently made me someone to talk to amongst the younger kids out here.

In fact, live music was to play a major part of my stay in Portland. It was everywhere. With the whole Brit pop indie thing going on back home, there was some great stuff coming out, but here I felt a little like I was revisiting myself a few years earlier, when new punk and its offshoot bands would be playing the live circuits and still sounding exciting. If that sounds like I mean they were behind us, then that's far from what I thought, but certainly the live music was in a different direction to what I had been playing in my club-nights and I really liked it. Not just the music, but the whole feel of an actual punk scene again, though I was certainly a fair bit older than most of the participants around. Still, I wasn't going to let a little detail like that get in the way of any shenanigans that would come along, and who knows, I thought, there may even be a chance of some female company!

This bit of wishful thinking actually came to fruition only a couple of nights later, when we headed to a little café next to the shop where Connie and Frank were launching their new band, Antiworld. I was to stumble across these by accident in Germany a few years later, but had forgotten till after the show that it was the same group, especially as they were made up in their stage personalities of Grandma Fiendish and Forty five Frank. As a debut gig, it was pretty good stuff, a kind of horror punk vibe mixed with a very theatrical stage show, and it came as no surprise that they had gone on later to build up a pretty good following across the world. This night, however, there were probably only about 30 or 40 people watching them, and some friends of theirs in another local Punk band, The Procrastinators.

Now here was a self-fulfilling prophesy in a band name if ever I heard one. The singer was a guy called Chris, who I got to know quite well. He had a somewhat symbiotic relationship with alcohol at this time, and even referred to himself as Chris Piss. Among the many local bands in Portland, it was generally agreed that The Procrastinators were one of the best, and everyone, including Connie and Frank kept telling them that they should really get a vinyl record cut, and get themselves out there, which Chris Piss

50

agreed with, but tended to go out drinking rather than get around to it. Talking to Neil on the phone a couple of years later, I gathered that they split up not long after I had left the states, without ever getting around to recording anything that he was aware of. This being the case, never was a band more aptly named. Though looking through some discographies for something else many years later, I did come across the name Chris Piss again. He apparently moved on to some other bands over the years, including Dead Conspiracy and Religious War. Curious if it was the same guy, I looked up some images of him, and the first one that came up was a picture of him holding a bottle of beer. I looked no further.

There was a house where himself and a couple of other members of the band lived, and after the show in the café, there was a bit of a party going on there. Neil didn't fancy it, but I had spent half the night talking to a young punk girl that Treeve and his girlfriend had brought along, who asked me if I fancied going, so dutifully I headed out there. She'd not known them for long, apparently, and was younger than them, maybe around 20? She sure wasn't 21 yet as she carried a fake ID with a picture of someone that could have been me, yet no-one ever questioned it. This particular night, she was dressed in leather jeans and came across like a younger Joan Jett. She seemed to have a permanent expression on her face of looking at you curiously, as if looking for your story behind your stories. It was a strange kind of look, but then I usually like strange. In any case, it was cool. I had stories. Chatting away to her at a gig was another reminder of my own younger punk days. I can honestly say I have been, physically, to hundreds of gigs over the years, but the figure is much lower of bands which I actually got to see. A bunch of us would turn up to a show, I would spot some cute punk girl in the bar beforehand, and get chatting. If I was lucky, I would sometimes catch the encore, but often as not I considered I had a more musical penis than I did ear, and that when it came to music being the food of love, I knew which one I'd rather stuff first.

"You must have seen lots of great bands", people would say over the years, in relation to the old punk days. "Did you see the Ramones? Iggy? The Clash? X-Ray Spex?"

"Not really," I'd truthfully answer, "but I kind of heard them. However, I do have fond memories of those gigs."

"Oh yes? Did you meet the bands?"

"No, not at all. But at the Ramones I hit it off with the singer of the support band's wife in the toilet while he was on stage. At Iggy I ended up snogging a certain female punk singer who went on to become pretty famous, but shall remain nameless, The Clash gig got me my first threesome, and at X-ray Spex I got chased out by a group of skinheads with knives who caught me about to leave with one of their girlfriends."

I got to see most of these bands again later on over the years, but could I say I was part of the gigging scene in the punk heyday? Well, I was at the gigs, but clearly not embracing the whole 'couldn't give a fuck' attitude, judging by how much time I spent trying to do just that.

"So, Mulligan, that's an Irish name? Are you Irish then?," the strange little girl had asked me at the gig.

"County Coundon born and bred," I remarked, in reference to the predominantly Irish district where I was born in the heart of England. But it got us talking and laughing, till eventually we went along to the party in the procrastinators house. There seemed to be plenty of beer around, and I had figured that my luck was in till the party had emptied out and I mentioned what a funny guy I thought Chris was.

"Yeah, me and him have had a few flings now and then." She mentioned. "I've stopped over in this house a fair few times. Actually, are you staying the night, or do you have to get back to Neils?"

"I'm OK for the night here. No idea how to get back, anyway."

"Well, I'm sure they won't mind you sleeping on the couch. I'm going to find Chris."

And with that she got up and left the room, leaving me sitting on the couch with a full bottle of beer and another guy on an armchair looking at me with an amused grin.

"Well, that went shit then," he observed.

"Yep. I'd better find a blanket. I hadn't noticed how cold it was in here."

"You want a ride back to Neils instead?"

"Yep. That's a much better plan."

In between gigs and a few lazy days in the apartment, Neil had came up with an idea that we could travel across the states back to his parents' house in New Jersey, as he had a good carload of stuff he needed to pick up, but it would have been $800 to get it shipped over to Portland. So as the idea of a road-trip sounded like a plan to me, we agreed that if I paid the fuel, he would drive, and that way he'd save a heap of money and I would get to see a bit more of the US. Firstly though, he needed to get some kind of registration documents, which he had recently applied for but which hadn't come through yet. This began to turn into a bit of a farce after a while, with Neil constantly calling the Post Office, and the trip looking less and less likely.

However, That meant hanging around Portland more, where I was getting to know more and more people, and getting quite comfortable. During the day, I'd often pop into the shop, and chat with Connie or Frank, and they always seemed to know of every event going on. So one day I'd pop in and later that night I'd be watching the Voluptuous Horror of Karen Black, and another day I'd pop in and get a free ticket to the Flapjacks or whoever was playing.

If not a gig, there was an English style pub called The Brass Horseshoe which was just a short walk away from Neils which became a nice place to hang out as well. There was an incredible amount of darts boards in there, which were always in use, and a couple of times, people, on hearing my accent, would ask if I fancied playing Cricket. This struck me as a bit odd, and I wondered if there were some kind of wickets out the back or something, till I found out that it was the name of a type of darts game they played. I'm not sure if I had ever thrown a dart in my life before, but I soon found myself joining in and was highly delighted to realise that I wasn't actually bad at it. My lack of sporting ability had always been an ongoing thing, but it seemed that a sport that involved standing in a pub and drinking brought out the athlete in me. In fact, I took the rules of the game back home and taught it to various people I knew, till there was quite a crowd of us eventually playing the game, which involved a number of tactics, and blocking the opponent's wickets and what not, till someone eventually won. They actually had local leagues in the states for this game, and the Brass Horseshoe apparently did quite well in these.

Fancying a change one day, and with Neil tied up with getting his car fixed in case we ever got on this road trip, I headed off with Chris one day to another pub he knew called The Vern. Or at least, that's what it had become known as. It was fair to say that it was a pretty run down kind of place, that attracted pretty run down folk, but I like it as it had what we would call politely back home Character, a word used in a strange context in regard to drinking establishments.

"Hey, the barman just tried to stab me in this dump you have brought me into!"

"Yes dear, he's a bit of a character."

"There's mice in the cellar and this place hasn't been cleaned in years."

"Well, it gives it character."

"I've just seen Patrick Stewart dressed in Shakespearian clothes pretending to bum someone in the toilets"

"Of course, he's a character actor."

The last one is not true, of course, which is a shame as I always felt that Captain Picard could do with more depth.

Anyway, the Vern certainly had character. Originally called the Something-or-other Tavern, the letters had dropped off till only The Vern was left. So for years that is what it was known as. It kind of suited it. This first time when we went in, I happened to be wearing my 'World's Highest Bungee Jump' T-shirt I had purchased after my jump off the bridge near Victoria Falls, and it quite caught the barman's eye. It turned out that he had recently been over to Zimbabwe himself, so we immediately got to compare a few travellers' tales. By the time I got back to the table, it seemed that the strange little girl had also come in, and between Chris and her, they had nearly polished off the pitcher of beer on the table that I had bought, without actually pouring myself a glass. I thought, what the hell, and got my new friend the barman to send another over to the table.

"I'm guessing I'm not interrupting anything?" I politely enquired, though kind of hoping I was.

"Like what?" Chris asked, with a genuine look of puzzlement on his face.

"Well, the party the other night. I didn't realise you two had a thing going."

"A thing?"

I looked at the strange little girl, whose name I had now actually found out was Zena, who looked indifferent to the whole conversation, and just poured another beer.

"Yeah...I'd gone back to your house, remember, but I left after, ahem, a certain somebody went up to your room. I wasn't being rude, or pissed off, but it was bloody freezing."

"Someone came up to my room? A party?"

I was a bit stumped. I could tell by the look on his face that he genuinely had no idea what I was talking about. Zena still had no expression on her face that suggested one thing or another.

"He doesn't remember. He never does. Did you get home alright?"

I decided to leave the conversation there, and instead we chatted about gigs, and venues closing down, and various people would come in and sit down for a while, until it was nearly closing time, when she suggested to me that we got a cab to a party she thought would be on, if we could get in. Another guy who had joined us near the end said that he lived near Chris, and could drop him back.

"Don't you want him to come to the party?" I asked her, so as to save any mix ups later.

"Well, if he wants to come. But they probably won't let him in. It's in a gig venue and he fell out with the owners, I think."

I turned round to Chris, who was about to leave, and whispered,

"Don't worry, I'm only going for a drink. Not trying to step on your toes, or anything."

"Step on my toes? Why would you step on my toes?"

"Yeah, with, well, you know. I mean, if It is a problem, I'll head home. I get why you'd rather she was staying at yours again, ha ha."

"Why? Has she been at mine recently?"

I decided to simply say cheerio, and flagged a cab down.

We got to the venue, a place called The Paris which had just staged its last show. We bumped into Neil outside, who had also headed there with Treeve as they planned to meet Connie and Frank inside, but the place was locked, and no one had responded to their knocking. We were about to go, when the door opened and a half dressed Drag Queen peered around and told us it was closed. Forever.

But Neil persuaded him we were there by invitation – which we weren't especially – and he reluctantly let us through to the hall where a number of people were sitting around on the stage, drinking plastic beakers of beer. We were introduced to the owner, Veronika, who appeared to stare at us and weigh up if she should let us stay or not. She said nothing, so I guessed we were Ok, and we pulled up a couple of chairs and joined the others. Most of the conversation appeared to be Veronika explaining why everything had failed there, and how it was everyone's fault, mainly the landlord's. Someone later told me that it had been a fairly successful gig and theatre venue previously, then they had hit on the idea of turning it over to mainly gay cabaret events. This started off alright at first, but there was no shortage of such things in the city, and the footfall kept declining. Undeterred, they had tried to keep getting more exclusively gay till other customers were made to feel unwelcome. I don't know if this was true, but It was certainly closing and it was the first place I had visited since arriving where I did indeed feel unwelcome.

At one point a tall transvestite came and joined us, who had been her bar manager and assistant apparently, who did a good job of looking right through us as we were introduced. He also went into a list of complaints about how bad the landlord was, and I was really thinking it was time to go. Till he mentioned the beer.

"And all that in the barrels now is just going to go to waste," he stated, "It's ridiculous. I might as well just give it to the removal men when they come to clear out our stuff."

I felt helpful.

"Well, to be honest, I wouldn't mind a beer. Would it be possible to get one, save some of it going to waste. The others with me nodded and agreed. The tall transvestite looked at me like he had only just noticed that I was there and huffed slightly.

"I suppose so. I'm not pouring it though. Just go and help yourselves."

So we did, and it's amazing how having a beer in hand helped the conversation to seem a little less dull. In fact, I even found myself disliking their landlord in sympathy.

So a couple of beers later, they decided it was time to go home themselves, and told us it was time for us to go too.

"No problem. Thanks for having us, and I hope things go OK for all you guys. Nice meeting you."

The tall transvestite made a noise that sounded like he was agreeing, but also managed to make it in a way that made it clear he wasn't.

"Oh, just before you go……Could you put some money in this empty glass for the beers please? That would be cool….."

Goodbye, big spenders, your cabaret sure wasn't based on Sweet charity.

Good news the next morning! After much waiting, the registration documents for Neil's car had eventually come through. This meant that we were in fact good to go. He had a couple of things he was tied up with over the next couple of days, so it was time to make the most of the last of my time here in Portland, which was a shame as I had grown pretty attached to the place. And making the most of it involved playing darts in the Brass Horseshoe, or drinking with Zena in The Vern.

But finally we were all packed and ready to head off, and Neil headed out to see some friends at some place or other, where I was going to catch up with him. I did, though, head down the Vern early to have a last drink with her, Chris and some of the others who drank there, and probably stayed longer than expected, as the barman who had also been in Africa happily treated me to a good few freebies, which were more than welcome. Eventually I told everyone I really had to go and catch up with the others, as we were planning a reasonably early start the next day.

"Or," said Zena, "We could go to a gig that's on…."

And that is what we did. We headed off to a venue located on the corner of Southeast Ninth Avenue, and Southeast Pine Street, called the La Luna. I've always felt that this way the Americans have of numbering their streets and Avenues as being both incredibly practical, and incredibly cool sounding at the same time. Though I didn't realise at the time, this place was a pretty important venue in Portland's musical history. Founded in 1992, being previously known as Ninth Street Exit, it was as important to the Emerging Grunge / Seattle /Portland scene as CBGB's or Max's Kansas City had been to punk in New York back in the 70's. It played host, and helped to propel such bands as Nirvana and Rage Against the Machine, along with other alternative type bands from Portland and the surrounding areas such as The Dandy Warhols, Sweaty Nipples, Pond, Cherry Poppin' Daddies, Sublime, and Everclear amongst others. This was a pretty important venue indeed, though I wouldn't have guessed it that night as it was an all-age venue, a new concept to me, and pretty medium sized. There again, CBGB's had also surprised me just how small it had been.

On this night, there was some kind of ska band on, which was not really surprising as Ska seemed to be pretty big news here at the time. It was also only $3 to get in, so it was most likely I would do my trick of mainly being in the bar. We almost didn't get to see them at all. Whilst messing around in the bar upstairs, I had picked Zena up and pretended I was going to throw her out of an open window. Being a bit of a nutter, she responded by rolling down my arms till I was actually clinging on to her, and pulled her back in. We sat down with our beers when the security guys came running up, as they had been told that someone was, in fact, being thrown out of a window. I am still pretty surprised that they let the incident go. I was also glad that she was such a skinny little thing, as even another few pounds may have resulted in a whole new

58

meaning of dropping by a gig. Amusement done, we wandered down to see the show, as the barman was now keeping an eye on us.

I'd caught a lot of shows up to this point, but I have to say, these guys were pretty good. They were also fronted by an incredibly good looking girl singer, who couldn't half belt out some high energy tunes, and had the audience dancing around pretty quickly. At one point about half way through, Zena leaned over to me, and called into my ear.

"What do you think of that singer?" she asked.

"Yeah, pretty good. She's got a great voice."

"No, I mean, what do you THINK of that singer? Pretty hot, eh?"

I had to agree.

"Would you fuck her?"

Well, it was my last night and I had nothing much to lose, so I just laughed and said yes, of course I would.

"Yep," she went on, "I'd fuck her too."

"Hey, good for you. Now THAT I'd pay good money to see, ha ha."

"We've paid good money to be here. Do you fancy hanging around in the bar after the show, and seeing if she comes up there? We could give it a go, see if we can get her to join in with us. Would you be cool with that?"

Well, no need to ask twice. Though it struck me as a longshot, hell, there was no harm in trying. I was in the company of a good looking girl, and if this hot singer was into that kind of thing, well, boy, would that finish my Portland experience off on a high note.

So we did indeed go up to the bar afterwards but alas, the hot girl didn't turn up. No problem, we had a couple of beers, then headed back to Neil's apartment, where I pulled my mattress out of his room – we'd been sharing – and chucked it on the living room floor, where we proceeded to round off our shenanigans the way nature intended, which also involved a bit of talk about what we would have done with the girl from the group.

I always kept little journals on my travels, as any good traveller does, and due to the lack of technology at the time this was in notebook form. The advantage of a notebook was I could stick little things in them. Local beer labels peeled off bottles were common, as were maps, train tickets, or gig flyers. It was many years later, when looking through the journal I used for this American trip that I stumbled across the ticket stub for this gig. And there it was, for $3, the La Luna, on November 16th, 1995. A ticket for the then little known band called No Doubt. We had been watching No Doubt, and then had been hoping, it seems, to see if we could pull Gwen Stefani, as this was indeed her in her first band when they were not long after starting out.

It also struck me that the honest fact was, if we had actually had sex with the stunningly gorgeous Ms Stefani, then no one would ever believe me if I told that tale anyway. Not one person. It was years after they had had a couple of smash hits in the UK, and Gwen had gone solo before I stumbled across the ticket and realised who it had been. However, the fact that we did not have sex with Gwennie, or even got close, meant that it made a pretty good travellers story whenever the States pop up, and as I always say, it's always about the story.

Even so, to this day, I think it will always be the best damned threesome I never had!

VII

The Great American Road-trip. I defy anyone to say that even the expression does not get the imagination going, and conjures up a feeling of adventure and romance in even the most casual traveller's heart. Think of the literature over the years. From Mark Twain's Roughing It through to Bill Bryson's The Lost Continent, via On the Road, Travels with Charley, Fear and loathing in Las Vegas, Zen and the art of Motorcycle Maintenance, Blue Highways, and endless other books, memoirs and diaries, people have been travelling and writing about heading across this vast country since the pioneers. And that's only those that have written books about it. There are countless more backpackers journals, or holidaymakers photo albums containing memories of ordinary folks flirting with adventure and exploration. In most cases, this started with a dream, or an idea, or a plan, and thankfully it came to fruition.

In my case, it started with a kick in the ribs. The morning we were due to head out, Zena and I had crashed out on the mattress I had pulled out of the bedroom and really did not feel like moving. We'd clearly drank more than we should, and I could feel my head a little on the spinning side. She had missed work, it seemed, and was in no more of a hurry to get up than me. However, Neil was quite rightly in a hurry to get going, and called at me a couple of times to get up, which I kind of was unable to do until some strength would magically appear back in my body. Eventually, he gave me a kick in the ribs, which indeed magically made it do just that. I said my goodbyes to the strange little girl, and stood under the shower for a while, hoping that rehydration might work its way in. It didn't.

So rather than the early start we planned, we set off sometime after midday. This fact seemed to really piss Neil off, plus I'd used his apartment maybe a bit too liberally, so as we headed off, there was a bit of a chilled silence in the car between us. I'd love to say that I felt guilty about this, and to a point I did, but my head was way too fuzzy to argue with myself about it. Hence, I found myself nodding off over and over again, eventually giving myself a sore neck. Whenever I did properly fall asleep, Neil seemed to need to listen to the radio pretty loudly, waking me right back up again. Well, I guess I deserved that.

As a result, I didn't see a great deal of the Oregon landscape, but what I did see was a very rugged, quite mountainous land with Pine trees. A hell of a lot of pine trees. With hindsight, maybe I should have made more effort to stay awake. Apparently Oregon comes number six in the list of states with Bigfoot sightings. Granted, number six is a pretty piss poor placing in the sightings scale, but there could be very good reasons for that.

Oregon as a state has been part of the USA since 1859, after the area then known as the Oregon territory within the current boundaries were finalised in around the 1840s. Before that, it had been an area that had seen a fair bit of dispute between the US and

Great Britain for a number of years, both of who felt it was theirs, and neither being too interested in the opinion of any of the local Native Americans who, as it was back then, were not deemed to have an opinion on this. During the exploration of the coast in the 1790's, mainly by ships looking for the Northwest Passage, A British sea Captain, George Vancouver, had laid claim to some of the land he had arrived in via the Puget Sound for the crown. The Americans had come the other way, with the infamous Lewis and Clarke expedition reporting back about the abundance of fur opportunities. Of course, back then the respective Meat Means Murder and Anti-fur lobbies did not exist. Actually they couldn't have really, as they would have either starved or frozen to death, which is a pretty shit way of making a point. So numerous American and British settlers headed out that way, partly by a route known as the Oregon Trail, and began by at first living fairly peacefully together, working and living off the land, and being neighbourly and co-operating to scratch a living, until, as it does, big business stepped in to ruin all that.

In this case it was the fur trading companies, mainly based in St. Louis, who began formalising the trade there, until in 1830, a privateer trapper named Jedediah Smith wrote to the US Secretary of War for President Jackson, recommending that they terminate the treaty of 1818 that had led to both nations peacefully coexisting as it gave Britain too much freedom to exploit the resources in the south. He also mentioned that the native Americans favoured the Brits to the Americans, which may or may not be true, as I imagine they were a bit pissed off with both of them. So tensions began to arise, and British fur interests decided that the thing to do would be to create a fur desert, to halt their American counterparts, and set about trapping and killing all the animals along the southern and eastern borders until there was nothing left.

In the end it was futile, as during the 1830s thousands of Anglo-American settlers began arriving and occupying, and doing whatever things settlers did and dominating the southern regions, until the signing of the Oregon Treaty of '46. However, let's be clear; They had trapped and killed ALL the furry things they could find, meaning some bunch of jobsworths would no doubt have taken that instruction pretty literally. We'll never know, but Sods law would say that that would have been the time that a lost tribe of Sasquatch's may have decided to come clean and introduce themselves, resulting in a rather unfortunate culling. This is very likely the reason that Oregon comes a pitiful 6th in the sightings ratings.

Of course, I'd imagine that all that culling of anything with fur probably went down with the animal population about as well as the carve up of land went with the indigenous folk. In fact, there are clues that the fear of retribution became so prevalent in some communities that to this day it is against the law in Myrtle Creek to box with a kangaroo. This could be seen as worrying a bit too much, but then you can never be too careful.

Around about the time we crossed the state line into Idaho, Neil had begun to feel a little more cheerful. Or I was a bit more awake. Probably a mixture of both. The land appeared to change slightly as well. It seemed to be a lot more agricultural than where we had left. I mentioned this.

"Yep, that'll probably be potatoes. Last month and September was the big harvest time for them."

I had, as I tend to do whilst on the road, lost a bit of my sense of time, but a few weeks before we had left it had been Halloween, and I'd seen a hell of a lot of people out trick or treating. This had really only just begun to take off in the UK, as it displaced our traditional Bonfire night in the UK. Bonfire night, or Guy Fawkes night, had been a big thing when I'd been growing up. We kids would make a Guy Fawkes effigy out of old rags, and wheel him around asking complete strangers to give us a penny for the guy. This was totally encouraged by the same parents who warned us never to talk to strangers, though back then they never actually said why. I figured that it was because it must be rude, and found that when strangers spoke to me, I thought they must be being rude, even though they didn't sound like they were. But anyway, the run up to Guy Fawkes night was apparently a free pass to talk to strangers, and even ask them for money, which was something else that our parents told us never to accept off strangers, also without telling us why.

Then come bonfire night, the country would go out into their gardens, light a glorious fire, set off fireworks, cook baked potatoes on the fire, and maybe sausages, then a nation of fairly religiously tolerant folk who didn't really trust the government would throw the effigy of a catholic who tried to blow up parliament onto the fire, and cheer as he caught light. That included ourselves and the other good Irish folk of County Coundon, who would 'ooooo' and 'aaaaaaa' at the fireworks celebrating the failure of Mr Fawkes and his rebels to change the status quo. We couldn't stay up too late if November the fifth fell midweek, as everyone had to get to work to moan about their taxes, and the government, and all the other things Mr Fawkes had wanted to change, and we had just burned him for it.

So, with Halloween just behind us, I now knew it was November, and that meant, in Idaho, that the potato crops had been mainly harvested, and the local economy would be booming.

We eventually came across Boise, the state capital, and decided that it would be a good idea to get ourselves some digs for the night. The last couple of hours had looked like it was going to rain pretty heavily at some point, so we found a motel on the edge of town, booked in, then headed into the city to get something to eat. It seemed a pretty pleasant type of place, a lot of trees and greenery I noticed, though I would catch the odd whiff of something now and then I couldn't quite identify. We got a meal, then decided to have just a quick drink in a bar, as we planned on a long drive tomorrow.

The bar we walked into seemed nice and relaxed, and people nodded at us in a friendly manner. I liked this place. We sat on a couple of stools on the bar, and mused on the drive so far. My accent caught the bartender's attention, and she asked me where I was from, then told me it was England. She then announced to the bar that I was from London before I answered.

"So," a friendly looking old timer a couple of seats up began," What brings you to Boise?"

"Hey, don't worry, Jack. The British aren't coming."

This seemed to amuse a fair amount of people within listening distance.

"Do you know where my great grandparents were from?" He asked, and actually seemed to be waiting for me to tell him.

"No. No I don't."

"Cornwall. Do you know Cornwall?"

"Yes, I do. In the south. One of the few places in the UK that they surf."

"Do you know why they came here?"

Again, I didn't.

"Mining. Actually, it might be my great, great grandparents. I'm not sure. But the mines all closed in Cornwall, and lots of Cornishmen came out here. My family was in Silver Valley. Lots of mining work back then."

"Ok...So, what's your family name?" I inquired.

"Perrault."

"Perrault? That sounds sort of French?"

"It is. A lot of my family were French Canadians too. They came here first, the Canadians, into Idaho. Well, after the Indians I suppose. Do you know why?"

Ashamed of my ignorance about this charming fellow's family history, I decided to hazard a guess.

"Er, Potatoes?"

"No. Not potatoes. Do you know who brought potatoes to Idaho?"

I didn't bother to answer. He was going to tell me anyway.

"Missionaries. Christian Missionaries. Mainly a feller called Henry Spalding. A lot of folk assume he was a farmer, but he was actually a missionary. He brought potatoes to show the Nez Perce Indians that they could live better from agriculture. Made a bit of a bad job of it though, the crop failed the first year. I guess he didn't get too many converts. Trouble was, he was up north. The soil is no good up there. That's how you know he wasn't a farmer. But anyhow, the real farmers started improving the irrigation systems, and they planted even more potatoes. Soon the whole state was growing them, especially in the south and the east."

"And did the Indians begin living better through agriculture after that?"

Jack pondered this.

"Y'know, I really don't know. Railroads were being built then, by a lot of them Chinese fellers, and everyone was coming here. Germans, Swedes, you name it. Guess by that time it was too late to convert them. Though I wouldn't be surprised if the Mormons had a good go."

We finished our drinks, said goodbye, and headed back to the motel. Funny thing was, I woke up the next morning, and really fancied a baked potato.

Utah was our next destination, but a couple of hours drive down interstate 84 saw us pulling up in a place called Twin Falls. We figured we'd get some breakfast there and maybe get a look at Snake Canyon. This had sounded familiar to me, but it wasn't till arriving there that I remembered why. As a 13 year old lad, back in 1974, the world's imagination had been gripped by a motorcycle riding stuntman called Evel Knievel making an attempt to jump this canyon on what was called a specially adapted motorcycle that in fact appeared to be a kind of rocket. Evel held a place, and maybe still does in the Guinness book of Records as having the most broken bones inflicted by himself in a single lifetime.

That does, with reflection, make you wonder if he was a very good stuntman, or just a famously clumsy one, but nevertheless he was a total hero to loads of us kids in school, all of whom were quite determined we would be like that when we grew up, and would ride our bicycles over all sorts of rough terrain as a kind of practice, though with none of us attempting anything really risky except for my friend Colm who once decided he would try to jump over the Coventry canal. Now, this was by no means any great wide chasm, but adults warned us not to swim in it, not so much as they feared us drowning – adults seemed oblivious to those sorts of dangers back then – but more that it was so dirty we'd probably be sick if we fell in. Being sick back then was, from a kids point of view, no bad thing. You got the day of school, a blanket and pillow on the couch, the choice of afternoon TV shows, and a bottle of Lucozade. There was always the bottle of Lucozade. This was well worth being sick for, as not only did it taste better than most other fizzy pops, but in the days of glass bottles it came wrapped in a sort of coloured cellophane wrapper. Only the folk we considered the rich people had coloured tv's back then, so we would wrap this stuff over our eyes and viola, out black and white telly's, were now in colour. Just one, mind, amber, but nevertheless a marked improvement we considered. Though our mothers would tell us to get it off our faces if they saw us, mainly as it was felt that Lucozade would cease to be a miracle cure for all illnesses if it was just sat in a clear bottle.

Anyway, inspired by Evel's failure to jump over the Canyon sitting on the back of a rocket – unfortunately the parachute opened up too quickly, and he kind of nosedived slowly down into the river, just missing the rocks – we set about building a kind of ramp out of any old rubbish we could find, intending to all jump over the canal, especially if Colm made it first. He did, after all, have the best bike, a nice new racer. So after some very badly planned construction work, our ramp was ready, and Colm took a few practice runs at the ramp to make sure he could get his speed up, then went at it with gusto. Deep down, we all figured that he'd probably not make the other side, but if he got over half way it would be a win. And who knows, he hadn't been stupid enough to put a parachute on the back, so he was in with a chance. Unfortunately, he kind of lifted off the platform and pretty much went headfirst into the canal after maybe travelling about 2 feet. We naturally all laughed, and abandoned our plans to have a go ourselves as the ramp collapsed as he left it, which for months afterwards he blamed the failed attempt on. Anyway, he wasn't in school the next day, probably due to swallowing a lot of the canal water, so I imagine he was propped up on the couch, drinking Lucozade and watching Crown Court in amber.

So a bit of exploring, and we aimed at Salt Lake city, but after crossing into Utah, we came across a place called Brigham City where we decided we would get a room for the night, have some dinner, and maybe a few drinks in town, then make a big push for the Grand Canyon in the Morning.

"You know, I think I might try my new trousers," I decided.

"The ones from the shop? Sure, why not!"

I'd found that being back in Portland, I'd really begun to get my punk on again. Though at home I still wore my jeans a bit tighter than what was the current norm, and alternated between short bleached hair and a totally shaved nut, there weren't really what you'd call punk places to go, and certainly not a scene as there had been back in the day. So I'd been pleasantly surprised how big it all seemed in Portland when I arrived, though of course it could be that we were based around Neil's friends and the Alternative States of Mind shop so it was right in front of me. But I liked it, and had spotted a pair of leather jeans in the shop that I bought on a bit of an impulse. I'd always wanted a pair when I was younger, but never really got round to buying any. I had no idea where I was going to wear these when I got home, but I was still Djing so I could afford to look cool anywhere. Or look like an idiot, depending on who was doing the looking. Apparently that's not all I looked like, as when we went into a bar after a bit of food, a guy at the bar sitting alone decided to enquire, as he eloquently put it, if we were a pair of faggots.

"Only when I wear leather."

"What?"

"Yes, only then. I'm completely straight in denim, but like to go looking for a bit of bum fun when I wear leather jeans. How about yourself?"

"I aint no faggot!"

"Oh? Then how come you're trying to find out who's gay or not?. Hey, don't be embarrassed, I'm in leather today."

"Fuck off, man."

" I will. Sorry, bud, but well….you're not really our type, y'know? We like our guys a bit more manly."

The bartender interjected and told the eejit to shut up and drink his drink, which he did whilst muttering something.

It had caught the attention of two girls who invited us over to their table, and introduced themselves as Kathy and Marie.

"And do I hear a slight trace of an accent there, Kathy?" I asked the young lady who invited us over, a pretty black haired girl in her early 20's who had the look of someone who had maybe been a bit punky herself at some time.

"You do," she said, "Irish, but I have been here since I was a little girl."

"Are you two Mormons?" Neil asked, smiling. Utah is apparently the only state where more than half the population are all members of the same religion. In this case the Church of Latter Day Saints, or Mormons as I know them by. The first Europeans here were the Spanish, who made it part of New Spain, but it later became part of Mexico. It was during this time that many Americans, particularly Mormons, began settling there, often to escape persecution in other American territories. It was after the Mexican-American war of 1848 that it was annexed by the US as the Utah Territory, though not allowed statehood till the practice of polygamy was allegedly abandoned and outlawed in 1896. It was this that Neil picked up on.

"No, Marie laughed, "we are not saints."

"We sure as hell aren't" Kathy interceded, and the girls began laughing. "Why, would it bother you if we were?"

"Hey, not at all. I like the idea of two wives," he joked. "I was thinking you two would be great!"

"Honey, then you'd have our two mothers as your in-laws. We wouldn't wish that on anyone."

We went on to have fun with our two new friends, and they asked us about going onto another bar. I wavered a bit, knowing I'd pissed Neil off on the night we set off, but he seemed pretty keen to go on so the girls took us around and showed us a few of their haunts, all of which were fairly quiet, till we got to a place where a local band were playing, and the atmosphere was pretty kick ass. Turns out that I was right, Kathy had been a bit of a goth in her teens, in Chicago, before moving out here. I'm guessing that it was not to escape persecution, as she was a pretty robust looking woman who looked like she could have your back in a knife fight.

By the time we left the gig, we had pretty much paired up with the girls, Neil with Marie, and myself with the Irish girl. We were also pretty drunker than we had planned, and pretty much open to suggestions. This turned out to be Marie going back to the hotel with Neil, and me going back to Kathy's.

"Now remember," Neil emphasised, "We have a long drive tomorrow, so you need to be back at the hotel early. And I mean early. I'm gonna head off at 7.00, and if you're not there, I'll meet you at the Canyon."

I naturally agreed, and watched as they jumped in a cab to our digs on the edge of town. We got the next one, and headed back to Kathy's, which appeared to be in the other direction. Time had passed by quickly, and it was already the wee small hours.

"How easy is it getting a cab from where you live?" I asked her.

"Oh, pretty bad at the time you're thinking. No one ever answers the phone, and there is nowhere to flag one."

I had a word with the cab driver, to see if he could pick me up at 6, which was only a few hours away it seemed, but he was finishing his shift."

"But my friend is on at that time. I'll get him to pick you up then. I can let him know on the radio."

"Cheers, mate. It's pretty important."

"You gotta catch a plane or something?"

"No, but things might come flying at me if I'm late this time." I was sure Neil wouldn't set off without me, but hell, you never know…

Getting out of the cab we walked to the door of Kathy's house, when she then decided to let me know that she lived with her mother, so we had to be really quiet. Damned, that really hadn't been my plan at all.

So we kind of sneaked in, and went straight to her room. I guessed a cup of tea was out of the question, though I did insist I needed a pee, which she sort of argued about.

"Well, don't flush too loud then."

I wasn't really sure how to flush quietly, so left that advice and tiptoed into the room. It was then I discovered that perhaps I had been a little hasty wearing my new leather jeans. It was a warm night, and I was a bit sweaty, and I suddenly found getting out of the damned things was not that easy, especially trying to be quiet. I had also somehow managed to get a knot in one of my Doc Martens laces, and seemed to spend forever struggling with these two problems. Finally, undressed, I got into bed where we began to embrace....

Creak.

Oh yes. The bed was some olde worlde thing with really creaky springs.

"Shhh"

I embraced slower.

Even louder and longer creak.

"Fuck. Shhh. You'll wake me ma."

Even slower embrace. In fact, slow motion.

A creak so loud it would awaken the dead. Or an Irish mother.

It was too late.

"KATHY? Is that you?"

She beckoned me to lie really still. Hell, that was no great leap.

"Yes, Mum."

"What's all that noise in there?"

It was the first Irish accent I'd heard in quite a while, and just to rub salt in the wound, sounded remarkably like my own mother. It took me right back to a similar situation when I'd gone back to my parents' house whilst they were out, with my first ever girlfriend and we'd gone to my room for a spot of loud noisy embracing. Being younger and full of laddish hormones, this had gone on for some time, till I heard my mother shout up the stairs to shut up, as we had company. I hadn't even heard her come in. We both sheepishly ventured down, to see my mother with a look of thunder sitting drinking tea with 3 elderly female relatives over from Belfast who beamed politely at me and said hello, cups and saucers in hand. I said a friendly hello and left, but boy, did I hear about that when I got home later.

"Nothing Mum, I just feel a bit sick."

"Have you been out drinking again?"

"Just a couple Mum. I'm alright."

I heard the mother wander off to the kitchen, as it was one of those American apartment houses and all the rooms were on one floor. Kathy told me that her mum would just get a cup of tea then go back to sleep, and she'd be out like a light.

She didn't. She seemed to wander around making odd noises here and there, quite clearly wide awake. I was aware that my taxi would be coming soon too. I shrugged at Kathy and decided to start pulling my clothes back on as quietly as I could. Clearly men were a no-no for Kathy, who by this time was beginning to drop off and snore anyway. I figured that I'd wait till the mum went back to her room, give it 5 minutes then sneak out of the door and wait outside.

Too late. There was a horn honking outside. Kinda rudely, I thought. And try as I might, I could not get the stupid leather trousers to pull up! They had been tight when I first put them on, but they seem to have shrunk completely now.

Then there was a knock on the door. I heard the mother mutter something, and go and open it.

"It's your cab. I honked, but maybe you didn't hear?"

"A cab? What would I want with a cab at 6 o'clock in the morning?"

"So not for you?"

"Of course not. What would I want with a cab at this time, for sure. I think you've got the wrong house, mister."

"Ok, sorry to trouble you. I'll check my pad."

"Shit," I thought, knowing I had to get out of there and back to the hotel. There was a knock on the bedroom door. Like in some poor comedy, I stood behind the door, trousers half up and clutching my Doc's so she wouldn't see me.

"Kathy," she called in, opening the door only slightly. "Did you order a bloody taxi at 6 o'clock in the morning?"

"No Mum. Of course not."

Then I guess my hiding wasn't so good, as the door opened wider and suddenly a very angry looking face on what must have been a remarkably small person was looking right up at me.

"And I don't suppose YOU ordered a taxi at 6 o'clock in the morning, did you?"

I sort of looked back at her.

"Oh. Is my taxi here then?"

And with that I kind of shuffled and bounced out, leather jeans still not pulled up, boots still in hand, and went straight out the front door. The cab was still sitting there. I bounced towards it, calling out. He looked at me getting in in a kind of disapproving way, took the name of the hotel, and off we went, as I finished getting dressed.

"You might want to consider a better pair of pants," he stated.

I couldn't really argue.

I met up with Neil back at the hotel, who was alone, but wearing a big grin. First things first, I changed out of the leather jeans and into a much more manageable denim version. I made a mental note to not wear those for the rest of the trip. If indeed ever again. Quick shower first, of course, and we were on our way.

We took Highway 15, and that took us straight through Salt Lake City.

"I have to say," I mentioned to Neil, "That considering how long we were out, you look remarkably fresh."

"That's because I switched to non-alcoholic beer at one point. I knew we had to be driving early. You kinda look like shit."

I did. I mentioned that a decent breakfast was probably in order, so we stopped at a truck stop somewhere outside a town called Provo, and sat ourselves down. There on the menu was something called the Mountain Man Breakfast, which struck us as a pretty good option.

It was. And here I found one of these giant plates of food that I'd heard all about in the states, once you get out of the cities. Now I can eat, but this meal was possibly the largest amount of food I had ever seen on one plate in my life. Still, we gave it a good go. By the end, neither of us could actually finish, but at some point we had ceased talking and began a sort of communication by sweat instead. This involved looking at each other, nodding whilst chewing, and observing how much perspiration was pissing out of each other's foreheads, suggesting that we were now eating not through hunger, but some kind of stubbornness and grim determination not to be beaten. Till we were. Finally, in silence, we both sat back and congratulated each other on how well we had done in eating what would feed a hungry family for a week.

"Are you guys done with those?" The waitress asked, and topped our coffee up before whisking the remains of our banquet away. We sipped our coffee, trying to digest our breakfast, and making odd huffing and puffing noises. We were just remarking how that would probably do us for the day when the waitress came back.

"Hi again," she said, smiling whilst putting two large plates with things the size of 12" pizzas down in front of us.

"Here's your pancakes. I'll bring the syrup."

We couldn't do it. We began to sweat looking at them, and decided to get back on the road before lord knows how many other courses came out. Mountain Man? Whoever could eat these must be man mountains, more likely. But hell, it was great food, and so set up for the day, we topped up on fuel, and Neil picked up a cassette tape from the little shop there.

"Now we're on the road," he said, putting it on in the car as we headed off and out came the familiar opening chords of Bad Moon Rising. Yep, he'd picked up a best of Creedence Clearwater Revival tape, and what a background that was. In fact, for the rest of the journey we would pick up more Creedence tapes, or Lynyrd Skynyrd, or anything else that screamed road trip. It really got the mood going.

We stayed on 15, which took us down past the Dixie National Forest, Cedar City and Zion National Park. None of these we actually entered, but I was impressed by the changing scenery along the route we were taking, and stopped along the way many a time to take in some pretty good views. We changed at Hurricane to Route 59, and just kept going till we reached the North Rim of the Grand Canyon, sometime in the evening. Which was great, except neither of us had realised that there was not actually a town as such there, and we would be needing lodgings. So we drove back to a place we had spotted, about 40 miles back, called Jacob's Lake Inn. I was beginning to get the differences between short American journeys, and short British ones. If back home someone said they had spotted a place about 40 miles back, this would cause a big groan, and seem like the end of the world. In fact, It's about the distance from the Coventry end of the West Midlands county and the Wolverhampton end, taking in Solihull, Birmingham, and West Bromwich along the way. Americans will just shrug and say it's only – only, no less – 40 miles and cheerfully head on. Which we did.

We got ourselves a room, and decided on an early night. Well I did, Neil was still a lot fresher than me, and the idea of a hot shower and a comfortable bed after last night's shenanigans seemed mighty appealing. It was about 8 or 9 hours after our enormous breakfast, and I did wish I'd brought those pancakes along now, so we grabbed some rather expensive dinner, and I decided on spec to give Zena a ring on the payphone in the lobby. We chatted for a bit, then she told me she was off to the Vern. I suddenly missed Portland. Just for a moment though. We were on the road, and would be staring into the Grand Canyon tomorrow. Life was good.

So it was back the way we came, and a nice early start took us to the North Rim of the Canyon. I hadn't, and I am not sure Neil had either, realised that there is quite the difference between the two sides. Apparently the South is where "All the action is", as someone later put it. But as we were coming from the North, this is the side we were on, and what a stroke of luck. There were hardly any people around. We were literally a day or so off when they closed access to the North rim in mid-November, apparently due to problematic weather conditions. Well, you wouldn't know it now. It was a glorious day, and the view was incredible. And the echo! We naturally shouted stuff just to hear it and with no one to disturb us.

I found myself revisiting an old feeling. There are two types of ancient places. There are the ones that our ancient ancestors built, and the ones that the earth created long, long before the ancestors of humanity existed. Both bring on a feeling of awe and a kind of peace that you can only feel in these places. You go quiet. You walk away from whoever you are with, and feel this on your own. Yet you're not alone at all. You're connected with those that came before, or with the Earth itself. I would say it was very zen, but I've never been quite sure what that is. But time stands still for a moment, and the feeling you experience burns into your soul. The moment will then last forever. I walked a little way by myself, and experienced just such a moment.

I was minded of other occasions during my shenanigans when that feeling happened. In Bethlehem. Ayers Rock. Swimming in the Barrier reef. Victoria Falls. The Pyramids. Looking into the Canyon brought it all back. There is quite a bit of debate on the actual age of the Canyon, as we know it now. For a long time, scientists have believed it took about 5 – 6 million years for the Colorado River to wear its way down to the depth of over a mile down where it flows now. However, recent tests on caves have placed their origins at about 17 million years old, and other experts have argued it's maybe as old as 70 million years. Either way, it existed before humans had evolved, but has been home, amongst the caves, to Native Americans for a few thousand years. The first European, a Spaniard, first set eyes on it in 1540. I'm not sure, but he probably claimed it. People tended to do that back then.

It opens the question of how fascinated and drawn to these ancient sites we are. Canyons, waterfalls, caves systems, mountains, deserts. Where nature has created, or let be created, these extreme places, people are drawn to them. Why? Maybe because they show us our place in the scheme of things. They weren't built for us, and could well outlive us. And over the billions of years of Earth's geology, how many other extreme places existed for millions or tens of millions of years before changing that no human, or in some cases, no animal ever saw. Not for tourists. Not to boost an economy. And thankfully, never were recreated in plastic in a snow globe. We'll never know. They weren't for us, hard as it is to believe.

Yes, this had been a good place to come to.

After soaking it up, we both reluctantly and excitedly left, and began the 200 mile plus journey round to the South rim. We were stopping off too, at Angel point, at Cape Royal, through the painted desert and past Marble Canyon, where we crossed the Colorado. Most of this falls in the territory of the Navajo Indian reservation, an area of some 25,000sq miles. It was along this route that for the first time ever in being in the US, on any occasion that I first saw an actual Native American. I hadn't realised this till we drove past a little stall by the side of the road selling nick-nacks. We pulled up, and a large guy and presumably his wife in what I took to be traditional clothing stood and looked miserably at us. I was quite taken with just how much cheap tack for stupidly expensive prices was on sale. I felt a bit guilty though, as no one else was there, we were in the middle of nowhere, and this couple looked, well, very solemn. I bought a dreamcatcher. This is a traditional bit of woven something or other with a kind of netting and a few feathers hanging off it that is hung over your bed, or a baby's cradle, allegedly for protection. Protection from what, I'm not actually sure. Maybe evil spirits or something. Though why an evil spirit, on sneaking up to you in your sleep to do mischievous evil spirity things, would spot a bit of willow with a kind of spider web on it and think, "Fuck me, a dreamcatcher...I'd better piss off back to the damnation from which I came" I'm not exactly sure. Unless, of course, they are allergic to the feathers, in which case a good feather filled pillow should pretty much have the same effect, though Mr and Mrs Grumpy probably aren't going to tell you that. Interestingly, as we drove off, a little way down the road we saw a sign they had put up on the other side of the road with LOOK OUT. FRIENDLY INDIANS AHEAD written on it. I'm guessing that the Navajo Nation didn't include a version of the trades description act in their local laws.

It was evening when we reached the other side, where we took a look at the falls at Desert View. This was completely different from our experience in the morning. It was absolutely choc-a-bloc with tourists and though the view was no less impressive, there was no real way that you could enjoy the serene feeling of communion that I had had on the other side, and we had paid a $10 entrance fee at the desert view entrance to the national park for the privilege. To be fair, this is a pretty reasonable fee which allowed for 7 days access, though I hope that doesn't apply to any Pueblo peoples who still make pilgrimages to the Canyon as they saw it as a holy site. I bet they didn't end up taking a bloody dreamcatcher back home out of guilt.

We headed up to Bright Angel lodge where we managed to get ourselves a damned fine cabin for only $30 each. Probably as the drive to here had been a nightmare, with the sun blazing in our eyes the whole way, this place seemed to be just what we were after. And just to add to the feeling of adventure, there they were.

Backpackers. The familiar look of young explorers excitedly getting themselves ready for their escapades brought a happy beam to my face. I smelt adventures.

We found a pretty decent restaurant there ,and splashed out on an expensive, but pretty fine meal of chilli, mashed spud and gravy, corn on the cob and a beef stew, all of which they called a bread dish. This was due to it actually coming in a dish made out of bread. Brilliant. The novelty of this really impressed me, and I considered that it was basically a fat bastard's dream. I've seen myself finish a meal off to the point of mopping up every last bit of food and gravy with half a loaf, and even use the edge of the knife to scrape the very last tiniest morsel. Oddly, if I was eating out and doing this, someone would still come over and ask if everything with my meal had been OK. I'd usually answer by showing them my bleeding tongue, and nodding whilst perusing the pudding menu. I was at this point still at an age where I could eat pretty much what I wanted and not gain weight. Boy, that was to change eventually. But here I found myself with a bread plate, and got stuck in, till not a crumb was left. My Mother would have been proud, as there was not a bit left to send to the starving children in Africa, that favourite old threat of mothers everywhere. Not so lucky for the starving kids, mind you, but I daresay the bread would be a bit hard by the time it got there anyway. A few beers, and we dragged our overfed butts back to the cabin and decided on an early start to cover lots of trails.

That was the plan anyway, but in actual fact we slept a lot longer than we figured and ended up wandering a couple of small trails till we picked up on the Bright Angel trail, which was in fact a pretty decent walk, though I discovered that the chilli seemed to have played a bit of havoc with my innards, and seemed to want to turn into unstoppable flatulence only as we passed other people. Still it was a beautiful sunny day again, and we got quite caught up with the amount of people heading off to go down into the canyon, something we hadn't planned on. We figured we would go just a short way down, just so we could say we had, as we were aware we were completely inappropriately dressed, with no walking shoes, hiking gear or even water. There were plenty of signs everywhere warning you not to go down into the Canyon without water. Or food. But down we went anyway.

"Hey," Neil enthused as we reached a rather scenic place to look at the other side, where we had been yesterday." We should turn back here…"

"We should."

"Maybe just a little way more?"

"Yep. Why not? Just a little way."

And so it went on. It didn't seem so bad, though by the time we decided that we really should go back up, we'd passed a couple of signs warning us about water. But hell, we were young (ish) and fit (ish) and knew we would be fine. So we took in the last view for a while, and then began to head back up. We'd probably been walking down for about an hour, and it really hadn't seemed so bad. We'd even chuckled at the people who were doing it by mule. Actually, I felt a bit sorry for the mules. There were some pretty large people on them, who looked like they had definitely eaten their plates over the years, whether they were made of bread or not. No way would I ride one of them, I thought, If I couldn't do it myself I wouldn't get on a poor creature to do it.

We'd been walking back up for only about 20 minutes when it began to dawn on us that we were not as fit as we thought – Something I'd found a lot on my shenanigans when it comes to climbing things – and that the elevation seemed a lot steeper going up. Well, that's a bit of a no brainer really, but our initial impulsiveness ignored that completely. We took a breather, and carried on. The sun had really come out, and it was getting hotter by the minute, it seemed. By the time we took another breather, we were covered in sweat, and I could really feel a thirst coming on. I remembered feeling just like that when climbing Ayers rock back in Australia, but at least there I was going up first, and could have turned back and gone down if need be. This was the other way round of course, so there was no option but to carry on. I'd say it took us probably at least twice as long to get back up, and never did a bottle of water taste so good as when we got to the top and bought a couple.

Though a bloody steep climb back, at least we'd seen a bit of the Canyon. So we sat for a while and I got us a couple of bottles of coke to continue our thirst quenching. We were sitting on a bench, still admiring the view, and I sat down next to Neil and handed him a bottle. I felt very content. Here I was, out at some amazing place I'd never been before, sat with a great friend, we'd been on the road, seen some things, had some laughs, done a couple of daft things which turned out OK. These were indeed the shenanigans that I loved. Only one thing missing from the usual adventures, or rather one recurring character, I thought…

I opened the bottle of coke, and somehow it must have been shaken up. All of a sudden our nice peaceful moment of reflection turned into the pair of us being covered in spraying coke, with us jumping up abruptly and uttering the odd swear word. And there he was. The missing piece of the adventure. Whenever a minor disaster befell me on my travels, there was always a large fat gay guy in a flowery shirt at hand to comment on it. Whether a wheel fell off my bike in Amsterdam while I was on it, or I fell out of a telephone box, or even tumbled off a dancefloor, he was always there. It was uncanny. And sure as hell, just as we stood dripping in coke, a large fat gay guy, but this time in a bright red gilet and a straw sun hat came trotting along in front of us on a mule and said, smiling,

"Ooooo. Well, that'll cool you down. You'll be ever so sticky in this heat though."

I nodded. I would be.

VIII

After a little clean up in the rather decent public toilets, it was back on the road. Headed down 64 till we reached a town called Williams, where we merged onto Interstate 40. The plan was basically a long drive now back to New Jersey, and a lot of it down this interstate. We had stopped to fill up with fuel in Williams, and picked up another Creedence tape for good measure. I was just putting that in the player as we took off when there, right in front of my eyes, was a road sign that made my heart leap a bit. It was a large sign saying Route 66. Well, it did at first glance. What it actually said was Historical Route 66.

I think it's fair to say that Route 66 is probably one of, if not the most famous road in the whole of the states. And it's almost equally fair to say that there is no way you hit that road without singing to yourself the Rolling Stones/Chuck Berry/ Henry troupe or whichever-version-you-know song of the same name. So though the original highway in its original form is gone, there are certainly some parts of it left in one form or another, or its replacements taking the same journey via the interstate network, a part of which we had just arrived on. Yes, there was something pretty cool about hitting Route 66 with your windows down, and the distinctive sound of John Fogerty and the boys blaring out, knowing you had a long road ahead. Though admittedly maybe it's not so cool in a Honda, but hey, you take what you're given.

Amazingly enough, the origins of this esteemed piece of American lore go back to 1857, when the war department commissioned a wagon trail to be built along the 35th parallel. One of the ideas for this had been to test out the feasibility of using camels as pack animals through the south west desert, similar I guess to how the Australians had imported this hardy beast to open up their own lands. This didn't appear to become a thing as such, which is a shame as the whole logo on that other American icon, Camel Cigarettes, could have had the dromedary silhouetted against the Canyon or something, rather than the Egyptian Pyramids. On the downside, the old adventure packed Western films may not have been quite the same with the cowboys galloping slowly along on camelback. However, it did mean that for 10 years, from 1856, the US army did actually have a Camel Corp, up until the civil war. They didn't seem to catch on with the military during this time, though they were used to a point in the war mail service. The bulk of them were at some point captured by the confederate army, who also didn't really get the hang of them. They were eventually sold off at auction, though to whom is a mystery.

Intriguingly, there had been a legend in Arizona of the Red ghost, the spooky apparition of a red camel with a ghostly human skeleton riding it around the borderlands. You can imagine the guys sitting round the camp fires, warning the children of this, maybe even telling them they should go and put their left hand on the skeletons shoulder and ask what in the name of God it wanted. But this legend only lasted till 1893, when a farmer shot dead a camel on his land, and actually found that there was a human skeleton strapped to its back somehow. I guess it didn't want much after that, and any hand laying would have been futile.

This early trail was to become US 66, where after 1913 was to become part of an expansion of roads and routes across the US. It was also the first of these highways to be completely paved. During the 1930's during the era known as the dust Bowl, many farming families used this in route on their way to set up new lives in California. As a result of this, and previous westward traffic, many small businesses set up along the route, which started in Chicago and ran through to Santa Monica in Los Angeles county. It was to provide a life line during the depression, with families making money from the travellers as other means failed. It lasted till the mid 1980's when it was decommissioned as an officially named route, and split into the various highways and interstates that exist in its shadow now. But what a history. And here me and Neil were, cruising along what may well be in the maps as Interstate 40, but as far as we were concerned was Route 66, and we had the music tapes to prove it.

Neil decided to put a good few hours in, and drove straight for 6 hours, taking us through flagstaff, through the Petrified Forest National Park, and over the state line into New Mexico. I think he was smelling home, but we had a long way to go, so we pulled up at a stop just inside Albuquerque. It had been 1926 when the first travellers along Route 66 began to make an impact, and of course the usual motels, restaurants and gift shops had appeared. So a good 70 years of trade had been enjoyed, but looking at the room we got, dusting really hadn't been one of them. Actually, we may have just caught the owners of the motel on a bad day.

"Hi, we need a room. Two singles," we'd asked on arrival.

"Si, sure," the young Hispanic girl answered smiling. She then went on to ask us to fill in a form and got a key ready. This was fine till she read our names on the form. Looking at us, she called out what seemed to be her mother, who came through from the back, read whichever form seemed to be the problem and then they talked in Spanish in a very serious manner whilst looking at us suspiciously.

"Er, is there a problem? I asked.

"No, no. No problem. One moment please.

With that they called out a man who seemed to be the owner who also came from the back, looked at the forms, then seemed to argue with the older woman. All the time we just kind of stood there. Eventually he said something to the younger girl who then smiled at us.

"Here," she said, handing us the key. "Have a great stay."

So with no idea what had just occurred, we went off to the dusty room, showered up, then went out to a place where we had the most fantastic chilli.

"Hey, Mulligan, are you still awake?" I heard Neil ask, just after I'd fell blissfully asleep back in the motel.

"I am now. What's up?"

"Look at that, on the wall."

I reached for my glasses. I was tired, it was dark, and all I could see were two stains in the direction he was pointing. Or at least I thought that's what they were till they ran round each other.

"What the f…." I called out, sitting up.

"Amazing. That's a couple of lizards. I've never seen a lizard before."

It was. A couple of some local lizards playing chase on the wall. I found myself watching them and unable to go back to sleep.

"I'm guessing they are the harmless type," I said to Neil.

There was no answer. Now he was blissfully asleep. Like he'd know anyway, he'd never seen one before.

We weren't that hungry in the morning, so we just grabbed a couple of bags of crisps, or chips as Neil called them, and hit the road. What we hadn't done was pick up some water, and along with the heat, munching on salty potato chips and taking in a fair old bit of flatulence that the pair of us seemed to have from the chilli, we found we really needed a drink by the time we reached

Amarillo, a little over 4 hours later. We had also crossed a state line again, and we were now officially in Texas.

I'd noticed that the landscape had seemed to be getting flatter. Apparently this is because this area of the state is part of the Texas Panhandle, and can be prone to some pretty severe tornadoes. Not so much, luckily enough, around this time of year. We were not going to be here for long, so we just stopped off for food and drink, made sure we had plenty of water this time and headed straight on without stopping till we crossed the line into Oklahoma, and kept going till we reached Oklahoma city. Got a decent room somewhere for the night, and decided to grab a couple of drinks in a bar.

We found a nice place that did a bit of food too, and grabbed a table. Though the weather seemed OK, we were hearing that things may take a bit of a turn for the worst, so we were chatting about this when a couple of guys who looked like a redneck/rock fan cross came over and sat themselves down at the table.

"Are you guys from Scotland?"

"Nope, a bit further south, England…Close," I laughed.

"Cool, man. Mind if we join you?"

We agreed they could, which was a moot point as they were already sitting down. In fairness to them, they even ordered a couple of drinks for us, and seemed friendly enough, though I couldn't help but notice that these were not the two brightest of folk I had ever met. They seemed to start every bit of conversation with a question.

"Hey dude, so the queen? Do you think that she got pissed off when she married her husband, and he automatically became the king?"

"Er, he didn't. He's a prince."

"What, he's like, her son?"

"Hey, dude, so I'm reading a lot about evolution. It's pretty clear that we are all descended from monkeys, but why do you think that someone would fuck a monkey in the first place? Isn't that how aids started?"

"So, have you seen that in Chinese places their menus are in English as well as Chinese? Yet Chinese is supposed to be spoken by more people than any other language. So why do you think they need to read English as well? My Dad thinks they just learn Chinese to piss people off."

I could see by the look on Neil's face that he was beginning to find this as frustrating as I was. I was considering that they were actually not this dumb, but in fact winding us up a bit, when my doubts were put to rest by the last point they raised, and began arguing with each other.

"So, what do you think about cloning? Do you think it's a bit scary?"

"Why?"

"Well, think of the implications. I mean, let's say you cloned yourself, and then fucked yourself and got pregnant. Is that baby going to be unique, or just another clone of you?"

"What? That's not really how cloning works……"

The other guy interceded.

"Yeah, of course it doesn't work like that. It would be two dudes…."

"Ok, I didn't mean that. Let's say you clone a female version of you and fucked her.."

"Oh. Well that's different. But I don't think you could get her pregnant."

"Why not?"

"Like mules. Because they are not natural, they are sterile. Clones are probably sterile."

"Don't be stupid. That's because a mule is a mix of a horse and a donkey. If you cloned yourself and mixed it with monkey DNA, it would probably be sterile, but not just a human."

"Then how did we evolve from monkeys then, if we were sterile. Fuck, man, you're so stupid sometimes. Think it through."

I had so much to say, and could see Neil biting his tongue too, so we decided to leave on that note. We shook hands and went back to the hotel. Last thing we heard the guys say to each other as we left was whether or not if you fuck your identical twin sister, would that be a clone?

We got outside and just began laughing.

The next morning we set off early, and Neil was good for about 13 or 14 hours of driving, stopping just for short rests and food.

We headed into Arkansas, and picked up on Interstate 55 at Little rock, , brushing past the West Memphis Suburbs. I'd have loved to have detoured into Memphis, maybe see sun studios and all the Elvis stuff, but by now Neil was on a mission. About the time we crossed the line into Missouri, the weather had begun to take a turn for the worst. It was getting Stormy, there were some incredible displays of lightning, and we began to get tornado warnings on the radio. Calling in for gas at St. Louis, the woman in the station advised us to stick to '55 as the better route, as the weather was getting bad. We pushed on, and got a room at another Days Inn Motel, and got some well-deserved sleep.

The world had turned white overnight. And icy. This was going to slow us down, but Neil was determined we could do one long drive and get back to New Jersey. I wasn't so sure, but I'd learned to admire his ability to drive for long periods of time. So we gave it a go. Worryingly, we were passing by a hell of a lot of accidents, where cars and even lorries had come off the road. We crossed into Indiana, where we passed through Indianapolis, and the Gas station's advice seemed to be true, and we had avoided the worst of the weather. We passed into Ohio and had just passed Columbus, when our luck ran out. We were on a stretch of the highway that seemed endless, when the snow came down heavier and heavier till we were in a full on Blizzard. We were crawling along, tempers getting a bit frayed between us which was in reality due to the fact we were getting scared. We literally could not see more than a few feet ahead of us, and were driving blind. We had crossed into Pennsylvania at some point, and mindful of all the accident aftermaths we had seen, decided to pull off at the next turn off. We weren't even sure where it was, but ended up behind a snow plough which seemed not a bad idea, but after crawling along for over an hour, with no idea where we were, or if anything was coming up, we pulled over, debating spending the night in the car. However, we knew that we would be covered in snow and invisible in no time, so decided to take a gamble and hit '80 again. Best we could figure out from the map was that we had been not too far from a town along the way. Aware we were in trouble, but running out of options, we slowly made our way back, and again, still driving near blind, found a small town about 4 or 5 miles along with a motel. It was 2.30am, and we had hardly eaten, as we'd been stopping for food rather than carrying any. The motel had a vending machine, so we ate potato chips and chocolate bars, and waited out till the blizzard stopped the next day. We were worried that we would be snowed in, but luckily the road was still usable by the next afternoon.

So we slowly and carefully made our way to the New Jersey border, where we let out a relieved cheer, and didn't stop till we reached Hasbrouck Heights, and Neil's parents' house.. What a relief. Apparently this was a bit of freak weather that had hit this part of the country, and knowing we were on the road they had been more than a little worried. I would be lying if I said that I hadn't been pretty scared during that last leg of the journey, but here we were now, and barely put our stuff down, when we were asked,

"So….you two hungry?"

We were. We really were! So we were whisked out for a great meal, and on returning I think we both slept through till mid-afternoon the next day.

The original Route 66 was 2,448 miles long. People still follow as much of it as they can to this day, as it is embedded in modern American culture. Like so many of the world's great trails, both ancient and modern, it opened up opportunity. It created work. It changed lives. It was, and the route it took still does, create history. We didn't plan to 'do' Route 66. And technically we didn't. But in fact we drove around about 1,180 miles of that journey, from where we got on at Williams after leaving the Grand Canyon, and splitting off at Springfield. And we listened to country rock, we met people and nearly met our maker in the worst storm I had ever seen. We bought trinkets off Cherokee, we slept in motels, and we got to where we were going after a long old drive. So as far as I am concerned, hell yeah, we took Route 66. Hell yeah indeed.

I had my ticket changed to fly home from New York, and spent a couple of days letting Neil catch up with his friends and folk, and found a comfy stool in Monahan's bar again, a place I had visited on my last foray over here. I found I was already looking forward to the coming adventures I was planning. South America was a must, China, and maybe some South Sea Islands. In fact, as ever, I had multiple journeys planned out, that I would scribble in notebooks, or on bits of paper.

And finally it was time to leave and head home. It had been great to see Neil, share a part of his new life in Portland, and feel the warmth of his family again. And shenanigans galore between the two. I did make a last phone call to the strange little girl back in Portland, but her mom told me she was out somewhere. I'm guessing the Vern. Good for her.

I didn't know it at the time, but it would be another 20 years before I saw any of this wonderful, hospitable family again. That of course would be part of another story. Because it is always about the story.

PART 2

The Road to L

I

Arriving back in the UK meant addressing the small matter of employment. My master plan was to pick up whatever work I could to get enough funds for my next adventure out, and taking note of how many times I'd been offered work on my shenanigans – even in Portland a guy in the Vern had said he could fix me up straight away with some building work – I figured it was time to start looking at getting work visas sorted just in case, with a view to maybe heading off on the road for at least a few years, if not forever.

This seemed like a great idea in principle, but to quote good old Rabbie Burns, The Best Laid Plans of Mice and Men. And all that. Now, I'm not sure exactly what sort of plans mice make. Perhaps to go off for a wander around someone's kitchen that they have sneaked into, piss all over the remains of the food that they ate and then leave a few droppings near to where they got in. As plans go, this is a pretty stupid one, as the first sign that we have a vermin infestation is when we spot horrible little pieces of shite lying around the place, and so start getting the traps and/or poison ready.

Clearly mice are not aware of the good old human slogan of don't shit on your own doorstep. Though tending to apply to people who have affairs with their wife's sister, or causing problems for a relative who works with you, it may very well originated back in the day when larger beasties, rather than the wee sleekit, cowrin, tim'rous kind, would sniff the said shite and know where you lived. That plus your wife – because I assume that it would be the bloke who would be more likely to take a dump there – would get pretty pissed at the thought of you treading crap into the carpet.

Not that people always had carpets. Or even floors. For most times, the poorer folk in the world built a shelter, but the floor was simply the ground on which it was built. I've been told this is the origin of the expression dirt poor, which kind of makes sense. Either way, it would have been heavily frowned upon to tread crap into it after letting it all out on the doorstep. In fact you may well have taken a beating with an old wooden broom handle by the missus, causing you to run out and seek solace in the arms of her younger, more attractive sister, and so starting the process of shitting on your own doorstep all over again.

So Mice, it seems, are not the best planners in the world, which is good because though you wouldn't really begrudge them a bit of food, especially scraps you forgot to pick up off the floor when you came in pissed and dropped kebab all over the place, their habit of peeing everywhere, and the horrible smell they leave behind does not make them very endearing. I could never really get why everyone loved Jerry mouse always coming out on top in the old Tom and Jerry Cartoons. It meant that the house and their food were covered in little droppings. More realistically would have been Tom trotting upstairs with the decapitated body of Wee Jerry, and presenting it to his owner as a bit of lunch. He wasn't going to eat it himself of course, because as a house cat he'd rather wait for a pouch of something with gravy to be opened, but it's the thought that counts. Of course, there is an argument that Tom and Jerry were ahead of their time, and Jerry Mouse actually identified as a cat.

My own plans involved neither bad toilet habits, nor decapitated corpses, but rather raising some funds to get back out there. I took on a bit more DJ work, and as is the way these things go, one of the venues I was working in found itself looking for a new manager, due to the last few they had had not getting on with the owners of the bar. It had been a busy biker bar in its day, with a lot of rock music, so naturally had been a place of mismatching furniture and terrible toilets. However, trade had died off, as a lot of the old regulars had simply grown older, and the bad vibe between various biker groups had split the remainder. Having harboured a notion for a few years of running a bar or pub, I stepped in. It didn't last for long, as like everybody else I didn't get on with the owners either, but it led to me applying to one of the big breweries, and I suddenly found myself a publican.

Not just a publican. I had started to see one of the younger punk girls who came down to one of my nights around the same time, and I found myself a dad-to-be. I already had at least two lads that I knew of from a couple of failed relationships, but never-the-less it was time to have another go, in spite of the 17 year age gap between me and my girlfriend.

It didn't last. I have concluded that I am not very good at relationships. Or rather, I'm good at them till you reach that point where you have basically become two people who live in the same house and most of the conversations revolve around asking each other what we should have to eat. However, we had two daughters before we broke up, and this time I was determined to be a proper part of their lives. This I did, even becoming a single parent for a while when they got older.

It also meant that all my travel plans went right out of the window. And rightly so, it has to be said. The pub career also didn't last more than a couple of years, I'd possibly gone in at the wrong time, especially with a baby, and so after a few jobs via agencies I finally settled at a place that was a feeder plant to Jaguar Land-rover. So that was it then. Unlike a lot of my friends whom I had grown up with in County Coundon, I had kind of avoided the car factories. By now, the Coventry car industry as it was in my youth was truly a long time behind us, but there were still a fair few places that were involved. So, long after everyone else, the career advice from school bit me right in the ass, and there I was in the glamorous world of wheel and tyre assembly, without a plane ticket to my name.

At the time, I didn't actually notice that my adventures and shenanigans had somewhat slowed down. The thing about raising the wee ones is that they take up quite a lot of your valuable time, and prove to be quite the distraction to anything else that you may have had in mind. When they were very young, we took them on holidays to English seaside towns. Whenever I hear about seaside towns, the word quaint tends to be prefixed, but this wasn't quite the way I'd describe them. On one such holiday, there was a typical amusement arcade on the front that had the loudest fruit machine I have ever heard, playing the opening bars from The Addams Family over and over and over again, all day until it closed. It could be heard wherever you were on the beach. I don't understand how this did not drive local residents insane. I cannot even remember exactly what town we were in, but I still hear that accursed machine to this day, whenever anything reminds me of the Addams family, or seaside's, or fruit machines. I swear, if I lived there I'd have bought a shotgun and destroyed the thing one day. We also went out to places like the West midlands Safari Park, or the Sealife Centre now and then.

"Hey kids, see those lions? I was trapped in a toilet by a lion in Africa once."

"Did it try to eat you?"

"Ha-ha. It would have liked to."

"Do they eat rabbits?"

"Er, I don't know. Probably, yes."

"Oh." Sad Silence. "That's a shame. Can we go to the petting zoo and see the rabbits now?"

"Hey Kids, see how big those sharks are? Well, I was in Portland a while ago, and we went out on a boat and saw whales. They are huge. Massive. I saw one come right out of the sea and stick its bum in the air."

"Are they bigger than dinosaurs?"

"Er, yes, I think some of them are."

"Have you ever seen a dinosaur?"

"Ha-ha. No, I'm not that old."

"Oh." Disappointed silence. "Can we get a goldfish?"

I have UK size 9 feet. I have had the same size feet since I was at school, so every bit of foreign soil I have ever set foot on and explored, I have done it with the same size feet. Buy a new pair of Doc Martens, they are size 9, trainers, size 9, work boots, size 9. They never vary. But though I wasn't particularly aware of the kids getting taller, I couldn't help but notice that they went through a remarkable amount of shoes.

"They need new shoes," their mother would constantly tell me, up until and long after we split up. "They have outgrown the ones you got them last month. So about 4 times a year, I duly coughed up for new, bigger shoes. Which was odd, as there are only about 14 sizes for children, so by the time they had reached a point where they no longer outgrew shoes, but simply wanted more expensive ones, my maths made it that my daughters must have had about UK size 25 feet, which would put them at sasquatch status, and about 8ft tall. They are neither, so I wonder why they kept on outgrowing shoes so often? I guess the only alternative to this would be if they were some kind of genetically footed clowns.

They were not. However, I myself did flirt with the world of clowning. Clearly with a lack of travelling shenanigans to occupy my time, I accidentally became an adult clown for a number of years. This came about as a result of Windows making computers accessible to pretty much anybody. Back in the early days of PC's for all, social media was still a long way off, and the servers themselves hosted message boards and chat rooms and such. If I'm being honest, I actually bought my first PC as a result of Lucky Andy and others telling me how easy it was to access porn, and so I got all the kit, installed AOL and needed a user name/Email address. The week before getting it I had been watching some channel 4 TV show about unusual fetishes, and my ears pricked up when an article about clown orgies came up.

Clown Orgies? How had I never heard of this before? Basically, all these people met up somewhere dressed as clowns, and you could be porking someone from behind when someone would come up and shove a pie in you or your partner's face. There was a lot of usage of balloons and custard too. Here was the holy trinity of everything I love - sex, humour and bizarre situations - all in one. This was, quite frankly, a game changer.

With this fresh in mind, my AOL identity became Frisky the Clown. I suddenly had a new persona, and hit the message boards as Frisky the clown, agony clown. People bought into it, and would send me their problems.

Dear Frisky, my girlfriend wants to try anal sex, but I can't afford the lubricant. What do you recommend? – Backman.

Dear Backman. Try rubbing your genitals with hummus or taramosalata. I think you'll find this perfect for a Greek dip.

Dear Frisky, My wife hates the hours I work, and has said it's me or the job. Which should I choose? – Milkman Mike.

Dear Milkman Mike, you need to think that if they both suck, choose your wife. If neither do, then it's your job.

These early message boards were great. People made friends, some met up, the only thing you had in common was the server, or a website with a group you had joined. It was great fun, and personalities shone through, without you ever knowing the other people in real life. We weren't to know it, but there were soon -to-be powerful people who meant well, but were clearly social inadequates jumping on this, preparing new types of social sites that meant you could start to connect with people you knew, hardly knew, didn't know but knew you, and other people that you had no idea where they came from. Everyone jumped on this, and the days of making new friends were left behind as people attacked each other, realised that outside of pubs their friends were complete dicks, bored the arse off each other with uniformed causes, and decided that birthdays were now not about getting them a drink if you saw them, but being guilted into giving to the charity of the said birthday persons choice. The world became a more horrible place, as friends set out to convince everyone they knew that their lives were awful, life was terrible, and everything they thought they liked was actually a blight on the planet. But this was still to come, and at this point, these early days were fun, and it was great while it lasted.

Then, in that way that one thing leads to another, a girl I was seeing at the time was working in a local alternative clothing shop and all the staff had been given free tickets to a new club that opened in Birmingham called Scarlet. Not just a club, but a fetish club, no less, that had an outrageous clothes only door policy, goth and dance DJ's, dungeon areas and live shows of all sorts. I had literally no idea of what to wear to such a place, so went to the first one in drag, complete with long wig, high boots, and had even decided to shave myself completely. Completely. That in itself turned out to be a particularly stupid thing to do, due to the itching as my body hair all grew back, but also because of the fact that I was not exactly what guys who dress as women regularly would call convincing. And I kept falling over – how the hell do girls walk in heels? - including falling down the stairs in the club. It was a hopeless attempt at being a drag queen, never to be repeated, probably to the relief of the genuine Drag Queens and transvestites who would view me as a complete eejit.

So the next time we went to this club – and I wasn't going to miss it as my outfit aside, it had been the best night I had had out in years – I needed a new look. So Frisky the Clown came off the internet, and became a real character. Bowler hat with flower on, string vest, face paint, a pair of long stripey socks, Doc Martens, lots of studded belts and wristbands and finally a pair of rubber pants with a dick in front that was the only thing I had to buy, which I got from local sex shop lite retailer, Anne Summers. It was an outfit hurriedly hobbled together, yet I felt a lot comfier and strangely, on checking the website for photos a week later, I found I had won the costume of the night prize, granting me free access to the next event.

This must have been quite annoying to all the people that had spent literally hundreds of pounds, maybe more, on some fantastic rubber and leather outfits. It certainly surprised me. But it had the knock on effect of me deciding that instead of a one-off fetish clown visit, I would stick to it as it seemed to capture people's imaginations. Plus I could get in free at the next one.

Interestingly, going to these events seemed to open up a whole new world of shenanigans as well. The club being in Birmingham, we'd get a hotel room for the night as there were no late night trains back to Coventry. At the very next one, I went over there and shared a room with Polly, a girl I had known from the punk scene for many years, and we dutifully got changed into our costumes in the hotel and headed off to the elevator, wondering what amusements would await us. It didn't take long. We reached the ground floor, myself in full and better thought out clown gear, Polly in full rubber corsetry and thigh high boots, listening to bad elevator music till the doors opened. Odd looks we were prepared for, but not the sight of 8 or so armed police pointing guns at us as we stood there. I don't know who looked most surprised, but a moment later they started laughing, no doubt due to the tension that must have been happening, and the doors opening to reveal us two eejits. To this day, I wish that some fat cigar smoking detective had said, "Get these clowns out of here," but they didn't, and a great observational comedy moment was lost, apart from the image I have of that in my head. We asked later, but no one in the hotel would tell us what we had been about. Still, getting guns pointed at me seemed to be becoming commonplace on my shenanigans so it was forgotten about as soon as we hit the club. There was a lot of shooting to be had that night, but not a gun in sight!

The time after that ,we took another girl we knew over with us, and the three of us shared a room. The cheap digs we had found had no on suite bathroom, just one down the hall, and whilst we were getting ready, Polly decided she needed the toilet, and opened the door to the corridor, then held it open as she remembered something she wanted to tell us. The new girl was pulling her fishnet stockings on, I was wearing a bondage harness, and Polly was already rubbered up. A young couple walked past and just stared in. As Polly followed them down the hall, she heard the girl say to her chap,
"Did you see that? That's disgusting."
Apparently the bloke verbally agreed, but had a look of longing and forlornness upon his face as he said it.
I met the guy who ran the club, and discovered that the reason I won the costume prize was because we shared the same sense of humour, and went on to become firm friends for life, with me

eventually being his best man years later when he wed a girl that he and his ex-wife had played with a couple of times. Isn't it amazing how love can blossom anywhere?

Polly and myself went on to start our own similar fetish club in Coventry called Twisted, which introduced a ton of naïve young rock and alternative folk to the world of extreme alternative nights that involved games such as Bondage Karaoke, Pin-the-tail-on-the-bunny girl, Twisted Twister, Strap-on Hoopla.....and many more, all pretty self-explanatory. The club ran for 10 years, moving from venue to venue, till Polly eventually got married and moved on, and Frisky became a name that stuck with me forever more. And this was all down to watching a channel 4 programme where a fornicating couple got hit with a custard pie.

So even though my adventures on the road had been taking a child-rearing hiatus, other shenanigans had not, all be them more local, apart from when I was paid to DJ as Frisky in fetish clubs around the country, with each and every event bringing its own bizarre and unexpected adventures. Naturally, the kids knew nothing of all this. During the part of the week they stayed with me, I was merely Dad, the feller who made the bad dinners, would race outside at the chimes of the ice cream van, and pretended not to be pissed off by the endless repeats of Hannah Montana, and the suite life of Zac and Cody. They did know of my Djing dressed as a clown, but bought the fact that I told them it was a fancy dress thing. I had to explain the red bowler hat on the hatstand somehow.

I wasn't completely confined to home during this time. Once the girls became a bit older, and my ex and myself were able to be more flexible in our routines – helped by the fact we only lived round the corner from each other – I managed to start getting back out there again, though not in the long journey type of adventures such as the bumming around Europe, Overlanding Africa, Backpacking Asia and Australia or driving across the States kind of way as before. But it didn't matter, each time I got a chance, I jumped at it, especially if it was somewhere I had not been before.

At one point, I took a couple of weeks out in Turkey with a girl I had been seeing for a while, Pinky. This was actually quite a first for me. In all the years of Shenanigans, I had never gone away on a holiday with a girlfriend. I had, during one of my earliest shenanigans, hitched around North Europe with my ex-wife before we were married, but I'm not sure that by any stretch of the imagination that that particular adventure could be called a holiday. This time, we actually booked a flight and hotel, and I found myself once again in not so much a holiday complex as I had with John and Lucky Andy, but certainly a resort town geared completely up for tourists. As we were heading out, I had convinced myself that I would hate it, probably down to the fact that it had been so long since I had travelled, that the idea of being stuck in one place seemed a bit frustrating.

Pinky had been to Turkey before, and knew just what she wanted to do. Beach. So she had booked us right by a beach in Marmaris, overlooking the rather beautiful sea.

"Is it a quiet, secluded beach?" I'd asked.

"Nope. It's by the hotels. We will have to pay for loungers, and there will be thousands of people there."

I'll hate it, I reiterated to myself.

"What about the hotel? Is it kind of quirky and local-ish?"

"Nope. Bog standard hotel, room service, breakfast and dinner extra, small pool with a bar.

Hate it.

"And who goes to this place? Do you get backpackers as well as tourists? So there might be some interesting little bars and stuff?"

"Not at all. It's all restaurants to start in, then lively karaoke bars and nightclubs. Loads of holiday dance songs everywhere, and big screen sports pubs so people don't miss any soccer games."

Please God, smite me down now.

In fact, in spite of myself, I found I really enjoyed it. We had an early flight out there, and had showered and were on the beach by the late afternoon. We secured a couple of loungers outside of one of the bigger hotels, ordered some chips and beers from a couple of guys who were employed to take money for just such things, and sat back in the sun and relaxed. I ate my small portion of chips, drank a few sips of my cold beer, and fell asleep.

It was possibly the best sleep that I had ever had. I think that we don't always realise just how hard we all work just to get by, and combine that with raising children, maybe an extra job – in my case Djing and running Twisted on top of my day job – then cramming as much DIY and socialising as you can in every weekend till you reach an age where you say fuck it, I'm staying in this Saturday, and add to that that you probably don't really get your recommended 8 hours sleep. Who does? I am always astonished when I meet people that get 8 hours sleep. How? How is it possible? Around this time I would get about 4 hours, if that, sleep a night. Maybe a lie in on a Sunday, but that was sleeping beer off, not really blissfully slumbering.

So I lay in the hot sun, with the sound of the sea lapping gently in my ears, and I slept away an accumulated tiredness that I did not know I had. It was like the weight of the last couple of years just drained out of me, home and responsibilities were far, far away, and I woke up, after only a couple of hours feeling like I had slept for a month. There is something about being near the sea that seems to do that. We eventually gathered our stuff, headed back to the hotel and decided what to do later on. Though when I met Pinky she was working in the same alternative clothes shop that a lot of my recent girlfriends, including the kids mother, seemed to work in, by the time we got out to Turkey she had moved on and was managing one of the bars that I was currently Djing in that was not my own club night, Twisted, a busy pub called The Golden Cross in the city centre. We were well aware that we were only a few hundred yards from the main party area of town, and that the pubs and clubs along there would be kick-ass. Yet, maybe because of our new found relaxed state, we realised that neither of us actually wanted to do any of that. Being a pub manager and a DJ, that would have been one hell of a busman's holiday. So we found another little part of town with a more relaxed vibe, and bedded into a cool little bar we found that suited us into the ground. As is the way of things, it became a kind of basecamp for the evenings.

The first few days were spent on the loungers by the sea, ordering the odd beer and maybe chips, and the evenings we would find a nice bar or restaurant before mooching to our new favourite haunt and ending the evening. We did the occasional explore of Marmaris, but there was not a great deal to see as such. Originally a small sleepy fishing village, a massive construction boom in the 80's has left little of that. The population is around 30,000 people, but this swells up to between 300,000 and 400,000 during the summer seasons, making tourism the major part of the economy. Even though that amount of tourists and holiday makers must bring some pretty irritating and boorish folk into the place, the people working there seemed genuinely warm and friendly, especially if you complimented the town.

Once the novelty of lying on a sun lounger began to wear off a little, we tried out a few new things. There was parasailing, which I enjoyed anyway, and we decided to try out a full Turkish massage, which we had seen advertised in one of the large hotels. We dutifully booked ourselves an appointment via one of the little booths all over the city where you can book anything, and turned up at a rather plush hotel where we were directed downstairs. There in the lobby were a few of the staff, both men and women, all looking toned and fit, and just the sort of people you would want to give you a massage, putting the health benefits aside.

"Do you think this is actually just a massage?" Pinky asked me, looking at the extraordinarily good looking staff. "Or do you think it's a massage with Extras?"

"Actually, I have no idea." I answered, honestly. "Shall we have the extras if they are offered?"

It was a fair question. I had in fact met Pinky at one of my fetish club nights, and though we were not what you would call hard core swingers, we did like to invite the occasional girl back to the house to play for the night. On such a scene, these sort of women are known as unicorns, as though couples are easy to find, single women who want a no strings attached rendezvous with a couple are pretty rare. But we seemed quite lucky on that front and though Pinky would never dream of going out with, or have a relationship with another female, she did get a yen for a bit of girl-girl action every so often, and that worked out pretty well for both of us.

As she asked, a pretty young girl took us through to the massage room, and directed Pinky to a table to lie on where a young muscular fellow was standing. She looked over at me and mouthed "Oh Yes' in answer to my question about if we should indulge if offered, and winked. The pretty young girl directed me to another table and remarked that I seemed very happy. She was not wrong. Well not at first, as this changed when she carried on out of the room and an older fat hairy bloke came in and said hello to me instead.

No bloody extras for me then.

So, after what I took to be some kind of exfoliating wash, we were kind of shoved into a sauna for 15 minutes or so. As we sat in there, Pinky started laughing.

"How's the extras?"

"Fuck off." I laughed too.

"Anyway, it's all legit," she told me. "I asked Yusuf."

"You're on first name terms? Boy, you got the better deal."

She did. After the sauna, I had the fat hairy guy pummel my body a lot, before I left feeling admittingly better, but not as good as Pinky did, I suspect. We left happy enough, even if extraless.

Veering off down a side street, I next spotted a barbershop full of locals. And I saw they were advertising shaves. This I had to have. I had seen these shaves with the old cut throat razors and always thought they looked pretty good. Most of my shaves on the road were usually done with cheap disposable razors, which really only give you half a shave. Especially as for the last few years I'd been sporting a completely shaved head, with all evidence of my punk hairstyles long gone, though in fairness it was nature that kick-started that one. It was one of the few joys of getting back from a trip to use a decent razor blade. But I'd never had a cut throat shave done before, so in I went, getting a number of curious stares off the locals who were sitting waiting. I imagine that there were places on the tourist trail and hotels that offered the same thing, no doubt done by young attractive staff, and involving a lot of ritual, a photograph and over the top friendliness for 5 times the price, but this was the real deal, hot towels and all, and for very little money I came out feeling cleaner than clean. Now that I really enjoyed! Steamed and beaten body, facial hair removed and a receipt to pick up a photo of us being massaged that Pinky ordered, off we headed for a night on the town. Or, at least, our favourite quiet bar.

Thoroughly enjoying our trip as I was, that urge to move on kept niggling away at me. It was looking at the little booths that I found a reasonably happy medium.

Excursions.

I hadn't thought of this. Pinky was happy too, so we began to utilise our days heading out to interesting places, such as the nearby Myra Necropolis, and other old and interesting ruined stuff. But then my itch was scratched when I spotted a ferry out to Rhodes. Yes, the chance to cross a border! We headed off early the next day, and enjoyed the one-hour crossing, pottered around looking at even more interesting ruined stuff, and browsed through the many trinkets and snow globes on sale, most of which depicted pictures or such of the legendary colossus of Rhodes.

This was my second time at a place of the seven sites of the ancient wonders of the world. The last time had been inside one of the Pyramids at Gaza, where my sense of awe was somewhat interrupted by a tour guide bellowing out a load of old crap in Italian, which really put the mockers on the mystique of the place for me. With that being said, at least it was actually still there, unlike the Colossus of Rhodes. Built around 280 BC, it was apparently built to celebrate the defence of Rhodes after a yearlong naval siege by the future Macedonian king Demetrius 1st who had been attempting to punish the Rhodians for deserting his cause in previous battles. Quite the clever lad, he invented a lot of new siege engines, such as a 180ft battering ram that required 1,000 blokes to operate it, and the Helepolis, a 125 ft tall siege tower. Amazing though these things were, the military failed to conquer Rhodes, and they eventually went away, leaving these incredible things behind along with much bronze weapons and armour, most of which was to be melted down and go towards the construction of a 33 metre high statue of the Greek sun god, Helios.

Not one to let a smug and gloating island with the tallest statue in the ancient world get to him, he then went on to unsuccessfully woo a young boy called Democles the Handsome, who kept refusing his advances. Possibly changing his name might have helped. Maybe Democles the Butt Ugly, or Democles the Foul-breathed might have not drawn so much attention, but I guess his vanity got in the way. This unwanted attention was rebuffed until one day Democles the Handsome found himself cornered at the baths, pulled the lid off a cauldron of scalding water and jumped in, his death being seen as a mark of honour to his fellow Athenians.

The Statue guarded the island, and caused much wonder for 54 years before collapsing during an earthquake in 226 BC. Apparently the remains of it sat there until the year 653, when an invading Arab army under Muawiyah 1st conquered Rhodes and destroyed what was left of it, and sold the remains, though no one is 100% sure who to, exactly. If that had been today, the Irish scrap metal guys that I remember still using horses and carts in my youth would have had that long before the invaders got there.

So, mimicked in snow globes with a plastic statue of a sun god and a bunch of tea towels aside, there was no colossus to see while we explored the island. In fact, oddly, considering how accurate they are with the dates of its construction, when it fell over, date of its selling off and such, no one now knows exactly where it was, so there is not even a monument to it to go and see. There is even some dispute if it was near the harbour entrance, or on a breakwater in the harbour itself.

The lack of a decent colossus to see, plus the incredible heat, meant that once we had looked at all the keyrings, replica vases and such, we sat ourselves down in a nice bar and looked at the one thing Pinky had bought, a beer glass shaped like a boot.

"I could get more of these for the pub," she mused. We had seen one being drunk out of at one of the bars in Marmaris, where the idea is to drink the beer in one go. This is complicated by its design, for at a certain point, the beer will gush out as it turns the corner of the boot, usually spilling all over the challenger's face

103

and shirt which naturally causes much guffaws and laughter amongst his or her friends. This can be repeated all night, and never seems to get less funny, and there will always be someone who wants to drink it because it is in a glass shaped like a boot.

It reminded me of a challenge my Dad had told me about in one of the Irish pubs in Coventry which was known as downing the Golden Wellie. Here they had actually got an old workman's wellington boot that had served its owner for years and painted it gold. The idea was to fill it with beer and drink it down, much the same as the glass boot challenge, but with bits of rubber and crap floating about. My Dad bragged that he had completed this challenge once. I kind of believed him, but vowed to myself never to get drunk with him in that particular pub.

This was actually the first time we had mentioned the pub or work since we had got out here. Still, it was not in a negative kind of way, and we were having a laugh about some of the regulars and their antics. There was an older couple in their late 60's or so sitting at the next table, who seemed to be chuckling at the stories.

"I know what you mean there," the white haired old feller eventually said to us, smiling. "That used to be our old trade, the pubs. Ran them for years, till we retired. I know just the sort of customers you're talking about."

We had a bit of a laugh about pubby kind of things, then I eventually asked him where he had run pubs.

"Coventry at first, then we moved to….."

"Coventry?" I interrupted. "That's where we are from. Pinky here runs the Golden Cross."

"Really? I know it well. Small world. I used to love that pub."

"Which pubs did you have in Coventry then?"

"Oh, I ran the old white Swan. I had it when all the punks used to…….."

"Your name's Colin!" I interrupted again, this time with a huge grin. The guy looked surprised, and acknowledged that it was indeed him.

Just after I left school, and while I was still living with the family, my parents left County Coundon and moved to the Hillfields district, a notorious red light area by night, but a busy shopping area by day. My old feller, deciding he was a businessman now, had invested in a second-hand and pawn shop, and we rented a house round the corner from not only the shop, but the White Swan pub. This was great for me, as back in those days very few pubs actually allowed punks in, but the Swan was an exception. The downside from my parents point of view was that after many a drunken night, they would come downstairs to find numerous punks and skinheads lying asleep in the living room,, which would end with my Mum bringing a huge plate of toast or bacon sandwiches, a huge pot of tea, and telling everyone to get that down them and be on their way.

And the gaffer of this pub, one of the few who actually let us in, and even had bands on, was sitting next to me in a bar in Rhodes, no longer a big sturdy black haired man, but a white haired somewhat frail fellow, but with the same loud voice and sense of humour I remembered from the day.

"You owe me a pint," I laughed.

"Really?"

"Remember the old space invader or some such you had? You got a free pint if you beat the high score..."

"Oh fuck, yes....I remember that..."

"Well, I beat it once, and you didn't give me the pint."

"And you're not getting it now, either."

We laughed again, reminiscing about some of the characters that used to drink there that we both knew, and he told me how he'd eventually got a bar in Spain, but had recently had Cancer and had to give it all up. It's funny, I'd never really spoken to him that I remember way back in the day, but here we sat like old friends, two guys from an old punk bar enjoying a drink in the sun decades later.

"I miss those days, you know." He said. "Seemed a lot more carefree."

"I know." I agreed. "I kind of miss those days too."

Well, our adventures in Turkey eventually ended, and I had to admit that I had been wrong about being scared of a "Holiday" and that we'd had a great time. Except for the one thing we hadn't done. Just before heading out, we had decided that we would treat ourselves to sharing a hooker one night, but only if we could find a fat one, and her name was Fatima, or Fatma as I think it is in Turkish. This had struck us as a challenge we needed to do (And possibly more fun than the Golden Wellie Challenge), but somehow it never came off. In fact, I think we forgot about it till the last day, when we tried to look through the small ads in a local paper, but could find no advertisements for fat hookers. Or even any called Fatma. So instead we headed back home with healthier bodies and a glass boot.

III

Another little taster of getting out there emerged in the form of the stag do. Stag do's had changed remarkably over the years. At the point in time when me and my compatriots were in our 20's to 30's, and people began marrying off, they were still a local affair. Usually a pub crawl the weekend before the wedding, with all the lads hitting the pubs, then a club. Back home in Coventry, this traditionally involved what was known as The Gosford run. Effectively an area on and around Gosford Street in the city, where every weekend night at least one or two groups of merry pissed up blokes in fancy dress or drag would be drinking their way from the furthest pub out and into the city centre. On the other side of town was the Craven Street Run, a similar place where the Hen nights would do the same.

I had had a stag night of my own, just before I married Eva, the Swiss girl who was the mother of my first son. Having got pregnant in Amsterdam, we had settled back in Coventry in a failed attempt to raise the lad together. To do this we needed to be wed, so in full punk gear, and wearing handcuffs, we got hitched at the local registry office. The night before, myself, my old pal Brodie and a couple of others decided at the last minute that wedding of convenience it may be, but we should still have a stag do. We went to a couple of the pubs that would actually allow punks in, on a Tuesday night, ending up in one of the Irish pubs nearby that the punks used at the weekend, a pub called the

Brewer and Baker, where here we bumped into my Dad and a bunch of other old fellers, sitting in the lounge playing about with some guitars, and a drum. Though being from Glasgow, my dad identified musically as Irish, coming from that community there himself. A pub singer of some note in his day, he knew every Irish musician that ever graced the city, which at one point, in the heyday of the working man's club era, had been a hell of a lot of people.

We all drank together till the pub closed, got a big carry out of beer, and went back to my flat, which was only a few hundred yards from this pub. By this time I was living in the tower blocks in the Hillfields area with Eva and a few others in one large flat. Back at the flat were a couple of electric guitars, so the night turned into some drunken shenanigans of a mixture of Irish and punk music. I did not know it at the time, but of the group of men with my Dad, one was from the famed Irish folk band the Dubliners, and one of the others was from another famed band, The Fureys. I have no idea which was which, but with Coventry's huge Irish population, the odds were they had been visiting relatives.

So there we were, before the Pogue's had a hit record, and long before other Irish/punk crossover bands such as The Dropkick Murphys or Flogging Molly had picked up an instrument, sitting in a tower block playing Irished up versions of Blitzkrieg Bop and Complete control, and punked up versions of The Fields of Athenry or the Men Behind the Wire. In one of the very few "I wish" moments of my life, it is a crying shame that nobody stuck the cassette player on record, and got this recorded. We could possibly have claimed to have invented the genre. I'm sure that the miserable bastard upstairs never knew that when he came down to complain about the noise. He never knew he had that story under his belt, just one about being laughed at.

However, in later years the Stag and Hen do's left places like The Gosford Run, and went travelling themselves. Various European Capitals found themselves hosts to large groups of drunken lads or girls celebrating the last night of freedom for the Stag or Hen, which wasn't quite true as they were usually months before the wedding, and just years before the first divorce. And, always one to celebrate pretty much anything – me and some friends once compiled a list of every saints day so that we could get drunk for all of them – I merrily went out on every do I was invited on. Amsterdam cropped up a lot, which was never a bad thing. But also the chance to explore a couple of new places, and have a few shenanigans, if only for a long weekend, gave me a quick travel fix, just to tide me over.

Bratislava, the capital of Slovakia, proved to be a whole lot of fun. Located on the Danube River, the city has a ripe and fascinating history going back to the first known settlement there in 5000 BC, with the first significant settlement, a small fortified town built by a Celtic tribe in around 200 BC. The Romans controlled the area for 4 centuries, and the Slavs arrived between the fifth and sixth centuries. Known as Pressburg since before the 10th century, the area saw invasions, battles, conquests and settlements by The Hungarians, the Ottoman empire, the Habsburg Monarchy, and was a centre for the Slovak Nationalist movement. The Hungarian and German populations tried unsuccessfully to keep it a free city when it annexed into the newly formed Czechoslovakia after world war 1, and fell under Nazi influence in world war 2. Liberated by Soviet Ukrainian troops, it fell under the power of the communists in 1948 and became incorporated into the Eastern bloc. After the fall of communism, the city became capital of the newly formed Slovak Republic in 1993, when Czechoslovakia split during what was known as the Velvet divorce. All this has led to a beautiful city, rich in culture and history, with a diverse European population, and becoming one of the wealthiest cities in the European Union.

We, however, went there to drink lots of beer and look at beautiful women.

It was a friend of mine's stag do, a guy I'd known for many years from the old alternative club days, and who was now in a quite successful local punk band, Dragster. The weekend was organised by his best man, another old mate who had worked out in Bratislava and knew it well. He booked us all digs on a floating boatel, and, come the morning of us heading off, I woke up excited to be flying out, but also with a strange rumbling feeling in my guts. It seemed I had caught a mild dose of food poisoning somehow. However, no way was that putting me off, and I met the lads in a pub near the train station in the city centre, had a bad crap, headed to the airport, had a crap, caught a plane which I had a crap on, and so on. In fact, for the whole of the 4 days there, my time was dictated by making sure I was carrying toilet paper and that there was a nearby toilet.

It was a great place to visit, and I wandered off a couple of times from the pack to soak up the history. This was made easier by the fact I decided I could only drink very little beer, due to the effect it seemed to have on my guts. Even with all the history around, the lads seemed mostly impressed by the fact that they could smoke in the bars. It was not EU just yet, and so not bound to the smoking ban. This seemed to spur the smokers to smoke even more than usual because, as they explained, they could.

We caught one of the old punk bands from the 70's, the Boys, one night, as many of the old British punk bands had found a market playing over on the continent, even ones we had kind of forgotten about. Another club we visited the next night was a rock bar run by the Hells Angels, which was packed yet with no-one who looked remotely rock. We also took in a couple of decent lap dancing clubs. The best man seemed very knowledgeable about all these sorts of places. He also knew of a good club he wanted to try on the last night.

"Right, are we all set for this place then?" He asked after explaining the situation. Much to his surprise and annoyance, the majority of the lads seemed reluctant to go.

"Come on," he argued, "It's a bloody stag do."

The place he was talking about could best be described as a gentlemen only club. By all accounts, you went in, paid your entry fee, and it was much like another club, except you bought a special voucher at the bar if you so wished. The girls who worked the place would mingle about and talk to you, and then if you fancied going upstairs for business, you presented her with the voucher. The trick, the best man told us, was to buy a basic voucher and sort out any extras with the girl upstairs. This struck me as a damned fine arrangement, except for one teensy weensy problem.

"Come on, Frisky", he said to me as most of the lads, including the groom declined. "Surely out of all the people here you must want to come along?"

"Sorry, I just can't. I'd like to."

"Why not? Honestly, the women are outstanding there. You'll love it."

"I don't mean I won't. I mean I can't."

"Why?"

"Because of these bloody shits. There's no way I can confidently go up to a room with a girl. I've never shit all over someone during sex in my life, and on a hooker with 7 foot tall bouncers wandering around the place, it's probably not the best time to start it now."

"Damn. You're right. Shame"

In the end, just him and one of the younger lads went along. I was gutted. I looked the place up when I got back, and indeed the women were astoundingly beautiful. Still, I went back with both my balls and my dignity intact, so never mind.

Sitting at breakfast on the boatel on the last morning, the young lad was looking a bit uncomfortable.

"Look, I have a girlfriend back home, and I feel bad about last night. No one is going to say anything about that club, are they?"

We all laughed.

"Don't worry. Your secrets are safe with us," someone said. "Just don't give the game away yourself."

"Like, how?" he asked, looking puzzled.

"Well, when you are next in bed with your girlfriend, just don't suddenly ask her if she'll sit on your lap, put her legs behind her neck and swivel round 360 degrees."

Home it was after that, where the stag shirts were put away in all our drawers of unused clothes that we must keep together. Actually, these were good ones. The Best man used to run a rock venue in the town, and knew a lot of people through this, including Vince Ray, the popular rockabilly musician and tattoo

110

artist of some renown. He had actually designed a special stag logo for us, which was incorporated onto our matching bowling shirts. Approximately 1 hour after I arrived back in my house, I had my last crap of the food poisoning and was completely back to normal.

"Why didn't you just get some Imodium?" someone said when I was talking about the do to my friends on the weekend.

Damn. You'd think at least one of the 15 of us out there would have thought of that. Damn and damn again.

The next Stag do of note was a trip out to Hamburg with another old friend of mine. Off out we all headed for an adventure in this rather fine German city, the largest non-capital city in Europe, with over 1.8 million people in the city alone, another 5 million plus in the metropolitan area around it, and also Europe's third largest port, after Rotterdam and Antwerp. With over 2,500 of them, it boasts the most amount of Bridges in any city Europe (Who the hell compiles these kind of statistics, and why?), was the city that paved the way to the launch of the Beatles, and also is home to the notorious St. Pauli's Reeperbahn area, known for sleazy sex shows and a fenced off red light window area, Herbertstratte, barred to women and juveniles according to the sign on the entrance.

It probably doesn't take a wild leap of imagination to work out which area in all of Hamburg we stayed in.

For the first two days we were there, we basically found a decent bar we liked, and sat outside it drinking. There were a number of street girls who didn't work the windows walking up and down, and somehow we managed to amuse ourselves by giving them nicknames.

"Hey, its Pinky McInky again" (pink shirt, tattoos)

"Here's Plastic McFantastic" (Plastic mac.)

" Blondie McPondie" (Blonde hair.)

The common theme began with the first girl who walked past more than once, who happened to be wearing a tartan micro skirt, and got a laugh from the lads when one of them commented on Tartan McSpartan. This set the standard for hooker nicknames.

So those first two nights also meant visiting the legendary Herbertstratte, which was indeed a small street containing maybe 50 or so windows, where allegedly the best looking – and definitely the most expensive – prostitutes in the city work. The advice about women not entering was that there had been a history of the working girls frightening women off, mainly to stop the much cheaper street girls from working in there as well

We soon learned that at each end, outside of the fence, were two different rock bars, those of the dodgy seats, piss poor beer and awful toilet variety. So the routine became to have a drink in one of the bars, walk the street looking at the girls, and making all the appropriate laddish noises and comments. Then, have a drink in the other rock bar, then do it again. And so on. After a while, due to different drinking speeds, we would shrink in numbers each time we walked up and down the street.

By the second night I found myself wondering why the hell we were bothering. Same routine. Drink. Walk up street. Drink. Repeat. The lads were clearly too nervous to try out any of the fun in the windows, so I decided that someone had to go first, or they would be wearing their shoes out, so a quick word with a beautiful German girl in one of the windows, and in I went, to a cheer from the lads. By the time I came out, happily spent, the lads were in one of the bars, so I joined them and asked who was next. They all mumbled about different things, and it looked like I was the only one who was going to participate. In fact, I seemed to ruin their fun, as they didn't look half as keen on the next walk through. I gave up at that point, and stayed in one of the pubs instead.

I was up early on the last full day, and took a walk around the port and such. It was a nice place. I've always liked ports and harbours and the like. I bumped into one of the other lads who I didn't really know, but who was doing the same, and we went and got some breakfast.

"Don't tell the others," He said, "but I went into one of the windows last night too. I don't mind telling you as you popped into one."

"I popped while I was in one, ha ha. Why the secret?"

"Well, I've only just come out as gay. I made quite a big deal of it, and yet some of those girls just looked so hot."

I really did not know how to take this.

"Why don't you just come out as Bi, or whatever?"

"Too much pissing about. I think I'll just stay gay."

We met the others and all retired to the hooker watching pub, when the heavens opened and it rained solidly all day and night. We played a lot of pool, and nicknamed nobody. Not even a Molly McBrolly, which would have been great.

Next morning, up early for a morning flight, and off to the airport via S-Bahn line 1, where we all sat a little worse for wear.

"Well lads," I announced out of the blue on the train. "I think we deserve a toast. Here we all are, a group of men who didn't all know each other at first, but have left as friends. Doctors, factory workers, taxi drivers, plumbers and all sorts of blokes. We came here to celebrate with our friend, and visited this fine city. This city with its history, its culture, its art. We came, found a pub, and spent 3 wonderful days drinking cold beer and giving quirky Scottish nicknames to prostitutes. So here's to Pinky McInky, the groom to be, and the lads. Cheers."

I raised my Starbucks coffee that I was holding, and so did the lads, laughing. A German woman in her 30's who was sitting next to us spoke.

"Is that all you have done in Hamburg?" she said, incredulously. "Drank beer and looked at prostitutes?"

"Yes." I replied, honestly. "That's pretty much about it. It was great."

These were great shenanigans away of course, but as the kids were getting older I found myself more and more longing to get away on a proper adventure again, not just a flying visit. I found myself on a couple of occasions looking at the collection of embroidered patches I had built up over the years, wistfully remembering some of those great shenanigans away. I was also a bit niggled that there were a few gaps where I hadn't managed to get a patch in a country, or that some of them were quite frankly cheap and tacky looking.

Of course, there was now the internet, so I decided that I would fill in the gaps and replace some of the tackier patches. I didn't realise it then, but that was probably me trying to stay connected with my adventures. So I looked online and was able to replace a few and fill the couple of gaps for all bar one country. This was mainly due to the fact that Zaire, where I had sat with the mountain gorillas, no longer existed. Mobutu had fled the country leaving the rebel forces in control, and the name was changed back to The Democratic Republic of the Congo. With that also came a flag change. It struck me that to have the correct patch, it should be Zaire, with the Zaire flag, as that is when I was there, and so after a bit of searching the net I finally found one for sale in a Rastafarian shop in the States. It cost me 5 times as much in postage as the patch itself, but gave me a great sense of completion.

This came out in a conversation I had in the pub one night, standing with a group of the lads, after a good few beers. Somehow travelling came up. It often did.

"Y'know what?" I remarked, "When I got back from the states that last time, I thought I was going to carry on seeing the world. And look at me now. I turn 50 on my next birthday, and have hardly been anywhere since. You know why? The bloody kids, that's why. I thought by 50 I'd have hardly anywhere left to go. And you know what? The ungrateful little buggers have the cheek to tell me I don't do anything for them."

This, of course, wasn't true. It was just merry, if slightly forlorn banter down the pub. Raising them into the people they are now was well worth stepping out from being on the road. Though it was actually true of course that I had stopped in my tracks, and had taken a while to realise it.

"How many countries have you been to now?" Someone asked.

"Not sure. 30 or so, I think."

"Well, you like challenges. Why don't you see if you can reach 50 countries by your 50th birthday?"

I pondered this. You know, that wasn't a bad idea. Not a bad idea at all. We started to tally up how many countries I'd been to, and finally came to the conclusion that it was 39. This was, I thought, doable.

"In fact," the same guy said," Why don't you aim for making the 50th country on your 50th birthday, and we can all go out and celebrate it?"

There is something about a drunken plan made in a pub that beats most other kinds of plans. Mice do not get drunk. That is why they make such bad plans. Managers are sober (ish) at planning meetings in companies, which also means usually bad plans are made. However, stick a group of half-drunk people together, and there is no limit to the imagination that can be stirred up. It's how my club Twisted began. After visiting the more professionally ran clubs, Myself and Polly had got really drunk before catching the train back to Coventry, considered that Coventry was lacking in such a thing, so had wandered into a pub we knew with a large back room, and arranged to start a fetish night that involved bizarre and ridiculously fun games, outrageous acts, and would be hosted by a guy wearing clown makeup. We realised the gravity of what we had done the next day when we sobered up and groaned a lot, but we went ahead and it became a roaring success. There is no way on God's earth that we could have come up with that idea sober.

And now, in my Carling induced state, I had realised that there was no better idea in the world than meeting the fifty by fifty challenge.

It was game on.

IV

Most, if not all, travellers, no matter what they might tell you, like to keep a tot up on how many places they have been to. This tot up, however, can be quite speculative. Effectively, what defines a country? As I had found out before, the UK can be one country to some, which is what the United Nations would call it, but to Brits in the four nations, each one is a country. Having parents from Ireland and Scotland, I was always very aware of these being different countries from England, and that makes sense, each has their own flag, government and football team. To me, they are all countries. But if you were going by the United Nations, there are countries that are not on their list. Taiwan and North Cyprus, for example, are seen as occupied territories. Yet to others they are separate entities to the Republics of China and Cyprus.

To other travellers, the question is, are you only including countries as such? The Canary Islands are Spanish, yet are off the coast of Africa, have a flag and an autonomous government. Yet they are represented at soccer by Spain. Hawaii is part of the United States, but they are a group of islands far from the mainland with an indigenous population completely separate from native Americans. So the definition of destinations expands to some, meaning countries, territories and islands. I stumbled across a group called the Travellers Century club, which you can join once you have hit 100 destinations from their list. I liked this list. Having been to some groups of islands in the past, I cannot in my own mind see them as part of a country hundreds of miles away. They just feel unique. The Travellers Century list tallies with my own interpretation of how I see this kind of thing, but goes even further. To join, you can count airport changes, and Turkey for example counts as two places, if you have been to both the European part and the Asian part. In my mind I do not agree on those.

The bottom line to remember is that it doesn't matter. The tally up of places is, and should be, just for a bit of fun. When caught up in a debate about what or what not is a country, or whether or not islands count, just happily agree to disagree, get a beer, and tell a few disaster stories. One of my last trips was across the states, which was considerably a longer journey than an early trip around Europe, yet was only one country as opposed to six or seven. I had done a tot up purely because there was a challenge to be had, which was again just a bit of a fun excuse to get back out there.

So my next trip came quicker than I expected. One of my friends from that very conversation about hitting the fifty countries mark got back to me that very week, and asked if I'd been to Northern Ireland yet. I had not.

"Well, do you fancy coming over to see an Ice-hockey game? Tick a country off for you."

Clearly my friend, Wee Keith, was in the four countries in the UK camp then. Good. Now, I have always had zero to nil interest in sport, but what the heck, I thought. Plus, it would be nice to see Belfast. It was, in fact, where my mother and family had come over from, and whilst I was growing up various young cousins would come over, getting away from the troubles in the 70's. As a child, all I saw of Belfast was pictures of gunmen and bombs on the news, and it never really seemed to be a place that we were taken on holiday to.

The first thing I saw on arriving in Belfast was the world famous Harland and Wolff Shipyard. Now here was somewhere I had heard of, outside of the fact that the most famous ship ever made there was the Titanic, which was a shocking advert for unsinkable ships. Both sides of my family had a history of working on the docks. In fact, one of my great-grandads had actually owned tug boats in Belfast. However, the shipyards, and especially Harland and Wolff had had quite a history when it came to sectarianism. The majority of workers were Protestant, and Catholics were not welcome to work there. This took the form of threats and physical intimidation to keep them out in a country where Harland and Wolff were at one point the biggest employer. It was due to this history, long before the Troubles, that my Great Grandad, unable to get enough work for his tug boat from the Protestants, took it out one day and sank it somewhere in the harbour to cause a mighty blockage and quite a bit of work to shift it.

However, times had moved on, thankfully, and though there are still areas in Belfast that remain on either side of the divide, this did not affect us, and we had a fine weekend drinking and watching the Coventry team defeat the Belfast Giants. Or so Keith told me, as about half way through the game I'd kind of turned off and was wondering if the cold air in the stadium would make girls' nipples stick out more.

117

Well, that was a nice little jaunt, and it was nice to finally see Belfast.

"Would you look at that?" I pointed out to Keith as we walked past a theatre in the centre the next day. Keith laughed when he saw the poster I was pointing at.

"The Troubles (according to my Da.) A comedy."

So we'd reached that point. Now this would be fun to try to explain to my Mum. Though perhaps not as ironic as the fact that relating this somewhat amusing irony to someone back home, it was pointed out to me that a collaboration between Andrew Lloyd-Webber, (a kind of extremely talented yet chubby and odd looking rich musical maestro who not only produced fantastically worthy musicals, but in my mind hit the jackpot when he married one of the Hot Gossip dancers, a group of girls who danced in scanty costumes on TV in the late 70's and were the source of every schoolboy and their dads helping to boost the sales of Kleenex), and Ben Elton, (one of the original of the alternative comedians that appeared just after punk who seemed to spend a lot of time knocking the old school comedians such as Benny Hill. Oddly, I still to this day find Benny Hill a hell of a lot funnier), and these two had produced a musical called The Beautiful Game set in the era. I'm sure the songs were extremely amazing, and the script as right on leftish as is possible to get, but the title sure sucks. Now a combination of the two – The Troubles, The Musical – Now that would sure grab my attention! Oh yes. Preferably on ice.

Arriving back, I had little time to prepare for my forthcoming adventure, but managed to secure the time off work OK. I spent a good few days looking at maps, which I always enjoy, and realised that parts of Europe were open to travelling now that would have been more complicated before, mainly the old Eastern bloc countries. So I thoroughly enjoyed myself plotting out a route that would take in some interesting stuff and working out how to go about this.

My previous shenanigans and adventures had started with sticking out the thumb and literally bumming across The north of West Europe, living in squats and the likes. I'd been elevated to

Backpackers hostels when I went on a round the world trip, had overlanded on a truck across Africa, and we'd driven across the States, all of which were great ways to travel. For this adventure, I realised there was another option. Interrailing.

A favourite of gap year students, Interrail was a great way to travel from country to country across Europe. I was over a certain age, and no student, so I paid a bit of a bigger price for my ticket, but nevertheless the convenience and flexibility of a single ticket that I could use when I wanted to go on a certain amount of journeys wherever I wanted was a huge selling point. And it sold it to me via another new tool that I now possessed that was not available on my travels before, The Internet.

On previous adventures, finding hostels was limited to the rough guide books which floated around in hostels and other travellers backpacks – and, of course, good bookshops everywhere – but here now were dedicated sites for booking in advance. Hell yeah, that seemed like a great idea. I'd seen many a traveller who would turn up at a hostel at midnight after a delayed flight or something to find out the place was full, and they would have had to wander off to find another one. Or stood at a train station with a scrap of A4 paper that had a number of addresses and numbers scrawled on it, phoning around to try to get a place to stay. Now, here it all was at your fingertips. And no heading off to the train station on the first day of your adventures to get the times of the trains for when you wanted to leave, either. A website for DB Bahn, the German train company, actually had the times of every single train going across Europe, along with numbers to book them, and even platform numbers in most cases. This was amazing, I thought. So in one Sunday afternoon, I sat with the kettle on, decided on a journey, booked my flights, ordered my interrail ticket, worked out train times from one place to another, booked myself into cheap dorm shares in hostels, (making sure a couple of them had clothes washing facilities along the way), booked a coach down to Luton airport, and I was all set. I was remarkably proud of myself and incredibly pleased with modern technology, so headed off down to the pub to celebrate. This, I decided, was the way to go about things.

And so, just a couple of weeks later, I found myself at the local coach station, with only enough clothes and stuff in a bag so that I could take it as hand luggage on a plane, ready to head to the airport and fly out to Bulgaria, my starting point. And standing there, watching the coach pull in late, as they always seem to do, it was as if all the years of not being on the road just vanished. Just like that. The years of working, raising the kids, losing and making friends, buying a house and all other things that with the exceptions of a few great but short trips away had been my life for many a year now simply locked themselves in the folder of the mind that such things need to be in, and the travel folder sprang open and those memories jumped out like a jack in the box and were as fresh as if they were yesterday. I stepped onto the coach when it pulled in, found a seat, looked out at the permanent building site that is Coventry Coach Station, smiled and relaxed. Till the coach pulled off, where I let out an unwitting "YESSS!!" much to the surprise of my fellow passengers and then watched Coventry go past the window.

I was on the road again, and it was absolutely bloody great!

V

There was one amusing moment on the coach. I had been talking to a guy in the next seat who was heading off on holiday and was saying how great it was to just forget about work for a week or two. I totally agreed with him, and decided that I wasn't even going to talk or think about mine to anyone whilst I was gone. Which was great till we arrived in Luton and got stuck in some kind of traffic jam, right outside the Peugeot plant there, which is one of the customers my work services, and we have a lot of people down there. And sure as heck, I had to sit for a good 15 minutes with nothing to look at other than the logo of our company staring right back at me, and one of our lorries stuck at the gate. Well, there's a bloody good start, I thought.

Still, no point worrying about such comical things, and soon I had arrived at Luton airport, had the obligatory pint, and was soon embarking at Burgas Airport, destination Sunny Beach. Yes, I had decided that as a starting place I would treat myself to a decent hotel for a couple of days, with a pool and near the beach as my Turkey experience had taught me that I was not as adverse to this kind of thing as I had always thought, though a decided a few days would probably be quite enough which turned out to be exactly the case. Due to my hard learned mistrust of airport taxi drivers, I caught a bus for about £2 out to the centre of Sunny Beach, not bad for a fairly long journey.. Here I hit the first snag. I had changed up some currency before coming over for the first two countries on the trip, Bulgaria and Romania, with the idea that I would use cash machines once past them. As always, I carried a credit card as well, just in case. However, on presenting the bus driver with a banknote, she made very polite gestures that she couldn't take it. From what I thought I could make out, it was too big a denomination, which was a bummer as it was all I had. She tried to tell me something, and luckily an English speaker on the bus jumped in.

"She says that there are cash machines at the bus station in Sunny Beach. You can pay her when you get there."

That was pretty decent, I thought. And sure enough, we pulled into the bus station, where she came with me over to the cash machines. I took out the smallest amount I could, so as not to get big notes again. I looked at the notes as they came out, and realised that I had actually been a right eejit, and had tried to pay on the bus with Romanian currency. So I handed her a note the same as the ones in my other pocket, she smiled and offered me the change, and I offered it back as a tip, not because I was in the habit of tipping bus drivers, but because she had been really helpful, even though she thought I was some dumb English tourist who had just arrived from Romania, and didn't understand currency. Most of which, of course, was about right, but she didn't accept the tip, and I didn't tell her that I had plenty of Lev after all. So there I was, the seasoned traveller, being helped out by an elderly bus driver. Excellent. I had been on my adventures for all of an hour, and already felt like a newbie.

Bus paid for, it was time to find my hotel, which I figured would be a bit of a search as all I saw whilst driving into the town were hotels. Lots of them. Luckily, right by the bus station was a little bar called Sharkies, so I popped in, asked directions, and found that my hotel was literally on the other side of the station, so a cheeky pint and in no time I was all settled in the hotel. This was my nod at luxury, as for the rest of the trip I had booked myself into dorm shares in Backpackers hostels. But what could be wrong about a decent hotel, a pool and a beach nearby, I thought. What was wrong turned out to be the hotel experience.

Not that there was anything wrong with the place itself. Far from it. It was very nice, and my room was clean, comfortable and had come in at a pretty good price. The first night was fine, I had a walk around town and realised that as in other such towns I had been in, there were a massive amount of party bars which still do not appeal to me at the best of times, but even less so as a solo traveller. I went in one, found myself sitting in a corner surrounded by loud family groups getting plastered and considering that this wasn't the place for me. In fact, I thought the bar by the bus station seemed like a nice prospect. It was a smallish place, mainly open air, but had been playing some good music when I passed through and was near the hotel anyway. So I headed back there, and got a drink. Looking around, it seemed that there were a number of flags around it, including a large Glasgow Rangers flag, which I thought odd, as the guy at the bar, who seemed to be the owner, had a bit of an accent I couldn't place, but it sure wasn't Scottish. But I enjoyed a couple of drinks, felt a bit tired, and retired back to the hotel, deciding I would have breakfast there when I got up.

Which is when I discovered the plight of the older solo traveller in regards to hotels. Yes, I was to realise that I was a mature traveller now. I had already had a taste of this whilst booking. This was, of course, the first time I had ever really booked my whole trip online, and was impressed by how efficient it was. Except, of course, for algorithms. My self-image and my computer were apparently at odds with each other. There I was, looking at dorm shares across Europe, and comparing backpackers, but my computer kept throwing up adverts and pop ups for destinations clearly geared up for the mature traveller that the cookies considered me to be. Even Saga holidays popped up, and they are for the over 50's. However, they did keep asking me if I knew that I could go on one as long as I was travelling with someone over 50. All of these adverts included pictures of happy grey haired couples, in remarkably good shape and with excellent teeth, sitting by pools or on balconies overlooking beautiful seas, drinking glasses of wine, and smiling at each other in a way that said that there was no better experience than this. I disagreed. It looked like a vision of hell. Now, had they shown me a picture of some bald bloke like me sitting in a bar with a pint in his hand, and a sign saying "Strip club" above his head, I might have taken a bit of notice, but it seems these mature travel experiences are for silver haired people only, who never argue over if they should go shopping or to the pub, and enjoy fine wine on balconies. Bloody eejits.

Hotels, I was to discover, held similar views about me to my PC. When I went for breakfast, and in fact any meal I chose to buy there, the staff would kind of ignore me when I went in and sat down. This turned out not to be them being rude, but in fact assuming that I was waiting for someone. The staff were, as they tend to be, quite young, with no reason to know that I had been a solo traveller for a number of years, and apparently assumed that I had kicked off my slippers, brought in from the balcony and washed up last night's wine glasses, and was waiting for my good lady wife, no doubt a silver haired vixen with great teeth, to finish her toiletries and join me, before a day of walking past interesting things and pointing at them, whilst wearing jumpers over our shoulders in the sun, something else I noticed about the idiots in the picture in the ads thrown up at me.

Of course, the silver haired vixen was never going to show up, which was a shame, as my motto these days in regard to that type of thing is that many a good tune is played on an old fiddle. Even if she did exist, I would say that going by the adverts that I didn't have the teeth to keep her for long, though I'm making a good guess that decent dentures may be a factor in those pictures. So eventually I would have to call out to the staff, who would look around at me as they might do if a voice had come out of an empty space, and ask them for a menu. They usually brought two, then that was the last I would see of them till I called them again to say I was ready to order, at which they would look at the dining room door, ask me if I needed more time, then jot down my nutritional choices on their notepads, no doubt wondering if I was perhaps getting a little forgetful in my old age, and had failed to remember that my wife would be pretty hungry about now too, if I even remembered that I had a wife. Lesson one in how things were slightly different as an older traveller. No problems, I thought, It won't be like this in the Backpackers Hostel.

I spent the day by the beach, and as is the way with my Irish skin, managed to become as red as a lobster even though I had hired a lounger with a whopping big umbrella. I was a bit wary about leaving my money and phone by the lounger when I went for a swim, a second problem for a solo holiday maker, but had purchased a little plastic wallet thing for my pocket that assured me it was waterproof, and did indeed do the trick. Till the third swim that I took, that is, and hadn't done it up properly. For the first time ever, I had taken a phone on my shenanigans, and managed to drown it straight away. That was the end of that then. I ended up buying a little portable alarm clock instead.

It was a different set of staff when I got back to the hotel, and I went through the invisible thing again before getting some dinner. I headed out, and walked up and down the main party area, mainly wondering if there was likely to be a bar where solo travelling silver haired vixens hung out, but that didn't seem to be a thing. As it got darker, I was happy to see that the good looking young folk who give flyers out for clubs and bars were out in force as the streets filled up with revellers.

And here I learned lesson three of the world of the mature traveller. They don't give you flyers for clubs and bars very often. In fact, they even seem to hold back if you ask for one, and eye you up and down suspiciously, as if you had asked them where the nearest park was that you could watch children playing in. I wasn't completely ignored on the flyer front though. At least a few times I was given flyers for sex clubs and thinly disguised brothels. Unusually, this wasn't actually on my agenda for this trip, but at least I was grateful that a few of the flyer folk seemed to target single older males wandering the party streets of Bulgaria.

I had a couple of beers in different bars and decided that Sharkies was the place for me, and headed over there. Here I got talking to a number of people, including a group of Danish backpackers who had a whole bunch of flyers in front of them, and someone even ran in to give them a flyer whilst we sat there.

"Hey," I said, jokingly, "Can I get a flyer too?"

"Er, OK" the young lad said, "But there is a good sex club just next door."

This was true actually. I had clocked it, of course, and figured that if all else failed I might pay it a visit. The Danes pushed on to a club after a while, and politely asked me along, but I decided I liked the music here and would stay on. Going up for another beer, the owner looked at me and asked if I'd been in the night before.

"Yep. I'm a regular now," I jokingly told him.

"Travelling alone?"

"I am. From here to Copenhagen. Just having a few beach days first."

"Cool. I used to do that a lot when I was younger. Hey, come and join us."

At the other end of the bar were a couple of guys my age who turned out to be local bar owners. The Sharkies owner introduced himself as Marc, and the other two were an Irish feller and a German guy. Marc turned out to be half Swiss and half Scottish, hence the rangers and other Scotland flags around the room and the strange accent. And so it was that the rest of my stay here became about lounging on the beach all day, and enjoying a few beers with the "corner" crowd, which was just what I'd hoped. I'd also noticed a change in my feet. Over the years, a bit of the old arthritis had set in, not enough to be life changing, but enough to give me a good few pains and aches. I had noticed on my adventures in Turkey that this pain seemed to vanish, and lo and behold, in just a couple of days in the sun, this happened again. Humans are pretty resilient – well, some of them are – and you get kind of used to a permanent pain, not noticing how bad it has got till it goes. And with my feet suddenly having pain lifted from them, I found that I immediately felt a hell of a lot fitter, and lighter, and wanted to get out walking. I'd enjoyed my relaxing start to the trip, but it was now definitely time to hit the road. I had a good drink with the bar owners on my last night, shook hands, got a decent kip and was ready to go.

I took an air conditioned mini bus to Varna, and bought a train ticket for the night train into Romania. It was apparently the sleeper train to Moscow, so I figured that if it was like the Russian trains I remember, sleeping was probably a good bet and booked a bunk. I had a whole day to explore Varna which was good, ending up getting a meal in a pub near the station called the Three Lions which caught my attention by sporting a Coventry City FC banner, something I really did not expect to see. I asked about it, and though he was not there, it turned out that the owner was a Coventry bloke. Would have been nice to have met him. There was a surprisingly good chance that we may have known each other. Coventry is a bizarrely small town for a reasonably large city.

Seems the Russian trains had improved a little bit since my last journey on one. The toilet was still a hole in the floor at the back of the train, but they had at least put a kind of pedestal over it. The paper supplied was just as bad, though, with a kind of rough abrasive type that seemed to be still in transition from being wood. I had expected no less, and had brought my own. Hell, no flies on me!! Which is more than could be said for the toilet. Other Russian train customs remained too. They took both my passport and my Interrail ticket, which I found rather disconcerting, and kept it in a little office. However, it all worked well, and after a bit of an awakening crossing the border, I woke up the next morning to find myself ready to embark in Romania, and the 42nd country on my challenge.

VI

It was a glorious day. The bunk on the train had been OK, but not exactly luxury, and I'd had my sleep interrupted by the border and another point when some large guy with a breathing problem had come into the cabin for one of the other bunks. There had been two other people asleep the whole time I was in there, who didn't seem to move. Possibly dead, but you don't like to think the worst, really. I would be coming back to Bucharest soon, but figured I'd reserve a bunk on the next sleeper train I'd be taking, which would be to Budapest. The ticket covered the journey, but you still had to pay extra for sleeper bunks.

This Interrail ticket was striking me as a good idea at this point. It had been a good idea since 1972. That was the year when it was launched, to celebrate the 50th anniversary of the founding of the international union of Railways (UIC) and was originally planned as a one off that enabled young people up to the age of 21 the opportunity for unlimited rail travel in 21 countries for £27.50. More than 100,000 people took it up, and pressure was on to keep it going. After many requests, this happened and a new version of the Grand Tour was born.

It was almost a rite of passage for young gap year students or intrepid teens to get their ticket and take advantage of a freedom of rail travel never seen before. Year by year, the number of countries grew, and the age group kept creeping up until by the time I bought mine, people of any age could get them, so long as they were from an EU country, or if from outside the EU, you could purchase the equivalent Eurail pass. The idea behind it was excellent. 1972 was only 27 years after the end of World war 2. Anyone eligible to travel using it had, if not parents then definitely grandparents who had lived through Europe tearing itself apart. Memories can be long, but here was a chance for young people to get out and meet other Europeans like themselves, and to make friends and memories, and to take these encounters on through their life. Interrail connected the young people of Europe in a way never seen before. It was to eventually peak and drop off in usage, very likely because the internet, another great connector of people, if used correctly, made planning trips and booking ahead easy. However, that early freedom to get to a train station and decide there and then where you wanted to go, to change plans on a whim, or to pick up on travelling with new friends made interrailing exciting and affordable.

I, on the other hand, was a bit late to the party with it, having tended to use my thumb as a way of getting around Europe on earlier adventures. However, trains were always involved somewhere along any of my shenanigans, and quite rightly so. If there is a better way to travel, I haven't found it yet. Instead of flying over a country till you land, or driving along the uniform modern motorways, you can sit back, chat to people, read a book or just gaze out of the window at the scenery. I was to find that this was to be a joy of this trip. Often, a train can take longer than a car journey, as when the track was built it cut through mountains and forests, and when it couldn't it went round the long way. You pass by small villages and towns, and get a small glimpse of life going on that is oblivious to you. You see stunning landscapes for hours, then flat fields. You see, in fact, the country.

Once I had reserved a bunk on my next major train ride, I grabbed a bite to eat and boarded another train to my destination of choice in Romania, Brasov. I had picked this as the nearby Bran Castle is, it is claimed, the inspiration for Count Dracula's Castle in the Bram Stoker novel of some fame. And the reason for that was it bang slap in the middle of Transylvania. Yes, I was going to Transylvania.

No matter how aware I was that Transylvania is nowadays a region of Romania, it just did not sound like I was going to a real place.

"So, where are you heading?"

"You know, Transylvania. I've partied out in Narnia, and headed out to Atlantis, so I figured I'd try and hook up with some Vampirian chicks on the way. Hell, you seen that Elvira on TV? Now that's what I'm talking about."

Interestingly, Mr Stoker was not the first author to write about Transylvania and its association with Vampires, or the *nosferatu* of Romanian peasant lore. That honour probably goes to the Scottish author Emily Gerard. In fact, her novel, The Land Beyond the Forest published in 1890 is said to be part of the inspiration for Dracula, though the latter clearly went on to be a massive inspiration for both novels and films for generations to come. Though not the first actor to play the character, Bela Lugosi is amongst the most famous, and was in fact born in Lugoj in Romania, even though at the time it was called Lugos and was part of the kingdom of Hungary. Still it made for the accent we all know and love, even though it tended to get him second billing to Boris Karloff in many of the films they starred in together, which I imagine must have been pretty annoying for him. It makes you wonder if they ever called each other.

"Is that Bela?
"Yes."
"It's me, Boris."
"What do you vant, Boris?"
"Just refresh my memory. Who was the lead in The Raven?"
"I vas, Boris. You know that."
"But who got top billing?... Mwah ha ha."
"Piss off, Boris. And stop calling me."

Arriving at the train station, I decided to get a cab to the hostel, as the little map on the print out from the hostel booking site had not really taken into account the lack of street signs.

"Casual Hostel, please."

"Where?" The guy spoke English, which it turned out a lot of locals here did, due to it being quite the tourist hub, and was no doubt about to try to con me somehow. I told him the address which I had also got on the print out, and the name of the main road that it was off.

"Ahhh, yes, I remember it. There is a problem. That hostel closed down last month."

"Closed down, you say?"

"Yes, a shame. But I know another hostel near here, very cheap, very clean."

There it was.

"Well, they were taking bookings a fortnight ago. I tell you what, take me to this address, and if it's closed, we will go to the one you know."

Ten minutes later we were at my hostel, which had a huge OPEN sign hanging over the door. I still gave the driver a tip. It's nice to be nice.

It was indeed a nice hostel. The dorm share rooms only had 4 people per room, and a single bed each, which surprised me. There were a couple of French lads in the room already, who seemed quite friendly, and recommended that I try the cable car there. I had no idea there was such a thing, so after a quick shower I went for a bit of an exploration, and found it fairly quickly. Having watched the absolutely beautiful scenery passing me on the train, the idea of looking at it from above seemed quite pleasant. There was a bit of a queue, but it was worth going up in, especially as it took you up to one of the quirkier things I had noticed about the place. It actually had its own Hollywood-type sign that said BRASOV instead. It only took about 5 minutes or so to get up, but the view of both Brasov and the Carpathian mountains was stunning, and worth the money. Other folk chose to take a walk up instead, which I'm sure was even better, but I was all for the easy option.

"There used to be a citadel made of stone up here," a helpful fellow told me as we got off the cable car at the top. "It was built by the Teutonic knights. There were defence towers and all sorts of things."

"Oh?" I said, noticing that his wife was beaming at me through a large pair of thick glasses, as if she knew me somehow. "That's interesting."

"Yes," he carried on, "there wasn't always this sign either. 2014 they put this up. Do you know why?"

"Er, no….No I don't."

"No, nor me. It's good though, yes?"

"I guess so", I said, trying to show that I was very intent on staring over at the view. This seemed to work for only a little while."

"They built this cable car in the early 1970's", he carried on. I couldn't quite place his accent, but I was guessing Hungarian.

"There was a big singing competition here. So they wanted to impress the singers from all over the world. So they built a cable car to come up Tampa Mountain."

I couldn't help but wonder exactly what the connection was that they had made that to impress a bunch of singing contestants, they needed a cable car. Possibly a local business man who specialised in cables had come up with the idea. However, build it they had, and I was stuck up here with some Hungarian with a droning voice and a strange little wife who hadn't stopped beaming at me yet. I wasn't sure how her face muscles were keeping it up.

"Of course, it wasn't always called Brasov. The Russians were here for a while and called it Orasul Stalin. That means Stalin city. They changed all the trees on the hill to read S-T-A-L-I-N on the side of the mountain."

"Can you still see that?

"No. When it was returned to Romania they chopped all those tree's down."

I was just beginning to find this lecture on Tampa Mountain quite interesting when the beaming wife suddenly put her finger on my nose and squashed it in, saying something in Hungarian. The man laughed.

"She says that you have a very soft nose. She likes soft noses."

I didn't really know what to say.

"So," The man continued, "Are you here to see the vampires?"

I presume it was by accident, but this sounded so remarkably like Bela Lugosi in character that I actually found myself for a split second looking at his face, and trying to reassure myself that both Bela and Dracula had to be dead by now, not that that is particularly reassuring in a conversation about vampires.

"Well, kind of. I'm going to see Bran Castle tomorrow."

"Yes, yes. Belonged to Vlad the Impaler. A lot of them did. You will like it."

His beaming wife pressed my nose again. This time she left her finger on it, till I pulled back.

"Well, I'm getting the cable car back now. Goodbye, it's nice to have met you and your wife."

He looked at me with a puzzled expression. "She is not my wife…."

131

I had a quick look round, caught some more view, then went back down, determined to look up if there are any mating traditions here that start with shoving your finger in someone's nose.

Brasov was certainly a nice place to explore. At the centre was Council Square, which sits nicely in the old town, and surrounded by fine baroque buildings, and off running cobbled streets. I was genuinely impressed by the warmth of the local people I came across whilst there. That first evening, I found a nice place to eat, and noticed that there was fish on the menu, and also a side plate of chips. I obviously knew that it would be a nice fresh fish, not battered, but fish'n'chips sounded nice to me, so I asked for the chips instead of the potatoes it came with. With no hesitation they agreed, and when it arrived, I realised that they were American chips, not British. Hence, I had an absolutely delicious tasting fish with what looked like a pack of Walkers crisps shoved onto one side. They were, however, homemade rather than from a multipack and so I quite enjoyed it anyway. I made sure that I ate with confidence, so as not to look like an eejit who didn't know what chips meant here.

I mooched around a couple of places as the evening drew on, chatted to a few folk, all of whom asked me if I had been on the cable car. It was still hot in the evening, so I found myself sitting outdoors in all of these places. I eventually strolled back to the hostel, where something caught my eye. I had noticed that it seemed to be above another business that had been closed so far during my stay, but was now open. It had a neon sign saying nightclub, with an arrow pointing down some stairs at the side of the building pointing down to a cellar bar. I figured I would get changed and pop in, as the music sounded quite lively. I got as far as the lobby, where the French lads from my room and a group of Austrian backpackers of mixed ages were sitting chatting to the owner of the hostel, a pleasantly polite chap. I said Hi, and one of my roommates offered me a bottle of beer, so I sat and joined them instead.

The owner, it seemed, had not long bought the place, along with his business partner and old friend from school. The general

132

consensus amongst us was that it seemed a really nice place, and we hoped it worked for them. About half an hour into talking, he asked if we all fancied some wine, which we did, so he told us to follow him and led us straight down to the nightclub below. There was absolutely no one else in the club, and the guy behind the bar seemed pleasantly surprised to see us. He was also the DJ. True to his word, the hostel owner got a couple of bottles of wine between us, and due to the heat, we were kind of crammed in the small gap between the door and the staircase outside. A couple of other people passed through, mainly couples, but no one stayed long. We however, did, and were getting to know each other. The Austrians, it turned out, were a group of friends who had at some point in the past worked in the same place which closed down just before a trip they had planned together. After that, they never really saw each other apart from once a year when they would get together for a couple of weeks and backpack around a country of their choice.

The French lads were students who were formulating some kind of business plan for an internet idea, which they explained to me and it went over my head, though I nodded in complete agreement with them and knowingly said that I thought they were onto something. I would have tapped my nose in a knowing way too, but was wary that this could be some kind of sex signal that would lead to an embarrassing situation.

We were joined by others staying in the hostel as they arrived back from wherever they had been exploring, and in no time we were buying lots of beer from the smiling barman, and having a few interesting conversations about Romania, and places people had been.

"Did you know," I said to two Dutch women who had joined us, "That the Russians once shaped the trees to say Stalin on the side of the mountain there?"

"Really?" One of them said, "I didn't see that. Is it still there?"

"Oh no," I said, tapping my nose. "The Romanians chopped it down."

Interested as they seemed about the tree's story, there seemed to be no interest in my nose tapping. I was beginning to think that the beaming lady just liked soft noses after all.

It seemed to be one of those places that just shut when everyone had finished, so we were getting through a fair amount of the local beer, as the wine had been drunk very quickly. I took a guess that the wine was on the house for the hostel owners, to get them to bring people down from the hostel, which was a pretty fine plan. I had been getting on quite well with one of the Dutch women, who offered to buy me a drink and asked the barman if he wanted one, as by this time he too was standing in the crowded little outdoors bit, drinking a lemonade.

"No, no, I cannot, sorry."

"Because you're working? Hey, don't worry, we won't tell."

"No, is not that. I am driving taxi at 7.00 tomorrow."

This caused everyone to look at him. It was well past 3.00am.

"Really? Oh wow, we're sorry. Hey, we will let you close up."

"No, that's alright."

"Not at all. We'll go now."

So everyone drank up, and let the poor feller close up. This was probably a good thing, as my plan had been to get out to the castle quite early the next day. Naturally this did not happen, but I did notice a few pissed off looks when my trusty little alarm clock went off, in that surprisingly loud way that those little travel alarms can. I can imagine the younger backpackers cursing me for not having a phone and thinking that this must be something old duffers do, oblivious to the fact that I had, in fact, came armed with technology, I'd just taken it for a swim.

Next day, it was off to Bran Castle via the local bus, a journey of not much more that 45 minutes or so. I was quite excited, as after all, this was the place known outside of the region as Dracula's castle.

This, it turned out, was a remarkably good bit of imaginative marketing on someone's part. Apparently, there is no evidence that Bram Stoker ever knew anything about this place. In any case, it doesn't actually match the description of the castle in the books, aside from being a spooky looking kind of building. Even when it comes to links with Vlad the Impaler, a real life bit of work who was a kind of inspiration for the Count, there are very few links other than it's in the same region he lived in, and he may have gone there. However, never one to get put off by the details, I found myself enjoying the walk around the place, which is now in fact a museum dedicated to Queen Marie, the last Queen of Romania, albeit a consort, and apparently a bit of a drunk known for organising parties and orgies before and during the war. This, apparently ruined her once popular reputation, which is a shame as I for one would have been all the fonder of her for it.

So to anyone turning up at the castle hoping to find a kind of real life haunted house dedicated to Dracula, or even Vlad, a huge disappointment awaits. Well, in theory anyway, as nobody seemed to be disappointed. It's a good place to visit, set near some remarkable scenery, and hell…..you've been to Dracula's bloody Castle.

I had a wander around Bran the town after, which was much more vampire friendly. There was even a vampire themed bar which I felt obliged to go and have a beer in, and found myself sitting next to a group of fat German Goths clutching bags full of souvenirs.

"Did you visit the Castle?" one of them asked me in English, probably as he saw me watching him as he kept turning over a snow globe with a little plastic castle in it.

"Yes. Queen Marie sure liked her furniture."

"It belonged to Vlad the Impaler. You know him?"

"Not personally." I'm pretty sure I'd read that it had once been thought that he had been imprisoned there, but now they figure it was a castle in Budapest, but who was I to ruin these poor young Goths' image of the place.

"He seems evil, but he was fighting tyrants."

"Yes," I replied. "He was really sticking it to the man…"

This either got lost in translation, or they were true to the goth image of never really smiling much. I'd gone out with a couple of goth girls in the past and in fact really liked the whole goth look. I thought the goth girls looked hot as hell, and which was part of my attraction to them. But in all cases, upon dating them, they turned punk quite quickly, much to my complete annoyance, apart from they smiled more.

I had a beer, explored the town, and headed back on the bus to Brasov. I was all set for another night in the club below the hostel, but instead got talking to a couple of Finnish lads on the bus and we went for a drink and something to eat. As is the way with drinking with Finns, I have no real recollection of getting back to the hostel, but apparently tried to go to bed in the wrong dorm, much to the occupant of the beds annoyance, though he laughed about it when he told me the next morning. More annoyed were my roommates, as I went on to snore really loudly and was kind of unwakeable. My credit card, which I carried only as a back-up, was also missing, though a call to cancel it revealed no one had tried to use it, so it was no doubt behind the counter in a bar somewhere.

I slept for a good part of the day, which may well be the vampire influence beginning to kick in. It would not, in fact, be the first time that I'd been cursed by an evil cloaked vampire Count, if that was the case. No, that honour fell to Count Duckula, an old 80's cartoon character.

Though as punk as any of my 80's contemporaries, I tended to do things slightly off. So rather than the usual band logos on my leather jacket, I painted a cartoon picture of a fanged duck sporting two batwings on the back of my cut-off with the words Duck out of Hell written around this. This was a combination of an obvious parody of the Meatloaf album Bat out of Hell, and the fact that I had had a girlfriend who for some reason pet-named me duckling, which had caused the lads to rip it out of me for months when she let it slip in the pub one night.

This would be quite the talking point at gigs and such, and people would smile and say that they liked the picture. Or at least they did for a couple of years until a stupid cartoon show called Count Duckula came out, and everyone I met would see my highly original and self-designed motif and ask me if I'd based it on the newly arrived Count Duckula. Suddenly my charmingly witty character of Duck out of Hell had vanished, and I was now some twat with a bad rip off of a kids TV show on my jacket. The duck got painted over. I may have put a band's logo on instead.

Way too soon, it was time to head off again, for as beautiful as Brasov is, that excited feeling of moving on was kicking in. I had seen no vampires, unless they had moved down to pushing noses instead of biting necks. I had heard a lot about local hero/villain

Vlad the Impaler in regards to places he may or may not have stayed at, and considered that he is a surprising model for the template of Count Dracula. In most literature I have read, the good count never shoved whopping big spiked poles up his subjects' arses and left them to perish. Unless this is exaggerated too? Maybe he actually stuck things up, or simply pressed people's noses. He may, in fact, have been mistranslated and actually been Vlad the inhaler, more a clearer of sinus than anus problems.

I was booked onto the night train to Budapest, which I could get from Brasov. So on getting back from a last wander around on that last day, I sat in the hostel chatting to the owners and watching some cartoons in the common room, hoping to hell Count Duckula did not come on. It didn't, but eventually I dragged myself out, got myself a slap up dinner for a couple of quid, and boarded the train right on time. My standing in for Van Helsing was now over, and I felt my familiar tingle of excitement as I headed off to my next destination on the road to L.

VII

Well, this train was certainly a lot better than the previous sleeper I had been on. Fully expecting something similar, I was pleasantly surprised to find that the sleeping cabin, though a three berth, was empty but for me, and also contained a damned fine pull out unit that had a sink and water taps. Not only that, but there were free complimentary toothbrushes, paste, soap, etc. There was, a sign told me, a shower facility up the back, but I probably wouldn't use that, I thought. I would sleep well, but was not tired yet, so found myself standing in the corridor looking out of the window, though not being able to see much, when I spotted a guy about to enter another cabin with a can of beer.

"Hey," I called out to him. "Is there a bar?"

I let my hands sort of point at the can and made a questioning gesture, and he answered with a nod, and a point in the direction he had come from. This was getting better. I headed off in that direction, and there, only two cars down, I walked into what could best be described as a pub on wheels.

There was a bar at one end, and the rest of it was seats around tables. There were a few people in there, sitting around enjoying a drink, and eating snacks. I double backed to the room, got the current book I was reading, and returned and ordered a beer. They even poured it into a glass. The illusion of being in a pub was so complete, that I neglected to hold my glass of beer, and at one bumpy bit, it flew off the table and broke on the floor. The waiters came over straight away, apologised, and mopped up, but nevertheless, replacing the beer was down to me. I did, apologising. This was all very polite.

On hearing me talk to the staff, a couple of young lads, about 19 or so, introduced themselves as being English, and came and sat at my table. I put the book down. They were also travelling to Budapest, but had not booked a sleeper. Hence, they were intending to sleep on their ordinary seats, but had apparently become lumbered with some obnoxious local guy who was drunk and harassing them. These two had come to get a drink to get some respite, and were dropping hints when I told them I had a sleeper room to myself. However, and so it turned out, I knew that someone could get on at any point, so I pretended I didn't get the hint. They were also a bit worried about the guy harassing them.

They reminded me a bit of my early days of travelling Europe, doing it on a budget and getting into all sorts of trouble. My first instinct was to say I would come down and sit with their crowd for a while, maybe shoo the bloke off, but then I figured, hell, there are 4 of them, and they'll learn that you have to look after yourself out there sometimes. I did, however, tell the two lads I was talking to my cabin number, and told them that if things got a bit too rough, to come and give me a shout. The bar shut about half an hour later, we had enjoyed a good chat about our respective journeys, and how to deal with obnoxious twats on trains, and they said they would give me a shout if need be. I didn't see them again, so I assumed everything was OK and the drunk had probably fallen asleep somewhere on the train.

It turned out that I was right to have not sneaked them into the cabin, for at some point after I had retired, the door opened and someone came in.

"Do you mind if I turn the light on?" she half whispered.

"No, not at all. Please, feel free."

She did, and I found myself in the company of a rather stunning looking dark haired Romanian woman in her early 30's, wearing combat trousers and a Ramones t-shirt. My imagination, as it does, jumped into overtime, and by the time she had said,

"Oh look. free toothpaste," I was already pondering if these situations on pornhub ever come true, and wondering if there was enough room for the doggy position on the top bunk. I had, though, chosen the bottom one, which I tended to do when confronted with bunks, as I'd decided to make life as easy for going to the toilet as possible on long journeys.

"I'm sorry, can you look the other way," she laughed, then proceeded to lose her trainers and trousers, and went to climb up onto the next bunk up. I did indeed turn around and face the wall, and even pretended to shut my eyes, but was in fact unwittingly stretching my eyeballs round till they kind of hurt.

"Good night," she called down, and I just as I was about to say it back, she added,

"Oh, and I sleep with a knife."

I bade her goodnight and went to sleep.

The girl had gone by the time I woke up, and I hadn't heard a thing, so I guess she was a veteran of sleepers. Either that or I was more tired than I'd thought. I was awake quite early, got myself a coffee from a machine in the pub area and sat and enjoyed watching some beautiful Hungarian countryside going past, one of the absolute pleasures of train travel in Europe. It seemed like no time at all when the train pulled up in Budapest and I had arrived.

Here was another difference in travelling in the internet era compared to my previous trips. Before leaving, I had booked all my hostels in advance, and printed off the details for each one. These were great, and the printouts even had either a little map or a list of instructions on how to get to the hostel from the airport or train station, including any buses needed, or how to get there by walking. I usually opted for this last one, and this time was no different. I had booked into a hostel called Carpe Noctem, and it was only about a 20 minute walk from Budapest-Keleti, the main station where I had arrived.

I arrived at the hostel, and it was at the top of a mighty long, mighty narrow flight of old stairs. A young girl went to book me in, then looked at my passport and popped out the back for a moment. And here, for the first time ever, I discovered something that I didn't know existed.

The under-40's only hostel.

Yes, a young lad actually came out and politely told me that I was too old to stay at Carpe Noctum!.

"What?"

"Yeah, sorry. It's a party hostel. We've had trouble with older people before, so now we have a top age limit. It says so on our website."

I'm sure it did. But to be honest, I had at no point even thought of looking out for such a thing. I still have no idea what sort of trouble was caused specifically by older people, maybe some kind of rampaging pensioner mobs, or people upset by the sight of false teeth left in glasses in the dorms, but I figured that there was no point arguing, and asked him for the address of any other hostels nearby. He did helpfully tell me there was a good one round the corner.

So there it was. Before leaving, I'd been a bit worried about maybe being a bit older than the people I would be meeting, but so far, this had not been a problem. Till now. It would appear that though a seasoned veteran of worldwide backpackers hostels, overlanding by truck, couch surfing before it was a thing, and all sorts of roughing it, topped up with the fact that at this stage in my life I hosted and organised Fetish events and DJ'd in city centre nightclubs, I was, apparently, too old for what the lad told me in a somewhat, but not deliberately patronisingly way, was a "party hostel". Hell, I'd seen some of the people sitting around in there. I'm pretty sure I could have out partied any of them, and then got them home once they'd collapsed.

It felt, quite frankly, like a right kick in the bollocks.

140

I went off to the hostel round the corner, a place called Tiger Tim's. At this point, I wasn't so much pissed off with being rejected from the hostel - though I would in time. Backpackers and travellers are the very people I identify myself the most with, and to be rejected because of age, with my understanding and experiences of travelling with people of all ages, sexes and nationalities - but I was worried about how many of these places there were, and how many I might be booked into. I needed to check all my bookings now, and I had been to this point quite pleased at how well organised I had been so far.

Odd thing was, going into Tiger Tim's, I got the impression that it had a hell of a lot more life in it than the last one anyway. It was owned by an Irish feller, who was actually the Tiger Tim in the name. He got asked a few times why he was called that. He simply said that they should ask the three Croatian guys who tried to cause trouble in there one time. I did wonder if these were part of the marauding elderly gangs the other place was worried about, but decided to keep my mouth shut.

In fact, it was a pretty good hostel, with what appeared to be a pretty decent crowd, aside from one seemingly grumpy young guy who seemed to think that he was some kind of king of the hostel, and would put people down at any opportunity. He was, I was sorry to say, also English, and managed to show the worst traits of the cliche Brit abroad. We took an instant dislike to each other.

I was in an eight bunk dorm, with 5 other lads from various countries and two English girls.

"Are you coming on the pub crawl?" a girl who worked at the hostel asked me.

"Pub crawl?"

"Yes. We organise one most nights. One of my jobs here is to take people round the local bars and clubs. Fancy it?"

I did. I was also envious of anyone whose job it is to take people around on Pub crawls. If that had been an option on my last backpacking tours, I'd probably never have come back. I was to find this was quite common as I carried on my journey. Things seemed to be a lot more organised than I remember them being before. I'm not sure if this is a good or bad thing, to be honest, but

141

on this occasion I was thinking that it was nice to be asked, as long as they didn't plan on wrapping me in a tartan blanket and taking it in turns wheeling me from bar to bar in a wheelchair.

Like most hostels, there was beer on sale, and I'd been sitting in the common room having a couple of bottles with an American guy in his mid-30's who had booked in, and a couple of French lads from my dorm. The American, Steve, had been on the road for about 3 months at this point, and had earlier that day had had yet another argument with his girlfriend back home who this time had given him an ultimatum of coming back or they were over. He'd been planning on a 6 month trip all together, so this was a bit of a dilemma for him. The French guys, being younger, were laughing and telling him to tell her to go fuck herself, which I actually agreed with, but tried to offer some wise, sage like balancing advice and to ask himself what he wanted the most.

"Thing is," he said, "This is all timed to be before I start a new job I have lined up at a local university. It's always been my ambition to travel around Europe, and once the job starts, I won't get this sort of time again for the foreseeable future."

"Then I think you know what you have to do."

He was, as people do, only sound boarding. He was staying out here, he just needed it bounced back at him.

Later, the girl from the hostel announced that it was time to go on the pub crawl, which we did and had a pretty good time. I did notice the English guy with the attitude being quite condescending to bar staff in the places, and generally acting like a bit of a prick. Still, he wasn't my problem, and in any case, a few of us simply distanced ourselves from him. He did have a friend along with him who seemed OK, and looked pretty embarrassed a couple of times, and I wondered how long these two would stick together out there. Probably longer than you'd think. Loyalty can be a funny old thing.

Me and Steve got split from the rest of the group as we had got chatting to a couple of kiwi lads in one of the bars, and said we would catch them up at the nightclub we were finishing in. It turned out they were staying at the hostel I had been turned away from. I mentioned this to them.

142

"Really? I didn't even know there was an age limit. They do keep calling it a party hostel though."

"What does that mean, exactly?"

"No idea. They have a habit of organising drinking games, so maybe that's it. You know, beer pong and stuff like that, but it's only really the dead young backpackers that seem to join in. It seems to be the staff who get wasted the most, and you can't find them till gone midday. To be honest, you really aren't missing much. We head out when they start the stupid stuff."

This made me feel quite a bit better, it had to be said.

We headed off to find the nightclub, got to the address, and instead found a large department store in a block of buildings. There was nobody around, and we could hear no loud music blaring, though there did seem to be a bit of a noise coming from somewhere, that buzz of human activity, but we could not place where it was coming from. We were nearly about to go back to the hostel when we decided to go around the back, where we saw a couple of heavy guys in security uniforms sitting by a table in what looked like the bottom of a flight of emergency stairs. This, in fact, was exactly what this was. They saw us, called us over, and asked us for some money. I have to say, part of me wondered if this was a scam, or if the so called night club was just a crappy room in the building, but we were on a mission now, so paid, got a stamp and went in.

"Those are pretty mean looking dudes," I remarked about the security guys, who looked like they would be better suited to some mega dangerous drug work.

"Yeah, I was warned about some of these guys. A lot of them are ex mercenaries apparently, a lot of them Russian or Ukrainian, and are part of the biggest security firm here. It doesn't pay to cross them."

It never does. I'm sure there are plenty of totally legit security companies around the world that run the doors of nightclubs and bars and such, and haven't got fingers in lots of dodgy doings, but I personally haven't come across many after all the years of working in clubs. During the early rave days in Coventry, there had been one particularly famous dance club that served no alcohol, but did sell expensive bottles of water, and if you were caught selling any kind of pills or E's, or anything at all, you were not thrown out, but were taken to the manager's office by security. Word was, you were probably going to be carried back out, and would have trouble using your hands again. Naturally, the owners claimed that they had a zero drug policy, and wouldn't allow dealers in, but there seemed to be some selected dealers that somehow escaped the radar, which didn't seem to affect the sleep of the owners in their pretty huge houses in the wealthiest part of the city.

However, the place was not a scam at all. The stairs, though they looked bleak, took us up to the roof, where there was a fantastic open air bar area, full of plenty of people, mainly locals but with a fair few backpackers intermingled. We saw a group of people from our hostel and joined them. A bit of exploring revealed a staircase going down to the top indoor floor of the building which was also part of the club. Here was the hot sweaty club we had expected, with some pretty good techno DJs in charge of the room, and a somewhat more wide eyed clientele on the dancefloor. I left Steve dancing with an attractive Hungarian girl, and enjoyed the rest of the evening chatting to people in the beautiful warm night air of the roof garden. I noticed that the dickhead from the hostel was also up there at another table, and his friend was sitting looking quite cosy with one of the girls I recognised from the hostel. He looked a bit pissed about this, and went over to a couple of local girls at the next table. I have no idea what he said to them, but they looked pretty pissed off, and one of them went up to the bar and shortly after, one of the mean looking security guys went over and said something to him and he looked mighty sheepish and actually shut up. Steve eventually came back up, looking far more cheerful, and had a couple of lipstick kiss marks on one side of his face. I didn't tell him. Looks like he was getting over the split quite well.

So a good night had by all, and the next morning it was time to explore Budapest. Now here's an interesting place. It is split in two by the River Danube, and is in fact two cities, one on each side. I was staying in Pest. Much of the history of both of these cities, and a smaller third city called Obuda, involved much of the usual comings and goings of the various tribes and empires common to Europe in the past. There is Roman history, legends involving Attila the Hun, the Ottoman empire, The Habsburgs, and such. Reading a pamphlet I picked up in town somewhere, I also noticed a reference that for a time it had been bothered by the Mongols. Now that was an odd turn of phrase, I thought.

"Who is at the gates now?"

"It is the Mongols, m'lud."

"The Mongols? What do they want?"

"I'm not sure. I think they are selling something again."

"Really? Not conquering and all that? What are they selling?"

"Possibly rugs. Shall I ask them in?"

"No, tell them we are a bit busy, and in any case we've still got the carpets Attila left behind. Have they got nothing better to do than go round bothering people?"

Crossing from one side of the Chain Bridge, opened in 1849 as the first permanent bridge across the Danube, to the other, you can actually see the difference in the style of both of the cities as you look across from the other side. But all very beautiful. There even seemed to be a different feel depending on which side of the river you were on. I spent a nice couple of days just exploring on my own, stopping off at nice little cafe bars for a drink or a bite to eat, and soaking it all in. This was quite the contradiction to the hostel, that seemed perpetually lively. A couple of English girls were in the dorm room I was in, who seemed to constantly be asleep. In fact, I never saw them out with the crowd at all.

Unlike the two Swedish girls who booked in on the second-to-last day I was there, who caused quite the stir amongst the lads. They were both incredibly good looking, but also from the moment they arrived were laughing and joined in with the various drinking activities with gusto. In fact, on the last night I was there, everyone had headed to a kind of little island with lots of bars on, which turned out to be quite the area for having fun. Though a whole crowd of us headed up there together, we'd all gone our various ways, with the Swedish girls heading for the bar with the best music to dance to. Me, on the other hand, sat down with a group of young English lads who remarked on the CBGB's T-shirt I was wearing, much to my surprise. They were clearly way too young, in my opinion, to have heard about the place, but never-the-less we got chatting about music, and they were asking which bands I had seen. I initially was a bit wary about listing the bands of my youth, as I remember when I was young listening to old rock guys naming classic gigs they had been to see, and considering them to be the epitome of boring old farts. So I tentatively mentioned that the first band I had seen that was not a small local band in a pub had probably been Joy Division, fully expecting blank looks, but instead grew gasps of almost awe. They reeled off their big songs to me, all of which were released after I had seen them, and asked if I'd met anyone famous from those days.

In fact, I had. but usually before they were famous. Most of the folk in the punk bands were pretty down to earth back at the start of it, and I always seemed to have a mate who knew someone in a band and got us backstage. Contrary to what these lads might of expected me to say, much of the backstage meet ups I had with the likes of Stiff little fingers, Adam and the Ants, Steve Jones and Paul cook from the Sex pistols when they were in a band called the Professionals and such were not great raucous affairs, but instead watching the guys wind down. Seemingly disappointed by this, I brought up a story about Charlie Harper from the UK Subs.

Amongst punk circles, Charlie is a complete legend. He is possibly the only singer of a band I have never heard slagged off by anyone at all. Part of the charisma and persona of Charlie is his age. Most of the early British punks, either in bands or just part of it, were born mainly in the very very late fifties or early sixties. Charlie was born in 1944. The tail end, if you will, of World War 2. This meant he was 32 or 33 when he formed the Punk band, UK Subs, in 1976. At the time, this was pretty old to be a punk singer, and amazingly, as I write this in 2022, he is still singing with them. What a guy.

When I first got myself into the pub trade a few years before this particular trip, I had managed a pub in my home town for a while where the UK subs had been booked into to play. It was absolutely packed out, and the band were staying in the flat above the pub, literally in sleeping bags on the floor. There was a barmaid who worked there, Jane, who was young, pretty, clever and knew nothing about punk whatsoever, having missed it by a generation.

"So, this Charlie bloke: He's pretty famous then?" she said to me after the gig and we were cleaning up.

"Amongst punks and that, yes. A living legend."

"Yeah, everyone kept on about him at the bar. He's sleeping in the flat tonight, isn't he?"

"He is. why?"

"I might go upstairs and sleep with him. I've never slept with anyone famous before."

"What? No. Absolutely not."

"Why not? Is he married?"

" I have no idea. It's not that. I just can't let you sleep with him. Simple as that."

"But why not? He'll have a great time, I can tell you. I know my stuff."

"I'm sure you do. That's the problem. Hell, if you go up and sleep with the poor old geezer, you'll probably kill him. and I am not -NOT - going to be known as the punk responsible for the death of Charlie fucking Harper, I can tell you."

This story appealed to my new friends, and we drank merrily together till I headed back to Tiger Tims, and a few of the lads from my dorm were sitting in the common room, drinking bottles of beer. I joined them.

"It's annoying," one of the French lads said. "The other dorm has the two beautiful Swedish girls in there, blissfully asleep at the moment. We have the two grumpy girls who snore all the time."

After a couple of more drinks, someone suggested trying to swap their bunks. So with much drunken sniggering, a group of us tried to lift the bunks with the two girls asleep in our dorm, with a view to swapping these with the Swedish girls. It failed abysmally, of course, as the girls immediately woke up and began swearing at us, causing even more drunken laughter.

I believe that the person who suggested it may have been me.

Time to head off the next day, and I figured that I would walk to the train station as with a slight diversion I could see the famous musical fountain that I had heard about. It turned out that I had been informed wrongly, and instead found myself at a fairly normal, though quite ornate fountain instead. The Musical fountain, it seems, was on an island in the Danube not unlike the one where the bars had been. Now, I would have been disappointed at my own stupidity about this, had it not been for the fact that there, standing in front of the fountain on his own, was the annoying guy from the hostel. Though I hadn't really seen much of him the night before, we had had a bit of a row the evening before when he began trying to take the piss out of me for no real reason in a bar we had both been in. He was out of luck on that one, as I'm pretty skilled in that area myself, and when it didn't go his way in front of others, he got quite irate and began shouting a lot instead, as people like him tend to. I let him carry on, as he was making more of a fool of himself now than when I mocked him. Plus, the security guys didn't give the impression that they would ask us to leave quietly if it kicked off.

But here he was, in a quiet park, with no security around, and standing by a fountain of what I hoped was cold water. So I walked up behind him, tapped him on the shoulder and said Hi.

"Oh. It's you. Hi", he answered, looking very awkward about seeing me. Maybe in the cold light of sobriety he may have turned out to be a decent enough bloke, but I figured probably not.

I pushed him straight over the little wall of the fountain and into the water. He was surprisingly lighter than he looked, or just clumsy, and hit the water with quite the splash.

"Twat."

I walked on, bag over my shoulder, fully expecting him to follow me. He didn't. So I still had quite the smile on my face when I boarded the train to Vienna, the next city on my journey, and sat with a coffee ready to enjoy the view on my way to country 44.

VIII

It was not a long journey on the train, well under 3 hours in fact. This was lucky, as I had not allowed myself much time in Vienna. I found this a bit to be a bit of a mistake. I arrived OK, found my hostel, and decided to explore the city. I had just stepped foot outside the hostel when the sky opened and it absolutely began to pour with rain, a situation that carried on for the rest of the day. I had not, unfortunately, brought much in the way of waterproofs as my weather app had assured me that much of my journey should be hot and sunny. I did have a cheap roll up anorak type of thing which I put on and went wandering anyway. It's fair to say that I got incredibly wet, and did not particularly enjoy what I saw. This did not take away, however, the fact that the architecture was beautiful that I did see. When it comes to culture, you cannot really fault Vienna, or *Wien*, as it is in High German. Both Mozart and Beethoven made their homes here, as did Sigmund Freud who no doubt figured that the other two had been merely writing odes to their Mothers.

Finding myself in a cafe drinking coffee during one particularly heavy burst of rain, I read up a bit on the background history. We had the usual stuff about Celts settling on the site, then the Romans making it a frontier town called Vindobona, which guarded against invading Germanic tribes. They did, however, go on to retain contact with other Celtic peoples through their history, with the Irish monk Saint Colman being buried in Melk Abbey, and then in the 12th century Irish Benedictine monks founded a fair few monastic settlements. In 1440, it became the resident city of the Habsburg dynasty, and was the *de facto* capital of the Holy Roman Empire. During this time it established itself as truly a place of fine culture, known even then for its science, its arts and music, and famed for amazing cuisine. It managed to repel two invading forces of the Ottoman Empire, in the 15th and 16th centuries, and ticked along nicely till 1804 when during the Napoleonic wars it was declared capital of the newly founded

Austrian Empire, thus continuing to play a major part in European, and even world politics.

It suppressed a couple of uprisings against the Habsburgs, and grew as a capital after the compromise in 1867 that formed the Austro-Hungarian empire. All this time, amazingly, music was a major part of its definition, with other composers from across the region living, studying or associating with, such as Hadyn, Schubert and the Strauss brothers.

World war two took its toll however. It ceased to be the capital for a while, the Germans occupied it and shifted power to Berlin. It suffered much of the horrors of the deportations and murder of its Jewish population, then after the war was divided initially into 4 power zones, much as Berlin was. This in turn led to Vienna being part of the Eastern part of the 4 power arrangement, and coming under mainly soviet influence. During this time, the Soviets forcibly repatriated Hungarians, Czechs and Slovaks back to their countries of origin.

Politics was always going to be another of the great historical facts about Vienna. Hard as it is to believe, but in 1913, Adolf Hitler, Joseph Stalin, Leon Trotsky and Josip Tito all lived within a few kilometres of each other, and probably even used the same coffee houses. This is, indeed, one of the great European cities.

Except today. Today it was pissing down with rain, and I was stuck in a coffee shop, reading rather than looking.

I got back to the Hostel that evening, and realised that it was a bit more corporate than the hostels I was used to. There did not, it seemed, appear to be a crowd ready to go out partying. Not to worry. It was dark, so I headed out to find a bar to maybe have a quiet drink, and headed off in the opposite direction from where I had gone that afternoon. Now here was a culture change. The length of the road I was walking along appeared to be home to a large number of hookers, many of them appearing to be Romanian or Hungarian Roma girls, and as a single guy I found myself rather targeted. This wouldn't normally trouble me too much, but on this occasion I really wanted to just get a beer and maybe a light supper. I did eventually find a little place, then wandered back to the hostel. It was late, but I decided to call a girl that I was casually seeing back home.

"Heyyy. It's me. How's it going?"

"Great. Where are you now?"

"I'm in Vienna. It's lovely, but it rained all day."

"Really? I didn't know it rained in Europe."

"What? Well of course it does…How do you think people drink?"

"Well, it didn't rain while I was in Benidorm."

"You've only been once, you told me. And in the summer."

"Yes. And it didn't rain. Do the boats have covers? I presume you have been on one of the boats?"

"The boats?"

"Yes, you know, those gongadors, or gongalerios, or whatever they are called. With the guys with the striped t-shirts."

"Right. got you. You mean Gondolas. That sail on the canals."

"Yes, that's it."

"That's Venice. I said I was in Vienna."

"Oh. What's the difference?"

I began to remember that there was a good reason why me and the girl never really progressed into a more deep and meaningful relationship.

It was still raining the next morning, so I took the metro to the train station and waited for the train to my next destination, Prague. It had been a fleeting visit to the Austrian capital, and for once I regretted not spending the rainy day perhaps visiting a decent museum or something. Still, I thought, if I find myself with a girlfriend who likes art, and doesn't think that Vienna is covered in canals with gondolas on them, this would certainly be a nice place to revisit. This thought actually surprised me as I very rarely thought about revisiting places, as there was still so much of the world to see. And to think about coming back with a girlfriend? What was this? Was I maturing finally? I shook my head and put it down to tiredness.

It took somewhere around 4 hours on the train, but luckily the weather changed, and I found myself taking in some lovely

151

scenery as I attempted to read the current book I had on the go. This proved a bit futile as an oldish feller sitting opposite me seemed to keep staring at me, before eventually asking where I was from.

"Ah, England. A lot of history. Here in Europe we have history too."

"You do," I agreed, "And a lot of it is the same history."

"Yes," he laughed. "Were you in Austria long?"

I told him that I had literally flitted through, but would like to come back and see more of it one day, and added that I had started in Bulgaria, then came through Romania and Hungary.

"Ah, the lands of the vampires. Count Dracula in Romania, he was based on Vlad the Impaler, a bloodthirsty murderer. But there were real vampires, you know. And then there was also Elizabeth Bathory. She was from Hungary. Bathed in the blood of virgins. Or so they say….It was probably said to ruin her family. But who knows? And have you heard of Krivich? The vampire mayor of Sozopol. They dug up his remains, and he had an iron stake jammed in his chest. Though he may just have been a bad mayor. They think he was a pirate"

"I've been lucky then," I answered. "No trouble with bloodthirsty murderers up to now, ha-ha."

"Austria would have been safe. Not too many from here. I am from Austria."

"Er, no bloodthirsty murderers?"

"Not really. We are a country of art. Of Music. Of culture."

"Ok, I get that. But there was Hitler…"

"Adolf Hitler? Why do you say him?"

"Well, he was no angel really, was he?"

"He wasn't a vampire though. And did you know that he actually started out as a painter? In Austria, many people paint or compose."

I decided to leave this conversation, and go and see if I could get another coffee. So Hitler wasn't a vampire, and had painted. Well, that makes things a lot bloody better, doesn't it, I thought.

I arrived in Prague, and the weather had really picked up. I took a walk to my digs, a place called the Old Town hostel, that was just off the main streets. This was good, as these streets were packed with tourists. Prague, I was to find out, was a beautiful city, with much to see, and so draws in the crowds. But though right in the centre of the old town, my hostel was set a few side streets back, and it was a lot quieter. I threw my stuff in a locker, had the obligatory shower, and walked out to explore.

I got all of about 20 yards when I spotted a small bar on the next street. I always do spot bars, but this one particularly caught my imagination. It was called something like the Templare Bar, and had a sign with the Knights Templar cross over the door. The reason this got me a bit excited was that I have had since I was the young boy from County Coundon a bit of a fascination with the knight's Templars. This may have stemmed from the time at junior school when we all went on a bus to cheer on our school, Coundon Junior, in some kind of kids soccer league match against another school from the city, called Knights Templars. We were beaten about 4-0 and didn't do much cheering, but nevertheless I found the name of their school quite exciting, as I had done a couple of school projects on knights and crusaders. This was in between my usual school projects that were usually about monkeys and apes. Oh, to see an army of gorillas in full battle armour. Which I eventually did with the arrival of the Planet of the Ape films, mind you. In any case, it came as no surprise to me as a kid that a soccer team named after the SAS of the crusader world would easily win, and having no real interest in football anyway, I disappeared to the Coundon Library a few days later and read up on Templar history. Or at least the junior encyclopaedia version.

It was a nice bar. Far cheaper than I was to find the prices in the main street bars to be, and a nice relaxed atmosphere. In fact, whilst I sat there, a local policeman came up to the open window by the bar and chatted to the owner. The owner poured him a pint whilst they chatted, which he drank at his leisure. I was liking this place.

I sat back and enjoyed a couple of beers, a rather delicious dark beer I did not recognise. This took me till it began to get dark, where I left a tip for my host, and took a wander to explore the old town a bit more. This, I was about to find out, was to lead to one of the more unexplainable and mysterious happenings of the trip. I turned a corner onto one of the main streets, and felt a strange chill around the back of my neck. I had experienced this a number of times on my travels, usually when I have been to some ancient place, whether natural such as the caves that contained bones of long distant ancestors in Spain, or man-made, such as the Church of the Nativity in Bethlehem. From the pyramids to the Grand Canyon, from Uhura to the lonely deserts edge that is the skeleton coast, I have come to believe that there is an energy in these places that I don't claim to be able to explain, or can be bothered to argue with the naysayers about, but when you feel it, you feel it, and I had just felt it here and had no idea why.

Prague by night is perhaps even more beautiful. Less busy than during the day, you can really see the amazing architecture as it is lit up. Prague escaped a lot of the destruction of other major cities during world war 2, as Czechoslovakia, as it was then, had been ceding bits of itself to first the Germans, then the Poles and Hungarians in the run up, as its allied countries, such as France, attempted to avoid war with Germany. Weakened, it split briefly into the two republics it was to see again later in 1993, and was in no strong position to avoid the eventual German invasion. It has also been said a lot that Hitler also was rather enamoured with Prague itself, and felt the city - though clearly not the Slavs and Jews that lived there - was too beautiful to destroy. I have heard two very different opinions on whether this was true or not, but combined with its distance from the allied bomber bases, it certainly remains a beautiful old place, and a joy to visit.

After a decent night in the hostel, I went back to the main square that I had passed on my night wander, and went to look at the famous Astronomical clock. Well, me and hundreds of others. Starting construction in 1410, with later details added up to 1490, this clock is famous for not only its ability to tell the time - pretty handy in a clock - but the hourly show of Death striking a gong, and the movement of figures of apostles wandering about. These figures appeared around 1790 or so. In fact, lots of things were added over the years, which makes it worth a look. Back in Coventry, we have a relatively newer clock which features a life size statue of Lady Godiva coming out on the hour, and doing a kind of wobbly journey from one door to the other. Tourists gather to watch, and I never fail to stop there if I'm passing as it is due out to see the look of bewilderment and disappointment as the rickety old thing creaks its way round. This always cheers me up, oddly enough. Also a big grinning head of Peeping Tom looks out from above, a wooden character that is doomed to watch a sort of rocking horse with covered bosoms for decades to come.

The Coventry timekeeper is no Astronomical clock, which is probably lucky for the designer, as legend has it that the poor feller who made the clock was blinded on the orders of the Prague council so as he could not repeat his work. As an act of revenge, he sabotaged the workings even in his blinded state, and no one could repair it for a hundred years. This is how elaborate the workings were. And to this day, it still keeps great time.

Actually, so does the Lady Godiva clock in my city. The original designer, Edward Loseby had in his contract in 1870 that he would forfeit £1 for every second it lost in a day. He never had to pay the forfeit. And the clock ran smoothly with its wooden Lady Godiva for over 100 years, including it being moved after the bombing in WW2 to its present location. It survived riots, the Blitz, being rehoused, but did not, alas, survive the FA cup in 1987.

For the only time in its history, Coventry City FC won the FA cup, and the town went crazy. Possibly everyone except local burglars hit the city centre on the return to the city with the cup and jammed every vantage point. This, unfortunately included the part of the building where the horse came out of the clock. Presumably in one of those not really thinking it through moments, the people who had climbed up to this balcony were taken by surprise every hour, when the statue came trotting out and began to swipe people to one side, nearly knocking them off the platform. The good citizens of Coventry stood their ground, however, and the mechanisms were blocked and never really ran the same again. I have no idea what achievements the Prague Football team have made, but I will make a good guess that their fans have never been responsible for the breaking down of their world famous clock.

I gleaned much information about the clock, and other history of the city and its famed sons and daughters from a free walking tour I took. These can be pretty good in any city, depending on who you get on the day. They are not free, of course, you pay them what you think is right at the end of the tour. Sometimes the better story tellers are not always holders of completely accurate information, and on other times the actual holders of accurate information are not very good story tellers, and you nip off when they turn a corner. In either case, there is always a part of the tour where you visit their friend or partner's shop.

After a day of sampling local beers -all good - I walked past that same spot where I experienced the weird chill, and felt it again. This was strange and a little spooky, I thought, but didn't dwell on it and instead got my bigger spooky head on, and booked a midnight ghost tour around the city. This proved very entertaining, and I fell in with some German goths who were on the tour too. One of the girls was incredibly impressed by the fact that the guide would stop every so often and get us to take photos, where we would, she told us, see orbs that were the floating souls of the dead.

"Can you see one? Look, I have one" The German girl would keep saying. I could not see any on my camera, let alone hers, but as I sussed that she wasn't with one of the guys in the crowd as such, I decided to share her enthusiasm and said 'wow' a lot. You know, just in case. This tactic failed completely, but they did tell me they would be in a place called the Zombie Bar the next night if I wanted to join them.

This I did after a day of visiting a couple of Templar-orientated sites, including a church that promised an all seeing eye, high above the altar. In fact, it was so high above that I'm not convinced that I could see it properly at all. It may have been such an eye, but you'd think if it was to be all seeing, they'd have put it where you could at least look back. I also crossed a couple of amazing bridges, and was blown away at how brilliantly aesthetic whilst elaborate so many of the buildings looked. I really did like Prague, I decided.

I enjoyed a few drinks with the Germans later, and endured the pictures of orbs again from the excited girl which I still could see no orbs on. They were heading to Transylvania eventually, and I wondered what she would be like at Dracula's Castle. It struck me that if someone pressed her nose like they had mine whilst talking about vampires, she may just squirt, so it would be wise to take spare panties just in case.

Much as I would have liked to stay and try to get to know the German girl better, I found myself leaving their good company before the bar closed as I had read about an old Templar chapel underground, that now had a restaurant built above it, and used the chapel as a dining area. I have no idea why, but this struck me as the most important place I should visit. I was catching the train the next day, and got a bit panicky about missing my chance. I was truly drawn to visit this chapel. I found out the name of the restaurant, got out my trusty street map, and headed off. It wasn't far, it turned out, maybe a 10 minute walk. I walked along the street till I found it, and stopped dead.

It was the exact same spot that I had been getting the chill feeling.

This in itself caused the hairs to stand up on my neck again, and I just kind of looked at the place for a while. It was still open, and though I did not want a meal, I went in and asked if it was OK to have a drink and sit in the chapel part downstairs. They were fine with that, so I ordered a beer and sat looking around. The walls were still the original stone, but obviously the furniture was more modern. This didn't detract from the overpowering feeling of history I could feel, and I'm not ashamed to say that I felt a little awe struck. I even touched the walls. I have no idea what it is, and probably never will, but I could tell there was a story in this building. Maybe something dark, certainly something secret. I enjoyed my beer, and felt satisfied that I had come to this place. I still do not know why, but on leaving, there was no eerie feeling any more. I had felt a connection to the Knights Templars, and was strangely happy about that. I headed back to the hostel, and packed up for the morning. I wondered what the German girl would have made of that.

IX

The next day was to be a long, long day on a train. I boarded in Prague at about 08:00, and was to arrive in Copenhagen at about 10:30pm, all going well. I would be travelling through Germany for most of the day, changing at Hamburg. I made sure I took some food and water, just in case, but it turned out to be fine.

A lot of people I have spoken to about these sort of train journeys often think that it is a shame you lose a day. I do not agree. If you want to travel, the journey should be as important as the destinations in my mind, so I boarded the train wondering what adventures would occur.

They started more or less straight away. I was in one of those compartment carriages, sharing with a couple of Brits and some Danes. A row broke out almost immediately when a German woman entered the carriage, pulled the blinds down, turned off the light and immediately tried to go to sleep wearing one of those neck cushion things.

We were momentarily surprised at finding ourselves sitting in the dark, until a Danish guy opened the blind again, much to the woman's disgust. She went to pull them shut again, but the guy blocked her and an argument ensued. By the end she was arguing with and shouting at the whole compartment, trying to quote some imaginary regulation that only she knew. Much turning of the light on and off happened too. She eventually gave up, after at least half an hour of this, and stormed out, no doubt to go and surprise the hell out of another compartment of people by putting them in the dark.

However, this brought the rest of us a bit closer, and we found ourselves to be quite a friendly bunch, and laughing about the mad woman turned into interesting conversations. The Brit couple left us at Berlin, where they were setting up home. Apparently it was surprisingly cheap to rent apartments in Berlin, which I found interesting. By this time, we were taking it in turns to nip to the catering car and bring back coffee and biscuits for everyone, and we were all the best of friends by the time we arrived in Hamburg, where there would be two hours before the train to Copenhagen left.

About half an hour before arriving at Hamburg, I had a couple of thoughts about how to kill time rather than sit on the station. I was all coffee'd out by this time, and considered a beer to be a plan. That was one thought. The other was that I had been on the road for a bit and hadn't really had much to do with female company. The last time I had been in Hamburg was the stag do, so I was very aware of the Reeperbahn.

This thought stayed with me, and on getting off the train, I checked and saw it was only 4 stops away on the metro. I had no idea what it was like during the day there, but thought, if all else fails I can at least have a beer. In no time I was taking a walk down Herbertstrasse, where it looked like the windows where the girls worked were empty. Luckily, it seemed not all of them were. I spotted two windows next to each other that were occupied, both with nearly identical looking blonde girls, both smoking hot, who greeted me with that over friendly way they have till you hand your money over and they begin to look at their watches. I had no idea which one to go in with, and felt awkward about saying no to one of them, as business is business. In the end, I decided on the one who called herself Mandi, based solely on the fact that she had nicer shoes.

Going into her room, the mood changed, as expected from jovial to professional, which was fine as I was not on the hunt for a wife. In fairness, she didn't rush, which I guess was due to the fact that unlike the night trade, time isn't as much money as passing trade was slow, and I guess they get a bit bored just sitting in the windows with hardly anyone going past. In fact, a couple of times she suggested I slow down and I'd enjoy it more. However, she was not to know that unlike her, I was actually on a bit of a tight schedule, and couldn't afford to be late back to the station. It was on the third time that she said this, and tried to start giving me a massage again, that I said something that I never thought I would ever say in my life.

159

"Look huns, this is great, but we're going to have to hurry up. I have a train to catch."

Time killing done, I jumped back on the metro and wondered if I had time to get anything to eat, as I'd suddenly built up quite an appetite. I did, and found an all-day breakfast pizza on the station, which was a pizza but with scrambled eggs, bacon and sausage on it. I bought a couple of large slices which were absolutely delicious, and considered that I was having a great day indeed.

Back on the train, I found myself sharing a carriage with two of the Danes from the original group, a lovely retired couple who had been visiting relatives in Prague. For the rest of the journey we talked and shared coffees', and they gave me some interesting tips on places to go and see. It was a pleasant enough journey, which then went on to include something incredibly interesting. On reaching Puttgarden Station, There was an announcement that the train would split, so passengers to Copenhagen should remain in the front. Then one or two carriages were shunted onto the ferry. Once on the ferry, we disembarked from the train, the doors were locked and we were free to use the ferry facilities whilst it crossed to Lubeck. I found this incredibly exciting, truth be told. I have found out since that this service was retired in 2019, which I feel is a great shame, as it really was quite the experience, and at the time one of only 3 such shunts in Europe. I got myself a bottle of beer, and went up onto the deck. Along with some other people, I breathed in the sea air, and watched Germany disappear slowly behind us as we crossed the Fehmarn Straight, and soon, in the distance, Denmark began to appear. It was truly a wonderful experience, which culminated in an announcement to return to the train, where we were shunted off, and continued the journey to the capital, and my 46th destination.

The ferry only took about 45-50 minutes, excluding shunting times, and there was still another couple of hours of train till we reached our destination, a journey that had run well over time, as it was gone midnight when we arrived. There had been some kind of unexplained delay on the line, I gather. I bid farewell to my new friends, who were most concerned that I might not get to my hostel in time. They also gave me very wise advice on how to get there, which I knew to be wrong as I had my instructions on my printout. However, I felt that as they were so nice, I pretended to walk off the wrong way till I considered that they were gone, and headed back. It was also raining, which was somewhat annoying. It was only a 20 minute walk to my hostel, luckily enough, where I checked in, and found myself in a 16 berth dorm. A quick shower, and bed it was.

There are, as I say, people who see the transit as a bit of a wasted day. I had woken up in Prague after connecting with the ghosts of the Knights Templars, met new friends who I would never see again on a train, and watched the beautiful Czech countryside roll by, being only distracted by a mad woman and some jovial company. This had changed to dramatic German forest scenery, I'd been naughty in Hamburg, tried a breakfast pizza for the first time, crossed a sea via a train on a ferry and watched the countries change, and was about to bed down in Copenhagen, ready to go exploring the next day.

If that is not a bloody well spent 24 hours, then I don't know what is.

X

Boy, did I sleep like a log! By the time I woke up, there was a buzz of activity in the dorm, as people got ready for their planned days. I've noticed over the years that the bigger the dorm, the less likely it was to have a crowd that would get together as a group. This was no exception. There was next to me, however, a pair of bunks where the bottom one was completely covered in sheets hanging from the top one, with clearly no one sleeping on top. It turned out to be an Australian couple who carried a few thin sheets around to ensure they could sleep together in a kind of makeshift privacy. They were just getting up too, and we ended up in the communal kitchen sharing breakfast.

Most Backpackers hostels have a shared kitchen area, and most provide a free breakfast. This is usually cereal, or bread, cheese, ham and jam that you could help yourself too. I have met backpackers who had survived on Rice Krispies or Corn flakes, and the odd hard boiled eggs in more generous places. My new friends, who introduced themselves as Mark and Alice, were having a bite, then going for a run. They did this every morning of their travels, they told me and invited me along. I politely declined, and went back to my bunk with a cup of tea - also usually provided free - and read for a while. Once up, I picked up a free map from reception and went out to explore.

I found it very reminiscent, in my mind, of Amsterdam. A lot of the buildings seemed very similar, and it even had a kind of familiar feel about it. But it was a nice place to explore, and eventually I came to one of its most famous attractions, The Little Mermaid. Now here's a statue with problems. Commissioned in 1913 by the bloke who set up Carlsberg brewery, it was modelled on the ballet Star Ellen Price. However, she would not model nude, meaning the body was based on the sculptor's wife instead. I guess that's why it's got legs instead of a fish tail. You'd think a nice bronze statue, based on the delightful children's story by Hans Christian Anderson would have a fairly easy time of it, but no, it is permanently being targeted by vandals and political activists. Over its time it has had its head sawn off a couple of times, and also its right arm at one point. It is often defaced in paint, and once was blown off its base with explosives, and found in the water.

It is often dressed up, sometimes in football jerseys of the Swedish or Norwegian teams, or Christmas hats, and even in a Burqa to protest about Turkey's application to join the EU. It was once covered in red paint as a protest about whaling in the Faroe Islands, and on another occasion covered in green paint and a dildo glued to its hand, with March 8th daubed on it. This, it is speculated, was by a feminist group who used the date of international women's day to protest at its nudity. In later years, during the Black Lives Matter protests, it was again vandalised, with the words "Racist Fish" scrawled on the base. This caused much puzzlement, as absolutely no one ever can find anything racist about Mr Anderson, or his charming children's books.

The statue depicts the young mermaid transitioning into a woman, and perhaps tellingly has not been targeted by the Trans-Piscine community. Well, not yet.

I treated myself to a generous helping of noodles from a Chinese vendor in a market I found for dinner, enjoyed a beer somewhere, then wandered up to the Christianshavn district, which I'd been told was a pretty cool district to hang out. It seemed quite pleasant, but was caught somewhat unaware when I wandered into another area with a sign that declared that I was in the Freetown of Christiania.

Though apparently quite the tourist attraction, I had never heard of this area. It is, in fact, composed of an old barracks area, which is still owned by the Ministry of Defence, and some of the old city ramparts. It was created around 1971, and remained at odds with the Danish government about many topics, including their open drug trade. At the time I was there, they had, it was said, to agree to Danish law, but cannabis was quite openly on sale from stalls along the main road called, tellingly enough, Pusher Street. The resident population is usually between 850 - 1000 people, all of whom must accept the philosophy of the Freetown concept before being accepted. Much of this is the type of communal rules that mean you are responsible for yourself, and to your fellow residents. Hard drugs and biker colours were not accepted, possibly as a compromise with the authorities who at various times have tried to evict the Christianavites, but have usually failed.

It is regarded as the 4th biggest tourist attraction in Copenhagen, and even businessmen bring clients here, as to many it is seen as a reflection of the progressive Danish nature. Myself, I didn't really care for it. Not because of the open dope trade as such - and illegal it might be, but I virtually floated out of there later just from my usual act of breathing while I looked around - but because of the nature of many of the people I saw trading. They were polite enough, as I found out when purchasing beer, but reminded me of a certain point in Punk rock history, when the kind of fun loving gig going music orientated punks were being gradually replaced by a new breed of anarcho-punks and crusties, who seemed hell bent on being miserable about just about everything. They made clothes and food political, the music ceased to be fun, and became too preachy, (often ironically enough, about people who preach) and the original punk concept of do and think anything you want was replaced by think like us or you're a wanker. It wasn't my kind of thing at all, and these guys had that same, holier-than-thou look about them that took me right back. Still, it was an interesting place to visit, and I wish them well on their ability to build a new community. I had a drink with a guy who started talking to me for our whole conversation about the merits of cannabis, till I headed out of the community and found an interesting bar full of lively music, where I bumped into the Australian couple from the next bunks.

"Hey, you've been in the Freetown, eh?" Mark asked me.

"Yep. Were you there too? I didn't see you."

"No, we haven't been. It's just your eyes. Got wasted, eh?"

I laughed. Or more likely, sort of giggled.

"Nope. Just got high on the atmosphere. Literally."

We ate breakfast together the next morning, before they went for their run. A really nice couple, we decided that we would go out for drinks later that evening. I had another plan for the day, though, and that was to set foot onto country 47 on my trek. This was going to be in the form of a daytrip across a bridge.

I boarded a train at Copenhagen station and enjoyed the 35 minute or so crossing to Malmo, in Sweden. Doing this meant crossing the Øresund Bridge, a quite magnificent piece of engineering. On building it and having it opened for July 2000, one of the problems was that if it was too low, it would affect shipping, but too high and was risky for air traffic from the nearby airport. So instead, going in the direction I took, the first 2.5 miles, (4km) is in fact a tunnel running from the Danish island of Amegar to the artificially created island of Pemberholm. This was made of material dredged up from the seabed, and is now a nature preserve that is home to a species of rare green frog and multiple types of birds. After this, the bridge becomes a pyloned and supported bridge that continues to transport both road and rail traffic the remaining 5 miles (8km) into Malmo. It has effectively

164

created a region of some 3.5 million people, with people buying homes on one side of the bridge and having the ability to work in the country on the other side with a short commute.

Walking through Malmo, I was surprised at how quiet it seemed. It was, after all, a Saturday and I would have expected it to be busier. Undeterred, I thought to myself that I would make the most as I only planned on spending the day here. So maybe I would take a canal boat trip, which I had been told about by a young guy in the hostel. After all, it was only a day, I thought as I disembarked from the train, so I was hardly likely to have any serious adventures or shenanigans.

That being said, I was immediately impressed that on leaving the station, a huge- and I mean really huge - transvestite with a beard that would make Santa Claus jealous, had been wandering around with a toy fairy wand hitting people on the head and saying something that I took to be some kind of blessing. People seemed to ignore him, even if he tapped them with the wand. I had no fear. I was under the protection of the ghosts of the Knights Templars. He ignored me, however, so they continued to rest. Lazy Bastards.

I walked through a couple of the surprisingly quiet streets till I came across a market square, which was suddenly busier. I purchased a kind of hot dog thing from a stall, and was about to find a seat when a loud drumming noise caught my attention, and a drummer followed by a brass band suddenly walked round a corner and kicked into some pretty serious oompah type music. Everyone stopped to watch, and young kids seemed to be excitedly expecting something else to happen.

It did. Suddenly the square was awash with clowns. They were everywhere. I have no idea why they were there, but I was immediately saddened that I did not have my Frisky Clown make-up at hand.

I sat on a bench to eat my lunch, and an old looking clown sat beside me.

"What's going on?" I asked him.

"It's the annual clown parade in memory of Miko."

I was surprised to hear a Canadian accent.

"Yes," he went on, "He was really popular here. Has his own corner in the local museum. We are on the way to Folkslet park to celebrate. You should come. There will be a lot of drinking after."

Turns out that this Miko character died in 2005 and was so popular that they were holding an international clown's day for him here in Malmo. I looked around and saw all sorts of clowny shenanigans happening as these guys gathered up to head to the park. I wondered, would Coventry ever have a Frisky day when I pass on? That would be so cool, a gathering of fetish clowns from all over the world taking over Broadgate in the centre? The only rule would be that the Godiva clock should be spared from clowns standing on the platform and breaking it even more, though possibly dressing it in a red nosed gimp mask and bondage harness might not be a bad thought. And Peeping Tom could relieve his boredom by becoming Voyeur Tom for the day.

I had, however, a return ticket and was meeting Mark and Alice later, so decided not to go to the park, though I have never regretted missing something so much since. Quite happy that something reasonably daft had happened, I found a nice little outside bar near the train station, and enjoyed a couple of local bottles whilst chatting to a pretty clown girl about my own fetish clowning back home. I thought she might be a bit offended at this slur on clowning, but she was in fact quite interested, and I nearly changed my mind about the park until her husband arrived and cheerfully bought us some more beer. He was in one of the brass band costumes, so I figured that she would be more interested in his horn than any cream pie I could offer, so I just enjoyed the conversation instead. This was a good thing anyway, as apart from clown people, there just didn't seem to be many other people about.

They headed off to the park, and I decided to return to the station. I was on my way and within sight of it when I realised that I needed the toilet quite badly. So I was a tad annoyed that on going to cross the road to the station, a chap in a hi viz stopped me and anyone else from crossing. I was about to ask why when the answer became apparent. For the next 20 minutes, thousands of the missing Swedes came running down the road doing the Malmo Marathon. I was stuck. looking at where I knew there was a toilet, full of fizzy beer, and watching loads of the type of people who like to run for miles sweating and puffing their way past me. By the time I got across, I was nearly about to piss my pants so literally ran to the toilets on the station. Where, I found, I was blocked by the large bearded transvestite trying to hit me with his wand!

"Get out the way, mate," I shouted at him" Or do you want me to fucking piss all over you?"

"You'd do that for me?" he answered, but did stand aside.

Finally relieved, I enjoyed the return journey back across the bridge and returned to the Hostel. I got ready to go out, and found a perplexed looking Alice in the communal room. Mark had apparently been drinking all day, and was already incredibly drunk. She had decided to let him sleep it off in their tent-like bunk, so we got a couple of bottles of beer from the reception, and sat with some Asian-American lads who were playing board games. In the end, Mark didn't get up, but we had got into some pretty funny conversations with these new guys, who had some witty insights on being a young American with traditional Korean or other Asian parents. Alice also was from Irish stock, and we offered back our tales of traditional Irish upbringings in another country, and soon other travellers were getting involved, with similar tales of traditional parents and modern countries. The time flew by, and none of us ended up going out, but with dirt cheap prices on the hostel beer, no one minded either. It was a good night, and in the way that good humour can be, was very insightful into both the differences in cultures and similarities in challenges that we all share. I retired to bed in a good mood, I had a flight to catch the next afternoon, and decided a good kip couldn't be a bad thing.

Well, it was a good kip while it lasted! At some point I became aware of Mark and Alice getting up and dressed. I thought that this seemed pretty early, and whispered over to them if they were Ok. They were, but as Mark had slept for so long, they decided to go for an earlier run than usual. I didn't really get back to sleep, so I read for a while, then wandered down to the kitchen area and tucked into some corn flakes and a cup of coffee. I was sitting there when an angry looking guy who I'd seen in my dorm came storming into the room in his sleeping shorts and t-shirt and demanded to know where the Australian couple were.

"I have no idea," I answered, "Out for a run somewhere. Why?"

"Can you get in touch with them?"

"No…"

"Fuck. Fuckety fuck. I thought you were all together?"

"Nope. Just met them here. What's the problem?"

It seems that though they had gone out early, Mark had not unset his alarm for whatever time they had planned to get up. Probably as some kind of joke, he'd also got the Benny hill theme set as a ringtone, and not set to stop after a while. So for the last half hour, at regular intervals, a very loud Benny hill tune was ringing out across the room, and no-one could sleep. The bunks had a cage under them which you were given a key for, so he'd left his phone safely in there with his luggage, and no one could get to it. This struck me as too good an opportunity to miss, so I took my coffee back to the room and sat on my bunk. Sure as hell, the thing kept going off, and people were trying to bury their heads under pillows, or swearing loudly, and otherwise getting angry. The wiser people would give up and get up every so often, and head off muttering to the kitchen. I sat on my bed and whistled along to the tune every time it came on, which seemed to annoy people all the more. After about an hour, Mark and Alice arrived back, and the angry guy started yelling at them about the phone. Mark turned the alarm off, simply said sorry, then they went off to the kitchen for some breakfast, and you could hear a sigh of relief over the room. I gave it 5 minutes, jumped off my bunk, started whistling the Benny hill theme loudly and went down to join them for a coffee.

One last explore of the city, picked up my bag from the hostel, and had a farewell beer with everyone in the communal room, which included Mark and Alice, the American lads and even the angry guy, who was a bit more jovial now he'd had some sleep. There was a Johnny Cash soundtrack playing in the background. Perfect.

For this was the last destination for this part of the trip and I was heading back to Birmingham airport. I had used up my summer shutdown allowance and some unpaid leave and was back at work tomorrow. And that's what I did. This left me plenty of time to complete another 3 countries if I was to stick to my original plan of celebrating my 50th birthday next year in the 50th country.

But the travel bug had dug too deep. Hell, I'd had more adventures on a train in one day than I'd had in the last couple of months back home, and the rest of the shenanigans reminded me how much I loved being on the road.

I didn't last. I got back, dutifully went to work, and decided to bugger the plans for my birthday, and booked some more accrued holiday time and unpaid leave for a little later in the year. I also knew from experience that the next section of the trip would, in my mind, simply join up with the first one, which is indeed what happened. Hence, come November, it seemed that I had stepped onto the plane at Copenhagen, had a nap where I dreamt I was back home briefly, then stepped off the plane at Vilnius airport in Lithuania.

XI

It was cold. Snowing in fact. I, however, was wearing cargo shorts, as I always did when I fly. I didn't think it was that bad either. The ex-postie in me sees shorts as an option all year round. But armed with my trusty list of instructions on the back of my hostel details print-out, I had caught a bus to the centre of Vilnius and was plodding my way through to the hostel. The bearded guy behind the reception looked at me.

"Shorts? Really?"

"I'm waiting till it gets really cold. I have my fleece on though."

I booked in, had a shower and wandered out to get some food. It was afternoon, and there weren't many people around, so I put my head round the door of a couple of cool looking bars, then followed it in and had a drink. Back to the hostel, I thought, and come out later when there might be a bit more life.

This proved a good move as there were decent crowds sitting around in the evening, a mix of Aussies, Canadians and a couple of girls from New York. We all got talking and drinking, and were joined by a kiwi guy who looked a bit worse for wear. His clothes certainly hadn't seen an Iron for a while, and neither had his face been near a razor. He had obviously spoken to some of the others before, and said he'd be back in a moment, whence I commented on the fact he looked a bit rough.

"Yeah, he's the owner," one of the Aussies remarked. "He's married to a Lithuanian girl, but she threw him out of the house last week and has been sleeping here. He'll be back with a bottle of JD."

He came back with a bottle of JD. He was a nice bloke to be fair, but hadn't left the hostel since he had been staying here, other than to pop down the shop for his JD. Apart from that, it looked like he'd been living on cereal, bread and cheese, ham and jam, and whatever else was in the left food fridge.

Left food can be a real godsend in hostels. People staying keep their own food in a marked bag in the fridge, but there is always a shelf for left food. People have ended their trip, or moved on, and whatever cheese, or meat, or vegetables or anything really that they did not take were left as a freebie for anyone else. Similarly, the cupboards would have many part bags of pasta or rice, and on those days - or nights - you had been drinking and forgot to get anything, you could usually knock up something, so long as the skinny rat-like travellers hadn't got it all first. I suspect that Jimbo, the owner, had been his own skinny rat-like guest of late.

"Yum. Sweet Corn on toast. Ohh, and BBQ sauce. And is that an old onion?"

He was a trooper though, the owner, I'll give him that. He wasn't too generous with his Jack Daniels - Not a problem for me, for I never could take whiskey - and managed to knock a fair bit back whilst we sat and laughed and shared tales. At one point he got up and left the room, for about half an hour. We assumed at first that he had gone to bed and so were pleasantly surprised when he came back, shaved, better clothes and looking like a guy who'd just woke up after a great night's sleep. I'm sure this was entirely down to a hot shower and a Gillette blade, but there are those that might disagree.

"Right. We all ready? Let's hit Vilnius!"

And with that, most of us ducked back into our dorms, stuck a new t-shirt on and followed our host. It was already quite late, but naturally this feller knew the late bars. A young American lad had joined us, who knew the New York girls from a backpackers in Poland, and marched straight into the first bar that our host took us to.

"These are on me, guys!" He cheerfully announced. "I'm gonna show you how we drink in Detroit…"

Not too well, it turned out, though I'll put that down to age rather than location. He was good for a couple of drinks in there, loudly bragging about the life of travel he intended to lead, and even enjoyed a couple of shots in the next bar. But not so much in our final destination, a small, but red hot bar the host knew off the beaten track with no apparent closing time, loud music and - no doubt why we were here - a lot of pretty girls dancing.

"Mulligan, your name is, yes?"

"Yep."

"Well Mulligan, and oh, I'm Jimbo" he reiterated for about the 5th time since we'd been out, "Let's go and dance with a couple of girls."

"I'd probably better not."

"Ah right. Sorry, you're gay, eh? Sorry, I didn't think there."

"No, not that. But I'm twice the age of these girls at least, and lost the ability to dance when I had kids."

This is a medical fact. As soon as a man fathers his first child, he loses the ability to dance. This has baffled medical experts for a long time, but the proof is there, on every wedding dancefloor known across the world. Dad's don't dance like other men. They bumble about, with no idea what they ever did with their arms before, and sort of swaying whilst trying to hold their stomach in.

However, Jimbo wasn't taking no for an answer, as he felt the answer to his wife being angry with him was to try and commit adultery, so reluctantly I joined him as we went up to two lovely

171

looking girls and began to bumble and sway in front of them, whilst holding our stomachs in. We even kept this up when some of their friends joined them, and Jimbo started really going to town with some bizarre hand clapping whilst spinning thing going on, clearly having a different interpretation to the girls smiling than I had.

There reached, as it does, a time where I knew enough was enough. It's the time when you are more than aware that people are most definitely laughing at you, and not with you. The more I realised I was dancing like an eejit, the worse the dancing got. So, I hollered something about getting the drinks in and kind of side danced my way off the floor and up to the bar, a place I felt much more at home at.

"Great moves, Rich," one of the New York girls laughed, doing a remarkably accurate impression of a dad-dance briefly. I just laughed and bought her a drink.

I joined the others on a leather sofa, and asked how the Detroit drinking lesson was going on.

"Not so well. He's asleep in the corner."

I have no idea what time we left, but we got a cab as the young lad couldn't walk, and Jimbo seemed happy to pay, even though his plans of extra marital snoggery had fell through. A last drink in the common room, then I slept till well into the next afternoon, so I did no real exploring. The next evening I did get to go for a drink with the girl I'd bought a drink for, as her friend was pushing on to Latvia before her, as she was meeting a cousin to spend a day with, and had been picked up from the hostel, so that was pleasant.

I like being out drinking with a guy who's a bit more older and mature," she enlightened me at one point. "You know, been around."

"Oh yes?" I answered, liking the way it was going.

"Yeah. The younger guys just always hit on you eventually, no matter how they start off talking to you. It's annoying, sometimes. But you know what the score is, and are happy just having a drink and a great chat, without assuming I must be on the pull. It's refreshing. So cheers."

Damn.

I enjoyed my little taste of Lithuania. My time was a bit limited for this leg of the journey, but I met some great people, and enjoyed the whole vibe of the place. Jimbo made it up with his wife, and I caught a bus into Latvia with my new friend. She was meeting her companion at a hostel they had booked, and I would have joined them but for the fact I had, as on the last leg, pre-booked a hostel on the other side of town.

The three Baltic countries I was travelling through on this trip are not that big, and it was only about a 6 hour journey on the bus to Riga, the capital of Latvia. The buses are cheap, frequent, and rather luxurious to be fair. I'd only got three or four days in each country, so mainly I was going to be seeing the capitals and a bit of whatever I could find around them. But arriving in Riga, I was excited that I was hitting country 49 of my challenge, and my new friend wished me the best on that one, and said we should meet up for a drink in Latvia once we were settled. She told me the name of her hostel, which I meant to write down but didn't, and that was the last we saw of each other.

It was dark when I arrived, so I found the hostel, went out and got something to eat, had a drink and wandered up to the old town. I'd grown to like old towns in European cities, especially the further east you go. I like the quaint streets and cosy pubs. Always got some unique features to whichever country you were in. In this case, it was a bit quiet in the town, There just seemed to be a lot of drunken Russians about. I eventually headed back, and spotted a place called the Transylvanian Rocky Horror Bar which was shut, but I decided it should be on the plan for tomorrow night. I just hoped that no-one would press my nose.

The hostel seemed a bit quiet too, and I went out the next day to explore a few of the recommended sights, and could feel it had a much bigger city feel than Vilnius. There is an interesting history amongst the Baltic states, a grouping name that once included Finland before it eventually threw its hand in more as a Nordic state. Much of the occupations and political histories were shared, with the countries finally becoming separate from the Soviet Union in 1991. One of the acts of protest before this had been a 2 million person human chain from Vilnius to Tallinn in Estonia, known as the Baltic Way, part of the singing revolution that had been in progress since the eighties. USSR president Michael Gorbachev and his party had already by this time realised that the independence of the Baltic nations was inevitable, and began withdrawing Russian troops. Today, all three nations are part of the EU, and considered to be doing pretty well economically. This was evident in the rather fine infrastructure, and in the fact that everywhere you went, there seemed to be buildings going up.

I didn't see a lot of life the first night, and almost wished I'd taken up a friend's offer of meeting some people he knew there. Almost, but not quite. At this time I was working as a team leader in the same car feeder plant I had been in for a number of years, and at one point had a team of mainly Latvian lads on the morning shift unloading tyres by hand off lorries. It was hard work, but these were good strong boys and they were good at it. We got on well. Not so much the second shift, a less willing bunch of workers with a self-important chargehand who thought he was the CEO of the company. He and the morning shift chargehand detested each other. Half of my time was spent keeping the peace.

The guy on the first shift had been my team leader when I started at the company, and was a notoriously grumpy bloke nicknamed Digger, who was the scourge of management. In every factory in the UK there is a miserable old bastard who does actually know everything about the place. Managers come and go, they hate these old guys, but the old guys constantly prove they know more and are untouchable. Factories need these blokes more than they need managers. Digger was one of these. He simply did not take any crap from managers and made it clear about his low opinion of them. I really like the feller, and we got on well. So, it was a bit odd, when in the scheme of things I ended up in charge of him, a fact he said was not true and I could piss off if I thought I was his boss.

"Hah" one of the managers who he particularly disliked and had humiliated on a number of occasions said on my first day I was promoted. "You can deal with him now. see how you get on!! "

And that's when I promptly gave Digger the chargehand job, and let him run things. The bloke had taught me everything I knew in the warehouse section where we worked, and if there were new ideas to be brought, I got his opinion first and let him trial it. Hence, we carried on working just fine together, and by doing this wiped the smile off the faces of the managers who got a lesson in proper man management. I imagine most of them didn't learn it.

So Digger and the team of Latvians produced great results, and our section ran easily apart from at 2.00pm when the miserable folk of the afternoon shift arrived, moaning about everything. This was getting tedious, a fact I commented on during a break once, when Armands, one of the more articulate of the group, offered a suggestion.

"Hey, Richard, you have more trouble with the second shift, yes?"

"You bet. Pain in the arse, the lot of them."

"We have been talking. Do you want us to beat them up?"

"What?"

"Beat them up. Before work one day."

"What the....no, you can't just beat up another shift...." I began, but I have to confess, I did ponder if I could get away with this, just for a fleeting moment, but decided I probably wouldn't.

"You sure?"

"Yes. well no. but yes, we can't do that. Thanks though."

It's the thought that counts.

It was about six months later that Armands was called up to the office at the front of the building one day, and apparently there were three huge policemen waiting for him, put him in handcuffs, and that was the end of his time working there.

"What was that about?" I asked the others when we found out what happened, genuinely concerned, as he was a good bloke. It seemed.

"You don't talk about Armands and his friends," one of the others replied. And that was the end of that.

Well, till about a year or two later when I bumped into him on the main road in my district in Coventry. We greeted each other quite warmly, though I decided to not ask him about the incident.

Instead, we exchanged some gossip, and I mentioned that I was actually going out to Latvia in a month's time.

"Riga?"

"Yes, indeed."

He looked thoughtful, fleetingly, then told me that he could give me some numbers of people he knew there, who would look after me.

I laughed. "Thanks, but no thanks" I answered. "I'm guessing these guys would have some gifts for me to bring back to their old friend Armands, eh?"

He laughed too. "Of course. It's tradition."

I didn't take the numbers. But it was surprisingly good to see him again. Whatever sort of bastard he probably was.

The next day was somewhat different. All of a sudden the hostel, and in fact all the local hostels were full of Irish boys. It turned out that the Republic were playing in next door Estonia the next night, and being so close, hundreds of them booked into Riga for a night on the piss first. As most backpacker hostels are close to the good drinking areas, the pubs were packed with green soccer shirts that night. I ended up on the lash with lots of the lads, including two Dublin guys who actually ran a backpackers just round from mine. Living there, they knew the local unofficial late bars, so this turned into a momentous night of drinking. For once, my walk to the bus station to catch the 5 hour ride to Tallinn was not with a bouncy gait of anticipation, but rather one of pure pain and exhaustion. This was in spite of the fact that this was it, I was about to hit the 50th country, well before my 50th birthday, though I did decide that I would save my excitement for when I'd had a kip on the bus. Luckily, I had bought a ticket at the bus station when I arrived from Lithuania, as the place was full of hungover Irish guys all trying to make sure they got buses before the kick off.

Though I rolled up my fleece as a pillow, the fleece being the ultimate in versatile clothing and bedding, and tried to nod off propped against the window, this proved futile. The bus, including the lad sitting next to me, was full of song, and drinking, and loud merriment, as the lads headed to the tournament. After about 2 hours, I gave up, stretched a bit, and spoke to the guy in the next seat.

"You lads got tickets, or just chancing it?"

His immediate crowd around me stopped singing and looked at me in surprise.

"You English," he said.

"Yep. Been drinking with your boys all night though."

"Jasus, I thought you were just some local guy who knew how to kip on a bus. What are you over here for?"

"Just travelling. On a bit of a challenge."

He looked at me again, and handed me a can.

"Beer?" he asked.

And that was the end of the sleep. I suddenly became Irish and stayed drinking with these lads, via dumping my bag in my hostel, and even headed to the huge screen in the city square that had been erected for everyone with no tickets, which ran into thousands. Tallinn stadium is quite small, I gather, and was packed out. Though I have a complete lack of interest in sport, the atmosphere was fantastic, and I drank with the boys through the night.

So that was it then. The original plan, as discussed back in the pub back home, was to hit the 50th country on my 50th birthday, and take 50 of us along. Instead, it was just me, it was not my birthday, though I did celebrate my achievement by drinking with about 50 drunken Irishmen who really had no idea they were celebrating with me, but instead mistakenly thought they were celebrating winning the game. Or losing. I have no idea, I had more or less forgotten by the time I got back home. They all seemed pretty happy though, so maybe they were drinking to my success.

I liked Tallinn. The old town was great. The next day, most of the green shirts were disappearing off to bus stations or airports, and I finally caught up on some serious sleep. That evening in the hostel lounge, I got talking to some Dutch guys, and it came out about the 50 by 50 challenge, and they suggested that this was my real birthday then. This went round the hostel, and that night I celebrated again with a large crowd of backpackers and travellers, as this struck a lot of people as something they admired and wanted to do one day, then we hit some more of the fine drinking places in the old town, including a place called, amazingly enough, the Depeche Mode bar. Here was a bar, I was told before we went, where they played nothing but Depeche Mode, and the whole pub was dedicated to them. I thought this sounded absolutely terrible, but in fact I really liked the place. And it was true, it played nothing but the many more albums than I would have guessed by the band. I thought this quite novel, and remarked on it when we went in to the young barman as I got drinks in.

"So, what do you do when you get home? Listen to anything except Depeche Mode, ha ha."

It turned out that he wasn't a barman, but the owner, and he just glared at me.

"No!" he snapped. "I really like Depeche Mode".

Whoops.

The next couple of days were spent exploring and bumping into people who had been out on my big night, and some Irish stragglers including a couple of old boys I got talking to in a pretty cool bar called the Hell Hunt. It seemed that one of them, a self-employed builder, had never missed an Ireland game in 40 years. Even, he told me, when it had been in troubled areas, such as Iran or Iraq, and hardly anyone else had been there.

"And I've never had a bit of trouble," he confided. "Only problem is when you can't have a drink in the Muslim countries. But I like tea."

Fair play to that feller.

I wasn't finished yet either. I went down to the dock on the third day, and got myself a ticket for the Hydrofoil over the Baltic to Helsinki. Then it would be a flight to Amsterdam, where I was supposed to be meeting an old friend of mine, Del, who had never been and insisted he would definitely be there. I gave him the address of the hostel I would be at, and when I would be there, but had a strong suspicion that I wouldn't be seeing him.

I went on one of the organised pub crawls from the hostel on the last night, but found I split from the group when I met two very posh English sisters around my own age in a small wine bar, who were out celebrating one of their divorces. It turned out that she had honeymooned here, which struck me as an odd reason to go out there to celebrate divorce, but who am I to judge? In any case, I got to help her celebrate in a pretty pleasant way, and woke up in a rather splendid hotel, realising I had a boat to catch. We said our goodbyes, and off I headed to my hostel for my stuff.

"Well," she mused as I left, "That was certainly better than the first time I stayed here. Much better."

Boy, was she working through some issues.

I only had two nights in Helsinki, and figured that I would lay off the beer and just explore. I really did not like the hostel. It was a large corporate looking place, with no communal area, and basically only good for a sleep. I was even in a room by myself, though it had two beds and the guy on the desk told me anyone else might book in. Now that seemed odd to me, a two bed dorm, and a stranger arriving. No doubt it would be a snorer. Luckily, no one came.

Going walking the next day, I found myself in a rather cool area of the city, not far back from the harbour. I stuck with my no drinking plan till I felt I needed to go to the toilet, so popped into a Charlie Chaplin themed place called, I'm sure, Chaplins. I had a small beer, to be polite, then carried on looking at the junk shops and book shops that seemed to abound. This lasted till a mix of the small beer and fresh temperature drove me into another bar to use the toilet, and repeat the cycle.

Except, it wasn't a bar. It was a pub. An old fashioned English looking pub, complete, I was surprised to see, with proper handpull pumps on the bar itself. Real Ale, as it is known at home? Here? In all my years of travelling, I didn't really recall seeing hand pulls at all, a fact I hadn't registered till I saw them in this pub. They even had names like London Ale, or Buckingham Palace Bitter. Actually, they might not have been quite that, but along those lines. I ordered a pint of bitter, and sat down feeling quite at home. There were not many people in the place, as it was early afternoon, but there was a couple opposite me talking in English. After a while, I called over.

"Someone else away from home then?"

The guy smiled and told me that he actually lived there. He married a Finnish woman some 20 years ago and set up a business there. He had now retired, with no intention of moving back. They invited me over, and soon we were chatting about the beer. He told me how in the 90's a Finnish entrepreneur had found he enjoyed drinking cask ale in the UK, so set about importing it into Helsinki. It caught on, and soon a number of pubs began selling it across the Helsinki metropolitan area. Along with the rise of craft beer a few years later, microbreweries even began brewing their own.

"Let me get you a pint of something I think you'll like," he said. It was a stronger beer, but tasty. Naturally, I got the next round in, then his wife insisted on going to the bar and coming back with some kind of spirits. And so it began. If there has been one thing I have learned about the Finns over the years is that they can drink. Not only do they like to drink, they are freakishly good at it. Never, I have said to many a person, try to drink a Finn under the table. You won't. We had a good afternoon and evening, trying different things, till they had to go, and I decided to wander back to the hostel, as I was feeling quite merry by then. Naturally, I got about 500 yards down the road when my bladder reminded me of my existence yet again, so I popped into a rock bar on the corner, determined to just have a small drink, use the toilet, and head back. I had a flight in the morning. I was at the bar when a young Dutch lad began chatting when he heard me speak English. He told me he was with some friends, and to join them. It was a mixed group of a couple of Dutch guys and some Finnish rockers they had met. We had a drink, and they persuaded me to come to the next bar with them, another rock place. I did, and ended up arm wrestling with one of the Finns, a huge biker with arms twice the size of my head. He won, naturally, and decided this called for him getting the beers in.

"So you like beer?" he said to me. "Here, I'll show you a beer you'll like…"

I have no real recollection of much after that, though I recall being lost in a fog by the harbour trying to find my hostel, then waking up in it fully clothed. I checked my cash. Finland is an expensive country, and sure as hell, I'd spent maybe 5 times what I'd planned on. But, what the hell, it was one great night, I'd met some great people, and maybe - just maybe - kept up with the Finns.

XII

So it was off to Amsterdam. I still hadn't heard from Del, and to be honest was feeling pretty angry about that. Back in Estonia, when I went down to the harbour to get my Hydrofoil ticket, I learned of a little quirk in Russian visa law that would have been good to know in advance. It means that if you arrive in St. Petersburg by ferry, you have 72 hours that you can stay without a visa. It means you have to arrive, and depart by Ferry only, and be coming from Tallinn or Helsinki. With my limited time, I could have done this and flew home from Helsinki, if it wasn't for the Amsterdam thing. In fact, If my friend had let me know he wasn't going to come over, I'd have forfeited the Amsterdam flight and done just this. However, I felt honour bound to assume he was coming, and reluctantly passed on this opportunity. The last time I was in Russia it was still the Soviet Union, and it would have been interesting to get the feel of post-Soviet life. Plus, St. Petersburg is known for its beauty, and would have been a great addition to this part of my trip.

He didn't show up. I had known that would happen, truth be told, and wouldn't have been a big deal if I hadn't found out about the Russian visa waiver. Long ago, as a younger traveller I had learned that you make your own plans, and if anyone wants to come, tell them what you are doing. As soon as I would come back from an adventure, people would be telling me to let them know when I was going next, as they wanted to come. They never did. Indeed, this solo adventure was supposed to be 50 people, a suggestion made by a well-meaning friend, who had clearly never travelled much. When anyone suggested coming, I would always say sure, and tell them my route, fairly sure that would be the last of it. In fact, this was fine with me, as the truth was I enjoyed travelling alone. Or rather , I should say, solo. The important thing to remember when setting out on an adventure is that you may be by yourself sometime, but you will never be alone if you don't want to be. And that's a given.

I like Amsterdam, so it wasn't being there that was a problem. Plus, let's not forget, that I'd achieved my 50 by 50 and even beat it by one, so all was well. Plus, I met a great group from Wales who worked in a couple of the tattoo shops in Cardiff, who were staying at Durty Nellies, the hostel above a pub that I was staying in. They were out there for one of the girls' 25th birthday, and fully partying.

"It's a shame about your missus, though", the birthday girl said to one of the lads on the last evening I was there. "Still, someone had to mind the shop,"

"Yeah," he answered, mischievously. "We have to wind her up though…"

"How?"

"Hey, Mulligan, that's an Irish name. How's your Irish accent?"

It seems there had been a weird Irish bloke in the pub they drank in after work who had taken to staring over at the guy's wife, who also happened to be the owner of the tattoo parlour that he worked in. This had begun to annoy her, but with her apparently distinctive look, she was pretty used to it. So, half stoned and half drunk, he'd decided on a wind up, that involved me speaking like my Mum, and my phone on loudspeaker.

"Hello. Is that Janeen?" I began in an accent, whilst we huddled round my phone, the others suppressing giggles."

"Yes, are you after an appointment?"

"I am, yes. I gather that you might be able to do the mother stuff? How much is that?"

"Like a portrait? I'd need to know what size. I can fit you in for a consultation if you want, give you a price."

"Er, no, not a portrait. I mean, you know, roleplay."

"What??"

"Roleplay. You being my angry mother, and me being punished. Is that something you can do?"

"Who the fuck are you, you sick fuck. Who the fuck do you think I am, and where did you get my fucking number from?"

"Oh. I'm sorry. I've seen you in the Poachers pub, and heard you on the phone once talking to a client about doing the taboo stuff. The staff gave me your number and…"

"Taboo? Tab-fucking- boo?? I'm a fucking tattoo artist, not a taboo artist, you moron."

The others were stuffing their hands in their mouths trying not to laugh out loud. The girl was getting angrier and angrier.

"Oh. Oh shite," I went on. "Sorry, the hearing isn't what it was. I honestly thought that's what you said. I'm so sorry. Still that's saved me £200, which is what it cost me the last time."

"You paid £200 to be punished by someone pretending to be your mother? You sick fuck."

"200 for the punishment. It was another 200 if I wanted full sex afterwards. I quite fancied that this time."

The line went silent for a moment. Then the girl seemed to have calmed down.

"£500. And its step-mother. £600 with anal."

We all went quiet. I rang off. Everybody just looked at the girl's husband as a number of expressions flitted all over his face at the same time. He eventually spoke.

"She doesn't even let me have anal" he said quietly.

Well, that was pretty much the end of that evening, as the others unconvincingly sought to tell him that she'd no doubt sussed it was a wind up, and played along. Which I'm sure was what she was going to tell him. I had a last drink with the crowd, moved onto another pub, and exploded with laughter. I shared the story with some other Brits, and decided that this one wasn't going to get old soon. Mind you, I thought, that Irish feller in the pub they used was going to be in for a hell of a surprise when she finished work that day.

183

I caught the plane from Schiphol airport the next day. It had been a good trip, but I knew now I needed more. I was already planning a third part to this adventure. So much of the old Eastern Europe was open in a bigger way to when I started out all those years ago. I need to get a map and start looking at dates as soon as possible. It's only a short flight back to Birmingham, but I still got chatting to the guy in the seat next to me, who'd also done a bit of travelling. His plan was to visit all the major cathedrals of the world, and explore the cities they were in.

"I don't know if it's a cathedral," I told him," but I was very impressed by the church of Nativity in Bethlehem. I got a really incredible vibe from that place."

"Ah yes, Palestine. I do want to go there. It's not a cathedral though."

"What?"

"It's not a cathedral, it's…."

"No, I heard that. You said Palestine."

"Yes?"

"Because Bethlehem is in Palestine…Of course it is. Of course it is."

I'd totted up wrong. I'd counted my college days in Israel, and totally forgot that I'd gone into Palestine, which is recognised as a sovereign state by the majority of countries in the United Nations, similar to Taiwan, or Kosova. I laughed. I'd actually hit the 50th country in bloody Latvia, and not realised.

"Sir," I said to the confused looking chap next to me, "I owe you one. I've just been to 52 countries instead of 51 whilst flying into Brum."

So, there it was. My little play on country counting, and challenge completed way ahead of schedule!! And countries come and go. Centuries ago, I would have been born in a northern province of the Roman Empire. My country counting would be more I, II, III, IV, V, VI, etc than 1,2,3,4 etc. And Rome was soon going to feature in my Shenanigans, so it was apt that this set of adventures had seen me on the road to country L. Yep, I'd been to L and back, and already had itchy feet. This could of course be Athletes foot, but never-the-less it was time to get out the map.

Part 3

Drinking from the Powder Keg

I

There was a cartoon on TV in the 70's when I was growing up called Mr Benn, which I'm sure will be remembered nostalgically by many Brits of my age group. The premise of this very basically drawn kids show was that there was this feller in a suit and bowler hat who didn't seem to work, but spent a lot of time heading off to the changing rooms in a local costume shop without ever buying anything. This didn't seem unusual to us at the time, but we were at an age where we were not aware of gentlemen's private spaces or had any notion of the concept of gloryholes. Anyway, this well dressed chappie would go along to the shop, pick a costume, and get changed. He would then leave the booth and find himself somewhere else, and have all sorts of spiffing adventures before the shop keeper would appear, as if by magic, and the adventure was over.

And so it was that, as if by magic, my adventure on the road to L was over and I returned to 52 Festive Road - or would have done, if I had been Mr Benn - and went back to work. But the travel bug had become tick-like, and was burrowed well and truly into the wanderlust that resides within me and was gnawing at me before I got off the plane. I was already planning to get back out for adventures as soon as I could. And indeed, it was a different Europe to the one I had explored and had so many shenanigans in all those years ago. Many of the areas that we referred to back then as The East, in a political as well as geographical way were now more open, and just waiting to be explored.

I found myself drawn to the idea of the Balkans. In my early days of exploring, the majority of the countries that made up this region was still Yugoslavia, and though opening up then as a holiday destination to a point, I do not recall many travellers telling tales of hitchhiking or backpacking through there, though I'm sure some did. Like many of the eastern bloc or its associated countries, information about it was surprisingly scarce. Both History and Geography at school were, I have noticed with hindsight, remarkably lacking in what was relevant to the world we were living in then, especially Europe. Geography, which I loved in junior school, would teach us about the Swiss living in Chalets, or the French all being congregated around the Eiffel Tower. By senior school, this stopped, and we learned about coal mining, and various layers of the earth's crust in relation to minerals. History, which in junior school meant knights and castles, or Vikings, or the dark ages and other exciting stuff also changed and became very focused on the American slave trade. A tragic part of history of course, but in no way taught me about the build up to the atomic bombs on the other side of the Iron curtain, or why this had come about, especially with my school days being bang slap in the middle of the cold war. So we just knew that the Russians were the enemy, but not why.

However, the world moved on, The Soviet Union broke up not long after I left Russia many years previous, and Yugoslavia had broken up into it consistent parts, though had descended into some of the regions bloodier times in the 90's, as the Balkan wars came about due to a number of political, historical and ethnicity reasons, many of which have plagued the area for hundreds of years. At this time, the war was over, the dust was settling, and it was time to get out there and learn for myself more about the history and the people of this beautiful part of Europe.

So I worked in the factory, DJed in a nightclub, put the money away, and in no time at all, I put on my business suit and bowler

188

hat, then headed off to the costume shop to see what the magic booth had in store for me. But what costume to wear? There was no shopkeeper with a fez to ask advice, so I had decided on being a booted and suited Roman Centurion. My adventure this time was to travel between two of the great monuments of the ancient empires. I would travel from the Colosseum in Rome heading north, cross into the Balkans and head south again to the Acropolis in Athens.

The Romans were another piece of history that I had enjoyed learning about in junior school that were dismissed as irrelevant by Senior school. This is a shame, as so much about them is still here in Europe today, fifteen hundred years later. It's remarkable to think that the history of this vast ancient empire has shaped the very languages we speak, the borders we understand, the religions we worship or reject, and even to this day the roads that we travel. The Romans were good with roads. If you are going to have one of the best militaries in the world, you need to be able to move them quickly. And roads bring with them trade, migration, culture exchange and all sorts of other contributing factors to a strong economy. Those roads, many of which are the origins of roads that still serve as the backbone of nations infrastructures today, would have seen many oxen or mule drawn carts, much more in fact than the image of chariots charging along, going about their business, and transporting goods and people across the empire. The logistics behind the transportation of the military themselves must have been thought out in great detail, and acted out on with precision and highly skilled man management. but as remarkable the achievements of the Caesars were, and the admiration that I hold for them is, I instead opted for a flight out on EasyJet and another Interrail ticket. My lord, if they'd had cheap scheduled flights back then, imagine where else they would have conquered. Or at least they would have unless Ryanair charged them too much in excess baggage when they turned up with loads of shields and chickens and such.

So sooner that I thought, and as if by magic, I had landed in Rome, got myself to my pre booked hostel, and took a bit of an explore around the area near the digs which were remarkably close to the Trevi fountain, meaning lots of great stuff to see, and, naturally in no time I settled into a little street bar with some local bottled beer and enjoyed watching the world go by. Locals going about their business, tourists taking in the sights and nodding at the occasional backpackers that would stop to look at the beer list. It was summer, it was hot, and I was in no hurry to do anything.

The hostel itself was pretty good. After my warm evening in the city I headed back there after something to eat, and decided to plonk myself down in the pretty lively bar in there and see who or what would come along. I decided that the company would dictate my drinking for the night, as I had quite the day planned for tomorrow.

"Hey, OK if we sit here?"

It was two young lads. I had indeed got a whole large table to myself, and the hostel bar was filling up.

"Sure. No probs."

The lads sat down, and were a naturally friendly pair. I had learned from the last two parts of my current euro-escapades that though I was now considerably older than the majority of my fellow travellers, it was not necessarily a bar to socialising. I did learn, however, that the onus was on me to make the effort, and to balance it so that it did not seem like I was being desperate to fit in. That wasn't too difficult, as fitting in had never really been my strong point since I was a child. In fact, the older I grew, the more pointless the act of fitting in seemed to be. But though we all need human company, as do I on my travels, there are times when I can just sit back with my thoughts and musings, and just let everyone else get on with stuff. Learning the difference between being alone and loneliness is a key factor in coping with life, both on the road and back home, wherever that might be.

"So, where are you from, man?" one of the lads said, out of genuine interest as much as being polite to some old fart they found themselves stuck at a table with.

"UK. I just got here today. Kinda working my way across Italy and the Balkans, then heading into Greece."

"Cool. We are travelling Italy, then Spain and France and heading back gradually."

"Where's home?"

"Finland. You been there yet?"

"Oh, I have. Recently. I loved Helsinki. Drank some great beers out there."

"We come from near there. Actually, we have seen a really good beer behind the counter here that we know. We are about to get it now. Here, let me get you one and show you a great beer."

So then. Two Finns had spotted beer they liked. And at that point, it was pretty much decided whether I would be drinking or not.

There was certainly lots to see in Rome. I booked myself on a tour of the Colosseum, but found myself wandering off from it once inside. I find when I am at the ancient places of the world, being by myself lets me absorb more, and feel the history. Some people talk in terms of almost mystical energies in such places. Or of making spiritual connections. Others will say that such feelings are just overactive imaginations. I honestly do not know what happens, but I know I feel something. Maybe our imagination is a highly useful tool. We can fill in the gaps when something happens that we do not understand, or transport ourselves to ancient times without actually moving, like some kind of internal portal. Who knows, but if you let it, something happens.

Except, here it didn't. I fully expected to get my usual feeling of connection to something bigger than me, but it just did not happen. I wandered around, I was impressed at the size of the place, and learned a bit about the history of it, but I just did not connect. I was slightly disappointed by that. There was, as there always is at monuments, a lot of scaffold. I'm guessing that photoshop was possibly invented by travel agents. For in no publicity pictures do you ever see the incredible amount of scaffolding that surrounds most of these ancient places. Never mind the Templars, the Masons or the Illuminati, It would seem that the scaffolders are the true upholders of history. I wonder, when these guys are sitting with their arse cracks facing the Sphinx, or Notre Dame Cathedral whilst they eat their sandwiches, do these blokes realise that without them history would literally fall down? I think not. I believe that they are humble men, who worry more about the price of a pint, and care not for the frustrated looks on tourists' faces as they desperately search for the one spot that the scaffolding will not ruin their shot. Yes, future historians will mention these noble scaffolders in their writings, once the era of digital editing is long gone, and we begin to appreciate the beauty of a construction of metal poles and wooden planks with something famous stuck in there somewhere.

Similarly with visits to the Pantheon and the Forum Romanum, all were well worth visiting, but I just didn't feel the history as much. However, wandering around Rome itself was very pleasant, and I decided that this was a great place to start this adventure. It was amongst all the historical facts that I was trying to absorb that I also came across something unique compared to many of my other journeys. The McDonalds coffee was different.

As a rule of thumb, McDonald's coffee is a constant, decent tasting coffee where you don't have to go through a question and answer fiasco before you wrestle a plain white coffee out of the staff. You get a generic cup of joe with some squirty milk things, and that's that. Perfect. But here, I wandered into a McDonalds, ordered a coffee, and was surprised to be given a small cup of McDonald's Expresso. This was the first time this had happened to me anywhere in the world, and I could not work out if I was a little saddened, or pleasantly surprised. I'd already done disappointment over the lack of interest I received from the ghosts of Romans past and so was determined not to let a cup of coffee define my experience in Rome. I tried. I really did. But I remember to this day that small cup of coffee in far more detail than the colosseum.

The next day was an eagerly anticipated trip to the Vatican. I decided to ignore the skip the line ticket sellers, and just go early. That worked, I hardly queued at all. The Vatican, officially Vatican City State, is in fact an independent state totally surrounded by Rome. It is the smallest State in the world in terms of both size and population. Covering about 121 acres, it is home to a population of around only 450 people. I was surprised to learn that it only became independent from Italy in 1929. Growing up in the Irish Catholic area of the city that I did, and going to Catholic school, the Vatican was somewhere I had always heard about, but strangely not imagined going to. Before heading off, whenever I mentioned I would be going to visit it, people kept telling me that it was OK, you didn't have to be religious to appreciate it. That might well be so, but I'm catholic anyway. (Though granted, not a very good one. I'm sure if me and the pope had a chat about it, he'd probably headbutt me in the end). It would have been nice to see the Pope, but I have no idea if he was there that day or not. I guess he is not up for people popping in for a cup of tea, or even a small McDonald's espresso, so I just showed myself around.

It is a fascinating place to visit. I just lost myself soaking up the atmosphere, though still not feeling as connected to history in the same way I had at Ayers Rock, or the skeleton remains in Spanish caves, or the Church of Nativity. Maybe, I thought, I am losing my touch? Or maybe the cynics are right, and it was all just wishful thinking? It didn't really matter, as this was still amazing to visit.

The highlight was probably the Sistine chapel. And not just for me, clearly, as getting to this particular point meant joining an absolute throng of people, all aching to see the famous ceiling. Though the artwork and sculptures along the way and in the rest of the museums are quite amazing, everybody wants to see the chapel. Built between 1473 and 1481, the ceiling that everybody knows was painted over 4 years by Michelangelo from 1508 till 1512. Many of the walls had already been painted by the time Michelangelo was commissioned, with work by many of the most famous renaissance painters of the time. Even afterwards, more of the fantastically beautiful art was still being created, but it is the ceiling that caused the really craned necks. It's amazing to think that at some point, not only did the Pope commission so many of these fantastically talented people, but also had to employ some ancient guild of scaffolders to get them up there to do their work, showing that the scaffolders are not just the supporters and custodians of historical monuments and sites, but were also highly active in their creation.

Along with hundreds of others, at some point I found myself crowded into the actual chapel and looking up. All around the parameters of the chapel were security guys shouting out at regular intervals that there was to be no photography. This makes

193

perfect sense, but did not in any way stop people whisking their phones out and trying to take snaps. However, with the jostling and the shouting, it was never going to be a serene moment to stand back and admire the artwork above our heads, though I did try. It was at some point amongst this mayhem that I realised that was standing pretty close to one of the most famous parts of the famous ceiling, The Creation of Adam. I think everybody know this, the scene where God is giving life to Adam, and is in fact the fourth in a series of panels depicting scenes from creation. It is, i must be said, quite awe inspiring, and I tried to stand still and look at it for a while, but this was not possible. However, I also decided to be a bit naughty, and pulled out my camera, turned off the flash and holding it by my waist took a sneaky shot upwards. Of course it would be sheer luck if I got the shot I wanted, but once I had left and got to have a look, I had indeed captured it absolutely perfectly. I could not have aimed it better.

The next morning I set off nice and Fresh to visit another little Micro state within Italy, this time San Marino. This meant getting a train to Bologna, and changing to Rimini. From here there is a bus every hour going up to San Marino. I say going up, as the whole country appears to be a bunch of mountains. On the journey up I felt as though I was traversing some kind of giant Walnut Whip. The journey to get there was not, of course, uneventful. The train managed to break down on the way, and after quite a wait, we were herded onto some kind of cattle train to complete the journey to the boarding point for the San Marino bus. The journey up the mountain had seemed pleasant enough, and indeed, the actual city at the top was absolutely charming. Or at least it seemed it was until I discovered that I was actually booked into a hotel somewhere back down the mountain, my confusion coming from the fact that the little city at the top was also called San Marino.

For perspective, San Marino is tiny. It is, in fact, the third smallest country in Europe, behind Vatican city and Monaco, and is the fifth smallest country in the world. Its land coverage is only 61 Kilometres squared, (or 24 square miles) and has a population of about 33,500 or so.

It takes its name from its founder, Saint Marinus, who founded an independent monastic community in AD301, meaning that the country can lay claim to being the oldest constitutional republic, as well as the oldest extant Sovereign state. This community stayed steady till 1320, when the nearby community of Chiesanuova decided to join the country. I imagine that this would have helped the birth rate somewhat, from what had been effectively 1,000 years of monks. Then in 1463, four more communities joined them, and the borders have remained the same since.

There is always the question of why no one has conquered it, or why it remained independent for so long. There are a number of different suggestions, but basically it boils down to the fact that they were, and are, quite happy to not bother or be bothered by anyone, they are stuck up a mountain, and no one really could see the point of conquering them. They seem to go pretty much unnoticed, yet get 3 million tourists a year, have a very long history of not very collectible postage stamps, and have an army even though they have sat out through most wars and no one has really noticed. This includes Turkey, who when signing peace treaties with the allied forces after world war one, missed out San Marino, who also never bothered, meaning that technically, the two countries are still at war. No one had really noticed this till 1936, when a Turkish student was denied entry for being an enemy alien. My guess is they just didn't like the look of him.

There is also no border control as such, hence no visa stamps or the like. Anyone wanting a stamp for their passport can purchase a souvenir version from a shop somewhere in the capital. They also don't have a currency, but use the euro, even though they are not actually part of the eurozone. No one seems to question this, and yet head per capita, they are one of the wealthiest nations in the world. All in all, San Marino is a shining example of what a country can be like when you go through life just getting on with people and not pissing off other nations. I have no idea what Saint Marinus did to earn his sainthood, but I'm sure he'd be proud of the lovely little place today.

The capital which I had found myself in has a population of around 4,000 people, all of whom I believe shook their heads when I asked the whereabouts of the hostel I wanted before a kindly lady in a hotel reception informed me of my error. But there were buses going back down, so I had a couple of hours to explore the capital, full of long windy cobbled streets and a kind of castle, until getting the last bus back down to the small town I was staying in.

The bus driver dropped me off right at the hostel door, which I was pleased to see was above a pub. I walked into the hostel and was greeted by nobody at all. The place seemed empty. No-one at reception, no one sitting around, just no one. I looked into one of the dorms but it also looked empty. I was about to go and ask in the pub if it was in fact shut down, when a young girl came wandering through looking at a book in her hand.

"Hi," I said, from the other side of the room.

She looked startled, and looked at me for a while before speaking.

"Er, Hallo. Who are you?"

"I need to book in. Do you work here?"

"Me?"

"Yes, do you work here?"

"Work here?"

"Yes. Do. You. Work. Here."

"You want to book in?"

"Yes."

"OK." She stood and looked at me for a while again. "Hold on."

I waited for about 15 minutes in total at the desk, after she wandered off. Though she did come back after 5 minutes with an older guy, they both looked at me, then wandered off till she returned again, this time to the desk.

"Do you have a reservation?"

"I do. Mulligan. Just one night."

"And you want to stay here?"

"Yes. That's why I have a reservation. And am here."

"Ok. Here is your key. Checkout is at 10.00am. Have a good stay."

I wandered into an 8 birth dorm, where I saw luggage on only one other bunk. I bunged mine on the bed, decided it wasn't worth locking it up, and went to the pub underneath. It was quite OK, there was a blues band that turned up and played, though there were probably only about 20 of us in this place. Still, I had a couple of beers and a plate of pasta, and retired to my bunk. This was only a fleeting visit, though I did wish I'd been on top of the mountain to see a bit more of it. Never-the less, I had a good and undisturbed sleep, the other luggage was still on the other bunk untouched, and I got up and went to look for the free breakfast as advertised that came with the hostel. I found the kitchen, no one was about, but indeed there was the usual hostel fare of bread, cheese, ham and boiled eggs, plus cereals and free tea and coffee. I sat and ate, and had a couple of cups of coffee, and did not see one other soul. I eventually got my bag, put my key on the desk, and left. I heard the girl's voice call out goodbye as I went through the door, looked back, but could see no-one. Still, if I had to write a review on it - something I never really do - I could have written Clean. It was. There was a bus station in the town, but I figured if I stood where the driver dropped me off last night, I'd probably get picked up. I did, and it did. So I found myself back in Rimini, where I went for lunch by the sea. All in all, a nice place to visit, and I then headed off to catch the train to Venice.

II

Not an unpleasant ride on the train to Venice. Not far from the station I saw there was a boat going near where I was staying, but decided instead that I would walk. It turned out to be a fair bit longer than I predicted, but nevertheless, It was nice walking through the interesting Venetian streets, and soaking up the atmosphere. In any case, I'd started getting used to the warmer weather, something we Irish and Brits take a bit of time to do. We may moan about the rain and the cold, but our bodies are pretty good with it. I eventually reached my hostel, which looked rather nice, and the lounge was full of happy, smiling, chatty backpackers. Great, I thought, I'm going to like it here.

"You are in Room 14," the not so smiley or chatty feller at the reception told me.

"Cool. Where's that?"

He looked at me with a kind of puzzled look on his face that said he could not understand why a complete stranger did not know the layout of his hostel.

"Our other building. This one is full. Straight across the road."

I picked up my bag and wandered over the road. Surely he didn't mean this derelict looking place, I thought, but apparently he did. I walked up a couple of flights of stairs, and found myself in a six berth dorm, with a couple of people sitting in there that were clearly not part of the happy , smiling chatty people from across the road, who looked up when I entered with faces that seemed to be looking to see if I had brought them their bread and water.

"Hi", I greeted them. They didn't speak. I was no good to them - I had no bread and water. Nor, apparently, did the shower. The other prisoners watched me as I took my towel and toiletries into the shower room, and were still watching as after a few unsuccessful attempts to turn the shower on, got dressed and came back out.

"The Shower doesn't work then?"

"You have to go over the road," one of them helpfully told me.

I guessed that these would not be my drinking companions whilst I was here.

Anyway, eventually clean, I headed out to explore. I was quite hungry and wondered what delicious culinary delights I would find. I wasn't disappointed. Just a few streets down I spotted a street vendor selling what I can only describe as the greatest fast food invention since the Glasgow battered Mars Bar. The pizza-dog.

Yes, a pizza-dog. A large, tasty hot dog sausage wrapped in a specially shaped pizza of your choice. Well, of a choice of two, with pepperoni or not. I chose with. I had been planning on maybe sitting in somewhere and eating, but a little nearby wall did me well. I have always been, it must be said, a bit of a fast food traveller. Years of solo travel have made me more inclined to grab some street food rather than going into a restaurant of some kind. I treat myself every so often, but sitting around in restaurants on your own is not really much fun to be honest. It's not like a bar or pub where you can just get chatting to people. In this case, the pizza-dog was a find indeed, and after I finished I went off to find a bar. I didn't bother going back to the hostel to see if anyone wanted to join me. I was worried that if I asked the other cellmates in my dorm that they might say yes.

The children of the damned checked out the next day, and a young Filipino lad had arrived, who could speak no English, but we somehow talked more than I had to my other roomies. This occurred when we noticed that the balcony of our room was in fact a great place for cleavage spotting. In case of a lack of language skills, always find a common denominator where a series of grunts, laughs and hand gestures will begin to make sense, and the rest will follow. In the case of most men, this is relatively easy. Women, beer or soccer just about do it. Not soccer in my case though, but I'll bluff it if need be. We are, it has to be said, simple creatures.

I headed out for the day and explored more of this fine and ancient city. Venice has a fascinating and much varied history. It's no big reveal that it is famed for its canals, but what is interesting is that this means the city is made up of 118 small islands, which are linked by more than 400 bridges. These days, the majority of the population live on the mainland part of the city, but there are still about 55,000 on the island area. It is named after the Veniti people who inhabited the region, and for over 1,000 years it was the capital city of the Republic of Venice, till 1797. Over its time, it has constantly been a centre of finance, an art and commerce hub, and at points a major maritime power in the region. Its sovereignty only ended under Napoleon, and by 1866 had become part of the kingdom of Italy.

During its time as a major naval power, it established trading routes between Europe, the Byzantine Empire, and Asia, often because of its role in eliminating and keeping down piracy along the various coasts. It had regular alliances with Constantinople, even though its population was generally Roman Catholic. However, it frequently clashed with the Papacy, due to its religious tolerance, and refusal to persecute people of other faiths.

It embraced the arrival of the recently invented printing press in the 15th century, and by 1482, Venice was the printing capital of the world. A leading printer, Aldus Manutius, was in fact the inventor of the paperback which he designed so that they could be carried in peoples saddlebags. So if you are reading this book after pulling it out of your backpack or suitcase, you can thank - or curse - the imaginative Mr Manutius for this very information you are reading in a paperback. Unless you are reading it electronically of course, which is out of the hands of the Venetians. Eventually ,war with the Ottoman empire, the black death and new trade routes opened by Vasco de Gama amongst other things saw it decline as a major power, Napoleon made it a part of Austria briefly, Portugal took over as a commercial power in the area, and its oared ships left it behind in the rush of European powers to establish colonies anywhere they could.

Walking the streets here, I began to get a bit of the connection with the ancients that I had missed in Rome. Maybe the fact that here on these old, historical streets, ordinary Venetians went about their business, heading to work, trading, stopping to chat, in the same way that so many people for centuries before had done was a factor, rather than simply an army of tourists passing through with phones and cameras in front of them. Make no mistake, I am not judging. For though I might see myself as a traveller rather than a tourist per se, a tourist I am nonetheless. Just without the camera and phone as much. It is with a slight regret that I did not take more photos when travelling in the past. I was always more of a journal keeper. I have a few blurry badly taken ones, but even then, it's the photos of the folk I have met along the way that I wish I'd taken more of than buildings and such.

I was walking past a small cafe, when I saw someone who looked a bit familiar. I tried to place him, and where I had met him, but couldn't at first until it dawned on me that it was not someone I knew, but in fact a celebrity. It was, I realised, Gok Wan who I believe presented some fine cooking shows on British TV. I'd never really watched them, but he always seemed like a bouncy fun kinda feller. In this case, he was sitting at a table, seemingly enjoying a nice meal with a charming looking lady who smiled a lot. It was then I noticed that to one side was a whopping great TV camera which I had somehow missed, and they were clearly filming him enjoying a spontaneous and unscripted meal out.

I've never really got celebrity culture. There are characters alive and dead who I admire greatly for their achievements, but presenting TV shows is not one of them. Though I would probably have been a little awe struck had I met John Peel, the British radio DJ whose music show kick started my love of Punk and New Wave, and inspired me to take up DJing, which after, or maybe alongside, travel has been the other major passion in my life. I admire the wave of DJ's who came after my generation of alternative DJ's who developed dance music as a new form of the art, and in many cases were able to combine the two, as they took DJing to the same level as musicians, playing in packed clubs to people who came to hear their sets. I envy the fact that they didn't have to put up with pissheads asking for the same record over and over again too.

However, I knew that my daughters would be incredibly impressed, so I dutifully took the photo. I sent it to them as well, and as a bit of a wind up added, 'Guess who I am having dinner with?' to the message. It was then that I found out that neither of them actually read my messages. Good job I hadn't wasted money on postcards, though I doubt if they would know what they were if they came through the door.

I also decided it was time to do some laundry, and found a little launderette near the hostel. There were a couple of Elderly Italian women in there, and another backpacker. I tried to strike up a conversation with him, but he was not particularly responsive, just grunting when I spoke.. I figured that maybe he just didn't speak English, so gave up. I read a book instead. About half an hour later, his washing done, he stood up and said See you mate, in what sounded like a Yorkshire accent. He went to leave, stopped at the door, turned back and said,

"Gets very lonely, travelling solo, doesn't it?"

"I looked up from my book, grunted and nodded. This guy really wasn't trying.

Laundry done, I headed up to San Marco square, a very picturesque place indeed, and wandered around listening to various classical combos that were playing around the area. One small group were playing Strauss. I like Strauss. I'm not by any stretch of the imagination a classical music buff, but I do like Strauss, though I have no idea which piece is by which Strauss brother, so I just call them all Strauss. Vivaldi was another favourite of these little groups, as I believe he is in fact one of Venice's own.

All Classiced out, I wandered around till I stumbled across an open air jazz festival, so decided to make this my evening. Jazz is another music form I just do not get. But if I ever say that, people look at me in near shock and repeat back to me 'You don't like jazz?'

"I just said that.'

'And you say you're a DJ?"

Yes. Yes I do say that. And in all honesty I have never come across a DJ playing Jazz. In fact, my understanding of interpretation and improvisation would suggest that we shouldn't really ever play Jazz. However, I appreciate that lots of people do like it, and as far as I am concerned, the best music in the world is the music that you like the best. This also applies to Beer, food, places and Sexual positions. Any of these can also change through life depending on where you go, who you meet, and if you are prepared to try different things. Though at this point of my life, if anyone can top drinking a pint of Irish red beer in a hotel room by a beach, sandwiched between two girls of different races while listening to the Clash and knowing that Just Eat have assured you that your curry is on the way, well, I haven't met them yet.

However, I got chatting to a couple of Austrian backpackers who had also come across this festival by accident, and had a thoroughly pleasant evening. In fact, I was even incredibly impressed by the skills of one feller on a trombone who made that thing play notes a trombone should not really be able to do. I wouldn't say that I became a convert to Jazz in any way at all, but I could begin to appreciate what the people who did like it could see in it. Saying goodbye to my evening companions I headed back to my room, happy with my musical appreciation of the day, and deciding that it was a day that could not go wrong.

At least I did till I neared the hostel and got that horrible gurgle in my gut that you get when you have clearly eaten something with brand new bacteria that flex their national pride by letting you know that they are there, and passing through your body incredibly quickly. I just about made it to the room, squeezing my buttocks together as I walked up the steps. It was then I discovered that two Spanish girls had booked in whilst I had been out, got incredibly drunk in no time at all, and one of them was in the toilet bringing her own guts up. Her friend apologised, which was nice, but did not help my plight. I baby stepped my way over the road to the other part of the hostel, but my key did not work on the entrance fob, and no one answered the buzzer. It was getting too late. I attempted to get back up the stairs to my hostel, but unfortunately didn't make it, and gave in to the inevitable and took a shit half way up. By the time I reached the room, the girl was still hanging over the toilet, crying and puking, so I grabbed the bag my laundry had been in and some paper and went down to clear it up. It was, naturally, at that very moment that another couple of girls who must have just booked in came up the stairs, and walked up past me, frowning. Of course. The first time in my life I found myself the only male in the dorm, I was probably going to be known to them forever as the guy who shit himself on the stairs. Never mind. I had passed a place earlier that sold red ale, and could always listen to the Clash as some kind of compensation.

The next day, being both incredibly grateful I had washed all my other underpants, and also being moodily ungrateful for the way the two pairs of girls kept looking at me and laughing, I headed off to explore some more. Most of the shops, I observed, were mainly tourist based, with an ample supply of key rings, bottle openers and snow globes. I refrained from buying either.

I often wonder about the type of people who buy bottle openers. At some point in my earlier shenanigans in life I had eventually made my peace with snow globes, deciding that it was not my place to question plastic monuments in a perpetual winter, almost as if the pyramids, or St Pauls Cathedral were trapped in a white witch era Narnia. But who, I wonder, buys all the bottle openers? My guess is holiday tale bores.

"Everyone for another beer?" I can imagine some guy asking his guests at a party or barbeque.

"Shit," one of the guests will whisper to his or her spouse, "He's going to get out the bottle opener…But dammit, I need another beer…"

"Here you go" says the host, handing the bottles round, and ignoring the fridgeful of cans. *"Need a bottle opener, anyone?"*

Collective sigh.

"Here you go. I got this in Prague, you know. That's a picture of the clock on it. Remember, Gillian?"

Gillian did remember, and looked as hopeless as the other guests in the knowledge of what was to come for the next hour.

"You know the thing about Prague we found…."

I found myself looking at the fellers sitting in the Gondoliers. All stripey topped, and tourist ready. I'm not sure, but the gondoliers looked remarkably plastic to me. This struck me as a tourist gimmicky thing rather than something of genuine interest, but nevertheless people were getting in them. A few of them called out to me to get in. Seriously? Are there any single males in the world who want to get in a clearly romantic-themed little boat and be rowed around being serenaded by some Italian bloke in a tight fitting top? Actually, thinking about it, I guess there are.

I declined the boats, but did indeed get a bit of a cliché in by heading to the Rialto Bridge, buying a cornetto like ice cream, and taking a selfie. It may be the first selfie I ever took. I'm not sure if that means it was a proud moment, or I'd let myself down badly. Either way, I posted the image on Facebook and got lots of likes and laughing emoji's.

This, of course, is the difference I found between travelling now, and back in my Shenanigan days. Instant images. Instant posting them. The mobile phone changed travelling forever. Most – but not all – people no longer want to go and get lost somewhere. They want everyone to see their journey on a daily basis, if not more. And sadly for some, the photo has become more important han the experience. I've lived on both sides of the mobile phone divide, and can say that I fully understand the desire to share everything, but in truth I think I miss the disappearing aside from a few postcards, and coming back to tell stories, rather than remind people of them. But as with any technology, there is no going back, so I will, I have decided, leave the inner luddite buried deep, and share in my own way.

III

After a good sleep, apart from the odd giggles when I went to the toilet, I decided not to walk to the train station this time, but instead catch the river boat that was a 5 minute walk from the cowshed that had been my hostel, and I got to enjoy a lovely view of Venice as we went round it. I had to admit, it was a very beautiful city in its unique way. And contrary to what everyone told me in advance, I didn't particularly find it smelly, even though it was the middle of summer.

I was heading over the border into Slovenia, the first of the Balkan countries I would be passing through. It was a beautiful day, I was relaxed, and ready to enjoy the trip. I found myself at Venice St Lucia, the train station where I purchased my ticket to Gorizia Centrale, on the border. It was only a couple of hours journey then, so I sat back and enjoyed, as I usually do on European trains, some pleasant views and a decent coffee. This indeed happened. Arriving at the station, my next step was to get the number one bus to the border. On paper this looked simple enough, but a number of small mini buses were outside, all displaying either a number one, or nothing at all. The drivers all seemed to have new heights of grumpiness, and would just nod if you asked if they were the bus to the border. Finally one started up, and a number of backpackers climbed cautiously aboard, and we all hoped for the best.

Sure enough, it dropped us at a bus terminus on this side of the border, where we had to get out and walk up a road about 100m to

what seemed at first like an abandoned railway station. It seem
that Gorizia, or Gorica in Slovenian, is in fact one large town tha
had been split in half by the border at some point in history. Thi
had not really caused anyone much problems until the cold wa
when a large barbed wire fence was erected through the *Piazz*
Transalpina, and no doubt did cause people problems. Today, thi
no longer exists, and free movement is again possible. A larg
Plaque has been erected in the square to commemorate th
division. Plaque makers must just love it when terrible thing
happen. It's probably a close call if wars are started by politician
or plaque makers.

Myself and fellow backpackers walked into the station with th
caution of a group of survivors in a zombie movie. It was, it had to
be said, very quaint. That old, wooden style station that woul
look great in an old forties movie. There was a little kiosk with a
glass window with nobody in it. A waiting room with empty seats
A sign hung up saying NEXT TRAIN AT and then nothing. There
wasn't a platform as such, just the rails on the other side at groun
level. There were a couple of lists of train times up, and people
kept looking at them, then remembered that they couldn't read
Slovenian so wandered off aimlessly again. Everyone seemed
confused and frustrated, and the general opinion seemed to be tha
no one was sure if we were in the right place.

I decided to wander up the length of the buildings to have a look
It was a glorious day, and I figured that a train would come soon
enough. I had written down in a little journal a list of times I had
got from the DB Bahn website before I left. This was a German
train site, with times for all over Europe, and a godsend for
planning a trip. I figured there would be a train along soon
enough, so I might as well get on it, and worry about the
destination later.

The rest of the travellers were kind of huddled down near the
waiting room, still wandering in and out of the station, hoping
they would suddenly learn how to read Slovenian, so I was the
only one that reached the top of the station and spotted a door with
familiar sounds coming from it. I walked in, and sure as hell, it

was a bar. About 12 people, some in railway uniforms, were sat drinking and laughing.

"Train to Lake Bled?" I asked.

"Only one train. Lake Bled, yes. One hour", someone replied.

"Thank you. A beer, please. "

So, a glass of beer in hand, I wandered back to the lost boys and girls, to tell them it was confirmed we were at the right station. Actually, I got as far as a blonde Dutch girl who seemed to be on her own, and decided to just tell her instead. I also invited her up to the bar to get a drink, but she politely declined. It is fair to point out that at this stage in life I was carrying a bit more weight than I used to, and of course still had a shaved head, something I began to do as my once proud multi coloured hair from my glory days began to pack its bags and head off never to be seen again. So it was a beer bellied, shaven headed guy with a pint in his hand that had proposed we go for a drink, and not my self-image of a lean, travel hardened explorer that in my mind was also a good decade younger.

"Never mind", I told her," but there is a bit of time so I'll go and get another one while we wait."

"You know, you couldn't be more of the stereotype of your race" she said, but in a friendly enough way. Though I knew what she meant, I just said "Thanks."

I had a quick small beer in the bar, which was incredibly lively, then headed back to the crowd, who seemed a lot more confident, though a couple were still trying to interpret the timetable. Or at least the interrailers were confident. The others still had no ticket, and were debating just getting on. I sat down next to some older guy with a small bag, nodded hello, and got a warm smile back. And that's when I discovered why everyone was now more sure that they weren't at a ghost station. A young lad came up and spoke to this older guy.

"Hi. Are you the guy with the times?"

"Yes."

"Do you know when the train gets to Jesenice?"

The man next to me pulled out a couple of sheets of paper, print outs by the look of them, and told the young lad what he needed to know.

"Well informed?" I said to him, nodding at the paper.

It turned out that my new friend was Turkish. And though he looked like a bloke who was just popping to the next station to visit his mum, he was in fact travelling all over Europe. And in spite of all the technology around, he was the only person who had bothered to print out the information that he wanted. We got chatting about the various journeys we had been on, and when the train arrived, got a seat together to carry on chatting. This was no easy thing. Word had got around the train that there was a man who knew the times and changes, and a pretty steady trickle of backpackers would come up and ask him for details. Much to my admiration, he happily pulled out his pieces of paper and was able to tell everyone who came up what they needed to know.

"I get this all the time," he told me. "I really like it. Let's you get to chat to people and help them as the young ones aren't very good at directions."

He'd had an interesting life, had been divorced, no kids, and so would work for 8 months then go travelling somewhere. He'd been doing this for years. I was amazed at how little luggage he had.

"I use launderettes a lot" he explained. "They are actually surprisingly good places to get to know people. In fairness, I also found this to be true, and had, and still do, engage in lots of interesting chats with travellers and locals when my underwear and shirts begin to fail the sniff test, and it's time to find some washing machines. Since the practice of booking hostels online came about, I usually make sure that every third or fourth one has washing facilities, that usually means that you give them a bag of your smellies, and they wash them for a few euros, or whatever the currency. The real traveller knows to take advantage of this even if you don't have very much, as you never know when you might run out of clothes.

In no time at all we were at my station, and oddly I was the only one got off. I bid my friend farewell, and left him showing a

208

couple of Germans what time they would arrive at somewhere or other.

Bled Jezero was a fairly small station, as befitted a domestic line. I would be departing from a bigger station on the other side of the lake, but it was a nice place to arrive. The weather was still glorious, and I decided to walk to town, which was not too far away. I had a dorm booked at a place named after, surprisingly enough, George Best. Now, I've never been a football fan, but even as a kid I knew who George Best was. From Northern Ireland, he was one of the first of the superstar soccer players with a lifestyle to match. I couldn't tell you any of his sporting achievements, of course, but I do rather like the classic anecdote about him from 1973, or thereabouts.

A national newspaper had ran an article about how the great man was getting off form, and questioning his way of life in a somewhat negative manner. George was in Spain at the time, with his girlfriend, a former Miss world. After winning a considerable sum in a casino and leaving large denomination bills all over the bed, a waiter turned up with breakfast for the pair, and found George with his model girlfriend lying amidst wads of money, sleeping the night off.

"Ah, George," he said, quoting the headline in the national newspaper. "Where did it all go wrong?"

With no idea of where this hostel was, I nevertheless set off in a fantastic mood, and enjoyed the beautiful scenic walk into town. It took about 20 minutes maybe, and as I reached the edge of town, what was staring at me but the hostel, the first building I came to.

"Can this day get any better?" I thought.

The hostel was above a semi open air bar, it seemed, which was quite appropriate for a place named after George Best. I asked the barman where I booked in, and he told me he would do it.

"Great," I said," but first, I will have a nice cold beer, if that's Ok?"

A young Belfast lad was standing at the bar as well, and said Hi, and that there was a couple of them sitting at a table if I wanted to join them. It seemed, I decided, that this day could actually get better after all.

The lad's name was Joseph, and he introduced me to a young English couple he had teamed up with, Olly and Monica. I finished my beer, and decided to have another before checking in. This in fact went on for the rest of the afternoon, till we decided to go for a beer uptown and as it was getting dark, I figured it would be wise to check in and know where my bunk actually was.

Chatting to the barman who was also the guy checking me in, I asked him about the name of the place and if it got the right crowd in. It seemed that the original owner was an Irish guy and huge fan of George Best.

"As for the people," he said, "I have never had a problem with groups of English guys." It's worth remembering that, though the others may well hate it, a lot of people outside the UK consider English and British to be the same thing. Or at least interchangeable words. They don't always get Scottish and Welsh as being separate. Similarly, they don't really see the difference in the Northern and Southern Irish. To save pointless and endless arguments though, it's usually best not to bother mentioning this to Scots and such, as they will deny it to their death and go all Highlander on you.

"In fact," he carried on, "I don't mind groups of lads, or individuals from anywhere at all. There are only two types of people that I find troublesome. And that's groups of English or Irish girls. Now they are a pain when they drink."

Interestingly enough, there was a group of Irish girls there as well, who arrived while we were sat outside and looked like they were a hen party or something. They had seemed pleasant enough, I thought, but who was I to argue?

As soon as I checked in, we wandered up the street, till we came to a nice little bar, and indulged in some interesting cocktails. We popped into another place just up the road, where we spotted the Irish girls looking incredibly merry and laughing loudly with a table packed with even more interesting looking cocktails and shot glasses. They even waved a cheerful hello.

A last drink in a final bar, and we decided we were hungry, so we went back to the hostel to see if we could order pizza. We

:ould, and the four of us sat swapping travellers' tales, learning what we all did at home, and enjoying a last cold bottle of beer with the pizza in the beautiful warm night air.

About an hour or so later, we heard before we saw the Irish girls arriving back. Singing loudly, they headed straight up to their lorm, which I believe they were all in. From where we sat, we could hear them laughing a lot at first, then a bit of an argument seemed to ensue, with one of them shouting loudly to the others to chill the fuck down. Yes, that should do it. It went a bit quiet, then a lot of crying seemed to start, and finally one of them leaned out of the window not far above us and proceeded to vomit for quite some time out of it. More crying followed, then a little song, and finally I guess they began to pass out.

"Told you," The barman said as he cleared our table "Every time."

Next day we headed to the lake, and took our swimmers too. I have to say, Lake Bled is beautiful. Stunningly beautiful. There is a little island out in the middle with a church and a few buildings that date back a fair old way. The lake itself is a beautiful blue colour, which is due to it being formed from a glacier run off, and no motorised boats are allowed to cross. Small wooden boats that look not unlike gondoliers were the only vessels we saw. It was entirely possible to head off and walk all around the lake, and take in Castle Bled, which overlooks the north side, and even had a nice little museum. We stopped and swam at different points.

It was a long and interesting day, so we decided to head out to dinner later on. I really did like this group of people, and it was a shame we were heading off to different places in the end, but then that's the road for you! Even if it's a railroad.

Arriving back at the hostel, we were pleased to find out that the Irish girls had checked out meaning a more relaxed time could be had in the beer garden. There was, however, a group of Irish lads from Cork there instead who were all inexplicably bio-chemists. I'm guessing the George Best name attracted lots of folk from the emerald isles. Sitting with them was a very young English backpacker girl, who the guys had cheerfully nicknamed Babyface. Seemed she was in the dorm bed below me.

Monica was quite tired, so her and Olly were the first to hit the sack, leaving the rest of us to sit and chat. Babyface took a fair bit of winding up from everyone, but took it well and seemed to enjoy hearing the various stories being told. She told us that it was her ambition to get herself all around the world. I suspect that she eventually would

"I want to be where you are now" she said, in reference to me saying about the journeys that led up to my 50 by 50 challenge.

"You can be" I told her, and stood up and offered to change seats. It was that kind of night.

I'm not sure what time we all eventually retired, but Babyface was supposed to get up early for her train. However, I woke up to see her packing her bag well after she was supposed to be gone. That was the result of us all buying her a drink whenever we had taken the mickey.

"You gonna make it?" I asked her. "You need a hand with anything?"

"No, I'm Ok. Just got a headache. I think I will sleep on the train. Catch you round the world sometime.."

I hope she does.

We were all catching trains early that afternoon, but Joseph was on the one I had come in on and the rest of us were catching the same train for part of the way at the other station. That gave us just time to get down for a last swim in the lake. I had seen Joseph eying that island up, and debating if he could swim out there. He had that look in his eye again as we got in, then suddenly started to swim out. I looked at the others.

"Fuck it, let's go" Olly called, and we all headed out. Time was limited, so it was probably not a wise idea, but it was a pretty easy swim it turned out, and we managed to set foot on the little island. No time to explore though, and we headed back more or less straight away. The swim back seemed a bit more difficult, but we felt great when we got back, and even had time to grab some brunch from a pastry shop. We said our goodbyes to Joseph, and Olly, Monica and myself caught a cab to the station. We enjoyed a couple of cups of coffee together once on board , and then it was time to part ways, as they got off at Ljubljana. Great people, and

I'd miss them. However, no time to fret about that, I would be crossing the border soon enough, and heading into Croatia.

IV

Which indeed I did, and arrived in the city of Zagreb. Though the capital of Croatia, it still only has a population of around 770,000 people, though with the municipal area taking that up to about a quarter of the country's population. The city and country had had the usual history in the region of fluctuations between Ottoman, Hungarian, Hapsburg and German occupations and administration for over a thousand years until it became one of the 6 countries that joined the original Yugoslavia.

The concept of a state that united the southern Slavic people had its origins way back in the 19th century. The concept had been mulled over, discussed and put forward by a number of political thinkers, but it wasn't till 1914/15, after the start of WW1 that a number of prominent Slavic political figures from territories under the Hapsburg empire fled to London, where they began work on an organisation to represent South Slavic peoples in the Austro-Hungarian territories. And so it was that in April 1915, the Yugoslav committee was formed and began working on raising funds, mainly from Serbs, Croats and Slovenes living in the Americas along with other exiles living in Britain.

The prominence of this committee, due to the calibre of many of the people involved, they were able to take their concerns to the Allied governments who, worried about the weakening and uncertainties of the Austria-Hungary territories, began to take them quite seriously.

Though the fundamental aim of the committee was to unite the peoples of the Hapsburgs south Slav lands with the then independent Kingdom of Serbia, there was also an immediate problem with the possibility of Italian expansion into Dalmatia and Istria. This was due to the promise to the Italians by the Allies to look at territorial gains as a lure to bring them into the war on their side.

In 1916, the Serbian Parliament in Exile met with the Yugoslav Committee in Corfu, where they issued a declaration that laid the foundation for the post war state. It was initially to be called the Kingdom of Serbs, Croats and Slovenes, and would be a constitutional monarchy. This was followed in 1918, as the Hapsburg empire effectively dissolved, by a newly formed National council for Serbs Croats and Slovenes taking power in Zagreb, and declaring independence, and then two days later declaring its wish to enter union with Serbia and Montenegro. Not running so smoothly as hoped, massive civil unrest erupted, which led the council to request the Serbian Army to help restore order.

As is the way of all great and noble ideas, as soon as the union was officially declared, much in fighting and disagreeing about how to run things ensued, but eventually the territories that were to form Yugoslavia were finalised, and in 1922 the kingdom of Serbs, Croats and Slovenes was officially and internationally recognised as a sovereign state, and finally changed its name to the Kingdom of Yugoslavia in 1929.

But it is Yugoslavia no longer. After being under fascist rule during WW2, followed by communist rule from thereafter under Tito, the country eventually broke up under the climate that saw the collapse of communism in East Europe, German Unification, and the inevitable break-up of the Soviet Union. Yugoslavia, which had not been under the Soviet sphere during its time, saw a rise in nationalism in the various republics that had constituted it, and in the early 90's, during a series of bloody conflicts, split back into the 6 states that had made it up.

It was not wise, I had been warned, to get into any talk about the break up, or politics in general, with locals, due to the particularly brutal and complicated nature of the conflicts. I was to see this for myself.

On the first night there, I went out to have some food and a drink, as I tend to, and popped out on my own. The hostel I was staying in was quite quiet, and no one grabbed my attention as potential drinking partners. Sitting at a table outside a nice little bar on the main street, I found myself chatting to a young guy who was the waiter in the place, but was not particularly busy. His station was right next to my table, so the flow of conversation was pretty much uninterrupted. He told me quite a few useful and interesting things about life in Croatia, and about the current government.

As warned, I deliberately did not offer any opinions of my own, which was not too difficult as my knowledge of current Balkan politics was actually quite limited. In fact, I let the guy lead any conversation about the history elements of any kind. Eventually though, he did drift on to the topic of the war, and though he started by saying that the young people were putting all that behind them now, after he went into a bit more detail, it was easy to see anger welling up in him as he spoke about the Serbs. In fact, at one point I could see his hands were clenched so tightly that they were turning red. I decided to change the mood of the chat by asking about local beers. He almost immediately began smiling again and popped off to get me one he could recommend. It wasn't very good, but I feigned delight, and we left the topics of genocide and murder behind. The young may well be putting it behind them, but there is a way to go yet.

I said goodbye to my new friend, who told me he had very much enjoyed our chat, and took a wander around. Interestingly, there were a number of actual old fashioned gas lights that I could see, which I found quite quaint. I found a nice outdoor bar and sat and ordered a bottle of beer. Two odd looking men that could have been twins were at the next table, and seemed to be staring at me intently as I waited for my drink. This carried on as I eventually got my bottle and poured it into the glass that came with it. Though very warm, they both wore hats and coats, and both seemed to have exactly the same round spectacles that made their eyes look huge, which was especially annoying as they were staring right at me.

"Are you German?" one of them eventually asked me. But in English.

"...German?" the other one said, straight away.

"No, I'm from the UK."

"Ah, the UK."

"…UK"

They went quiet, but carried on looking.

"We have a lot of Germans come here. They like it for holidays."

"…Holidays."

"Oh."

"Are you here on holiday?"

I looked for the other one to say holiday, but he didn't this time.

"Er, no, passing through. I'm travelling from Rome to Athens."

"Oh, Athens. That's a horrible city."

"…Horrible city."

They went quiet again. I hoped this would last. It didn't.

"Do you know why Zagreb is called Zagreb? Well, there is a legend that says that once there was an exhausted and thirsty knight from somewhere far away, who eventually found a spring here. There was a young girl next to it, and he was so tired, he asked her to ladle the water for him. The Croatian word for this is Zagrabiti."

"…Zagrabiti"

"Oh. That's interesting."

"The city was built on a stream, but they buried it."

"Oh."

"Do you know another Croatian word? Medvjed. It means bear."

"…Bear."

"You'll find lots of bears in the names here. The mountain, the castle, even a pub. And streets. But there are no bears here. None. There used to be, but they all went south."

"Why?"

"The city got too big. So now there is not a single bear here, when once there were thousands. No, there are no bears.

"…no bears."

"Not even in the zoo?" I asked. "Isn't there quite a big zoo here?"

The brothers- or whom I assumed to be brothers – spoke amongst themselves for a short while, clearly debating if there vere bears in the zoo. I have no idea what they decided, as they then went quiet and resumed watching me.

"There are a lot of tunnels, you know."

"…Tunnels."

I finished my beer smartish and bade them farewell.

I had time to kill the next day, and decided to do very little with it. I would be catching an overnight train later, and in any case, I was feeling particularly lazy. I had some breakfast in the hostel, and retired to my bunk with a book. There are people I have met on the road who seem happy to cram as much into a day as possible. They come armed with to-do lists, and cameras, and sensible footwear, they get up early, head off, arrive back late and tell you what amazing things they have seen that day, and what they intend to do tomorrow. I really admire these sort of people, but at the same time would like to piss in their shoes at night as a kind of delaying tactic.

I am, needless to say, not really like that. There have been many a time I have just lounged around a hostel, reading, or watching TV, or having the odd yabber with strangers and ignoring the beautiful sunshine and amazing things to see completely. Often, I end up remembering these little snatched conversations more than some of the amazing things. This was one of those days. There was the usual free help yourself breakfast in the morning, and I fixed myself a bowl of some chocolate based cereal that tasted like someone had sprinkled some lumpy cocoa powder over some corn flakes. While eating, a young girl walked into the little dining room, who at first glance I mistook for Babyface, and waved over. It wasn't her, but she sat down and said hallo anyway.

"Sorry," I said, "I thought you were someone else. But Good Morning anyway."

"Who did you think I was?" she said in a French accent.

"Someone I met at Lake Bled recently. You have the same sort of hair."

" I was at Lake Bled. When was this?"

"Last week, but it wasn't you. Did you like it there?"

" I did. Are you sure it wasn't me?"

217

"Yes, it was an English girl. And in any case, you don't remember me, so it was someone else."

"Are you sure she was English? I am French."

"Yes. Yes, I'm sure, but it's nice to meet you."

She looked at my cereal.

"They have breakfast here? What do they have?"

"There is a bowl of hard boiled eggs. And bread, so you can make toast. Tea and coffee, of course, and this cereal. It's sort of chocolate."

She looked thoughtful for a while.

"Do they have Weetabix?"

"No, I don't think so"

This appeared to sadden her slightly.

"Oh. I like Weetabix."

We just sat till I had nearly finished my choco-stuff then she got up, wandered into the kitchen, and came out with just a coffee.

"They have no Weetabix," she told me, and sat down again. We didn't speak after that till I got up to get myself another drink, and she was gone when I came back.

Oddly, I have no idea what I did for the rest of that day, other than it was very little, but in the way that our brains retain the strangest of things, I clearly remember that girl not having any Weetabix. In fact, after I got back home, I mentioned this to my girlfriend of the time, just in passing, and every time I mentioned going travelling again, she would say, Oh, so you can meet the Weetabix girl again?

Yes. Yes, dear. I want to go and travel the world for no other reason than I can find a girl who doesn't want a bland chocolate cereal for breakfast.

V

Later that night I found myself on a very empty overnight train to Sarajevo. In fact, I had a whole carriage to myself, and was able to lie across the seats and get a decent night's sleep, only interrupted at the border as we arrived in Bosnia and Herzegovina, generally referred to as simply Bosnia in English. The trouble free journey meant arriving way too early to book into a hostel, so I decided to head to the bus station to get a ticket for my next destination, as advice on Trip Advisor had told me that getting a ticket could prove difficult on the day, so purchasing in advance would be wise. However, at the Central Bus station, which was handily close to the train station, they informed me that the bus to Montenegro, my next stop, actually left from a different location, the Sarajevo East Station. As I turned round to go, the guy behind me, an Australian, asked me if he'd heard right and we were in the wrong place, and cussed a bit when I said that we were.

He was leaving for Montenegro later, and had also decided to get a ticket early. We decided we'd head there together, and as it was stupidly early, we'd catch a cab, as we couldn't seem to find easy info on a bus to the other station, which seemed odd considering where we were. Both of us having been the victims of taxi drivers strange pricing policies before and after getting in and out of a cab, we made sure we got a firm price from the driver first, who then looked annoyed when my new companion, who by this time I had learned was called Matt, then gave him the exact money, plus a tip, in advance. No extra zeros this time then!!

It was probably only about 8 or 9 kilometres to the East Station, so it did not take long, but we noticed that at one point the driver stopped, got out, and took his taxi sign off the roof of the car. We asked him why, as best we could, but he just shrugged and said 'No Licence', which seemed to make no sense, but hey, we were getting to our destination so what the heck.

At the bus station we noticed that the buses seemed more likely to be heading to Serbia and Croatia, but also had different colours painted. It also turned out that whoever had written on Trip Advisor that tickets were hard to get was full of it. A very nice woman in the booth sold Matt his ticket, and as she gave me mine, she asked why I'd came all the way out there two days early as It was never a problem getting a ticket on the day. I guess the author of the wrong info had meant that he or she had not been able to get a booking online, so had to struggle with an actual person to ask for and receive a paper ticket. Poor love.

"I'm going to get a cold beer," Matt said, spotting a bar right beside the station which seemed open. "You gotta get back?"

"I'm in no hurry." He'd sold me at beer.

We sat outside, and Matt asked the barmen for a particular beer he'd been drinking in the city, but the barman shook his head and said not here. We got a couple of bottles of some other beer, and noticed that it was Serbian. We were sitting outside, and the only other customer was a woman in her mid-thirties or so, wearing a colourful headscarf , and looking at her phone.

"Is Srpska" she threw in, looking up from her phone as she saw us looking at the label on the beer bottle.

"Sorry," I said, "Is that the brewery?"

She laughed.

"No. Srpska. Republic of Srpska. This is where you are now."

This confused the hell out of me. I was aware that the country was composed of two major regions, with Bosnia being the larger one in the north, and Herzegovina to the south, but the Republic of Srpska? Seemingly, Matt wasn't as confused.

"Ah…This is Srpska too?"

The woman went on to explain. Apart from the two geographical regions, the country was also split into two distinct Entities, one being the Republic of Srpska, and the other being the federation of Bosnia and Herzegovina. The major distinguishing factor between the two, aside from the boundaries, was that Srpska was predominantly Serbian populated, whilst the federation was mainly Croats and Bosniaks. During the civil war in the 90's, the majority of non-Serbians were expelled from the territories of the Republic of Srpska, and a large inflow of Serbs from the other regions came in. Both entities, like both regions, though loosely coming under the same presidency, in fact administrate themselves in the main. I mentioned the taxi driver taking his sign off.

"Ah yes," she smiled, "He will not be licensed to be a taxi in this territory. Everyone knows that the taxi drivers from both sides do this, but no-one really cares. Still, it maybe stops policemen asking for a bribe…"

Enjoyed a couple of beers with Matt, till his bus came, then headed back to book into my hostel. A nice enough place, plenty of people milling around, but first things first, a bit of an explore. There were definitely still signs that there had been a war, even now. In fact, one building I saw still had a shell coming out of the side of it, as removing it would have caused more damage. I like to think it was defused!!

In fact, two things spring to mind when you think of Sarajevo. Most recently of course, is the siege of Sarajevo during the Bosnian war. Four years of a bloody part of its rich history – for here is a city where Austro-Hungarian architecture meets the beautiful mosques from the Ottoman era – where people waited for military vehicles to go up their streets so they could shelter beside them in the hope of getting food without being shot by the Serbian snipers that took aim from the surrounding hills. The other thing, of course, is that it is the place where Archduke Franz Ferdinand was assassinated, leading to the start of the first world war. This, amongst many other trigger events, is why the Balkans are often referred to as the Powder Keg of Europe, as the various conflicts in the region, both local and those caused by an entanglement of the superpowers of the region at the time, Russia, the Ottoman empire, Austro-Hungary and The German Empire. In fact, back in the 19th Century, Otto Von Bismark correctly predicted that the Balkans would be the source of major conflict in Europe.

Of course, this was all before I arrived. At this point of my life I had never remarried after my accidental wedlock with Eva, my Swiss punk bride whom I had married wearing handcuffs in what seemed like a lifetime ago. This was probably a good thing. I found that in general, my married friends often complained that they were permanently being blamed for pretty much everything that their good wives didn't approve of. This I found to be true of my various girlfriends as well, but though their memories seemed to last forever, my relationships tended not to, so the blame for whatever I allegedly had done would disappear once we agreed to "Still be good friends" then never really speak to each other again. Had I been married, however, and maybe would be over here with the no doubt beautiful Mrs Mulligan, I somehow suspect that Gavrilo Princip and other members of the group of assassins that took out The Archduke and his wife would be somewhat excused of their responsibility for World War 1, and somehow it would have become my fault. I guess I dodged a bullet there. Which unfortunately for a lot of people, is more than could be said for Franz Ferdinand.

They like their coffee here, I noticed. Everybody seemed to be drinking it in numerous little coffee places. And there was a pretty cool old style bazaar kind of area called Baščaršija. This was a nice place to explore, with many traditional Bosnian clothes and craft shops, and both an ornate Mosque and an old synagogue. I indulged in a rather fine coffee, then headed back to the hostel where I overheard a group of backpackers sitting around discussing going to the bars later, and inviting each other. I was mindful that being older they would not invite me, not out of rudeness, but because they tend to not really see you, or if they do, they assume you are waiting for your equally elderly wife – who had no doubt just dropped out of the Saga ads – to turn up, so you could go out before it was dark and visit elderly people things, and get back before catching a chill. I had of course learned that it was up to me to ask, so asked the lads that were talking if I had just heard they were going drinking, and would they mind if I tagged along. They looked surprised, which I guess is because they hadn't realised that anyone was standing where I was till I spoke, but said sure, quite genuinely.

So later off we all went. I have to say, Sarajevo really did have some great lively bars. It felt to me as if a place with such a brutal history had chosen to get through it by throwing regrets to the wind, and just started to party.

We were in about the third bar or so, and I'd been chatting for a while to a young Austrian lad who mentioned that he had taken quite the shine to one of two Polish girls who were with our group. They were both very attractive, it had to be said, so I suggested to him not to worry about being stuck talking to me, but to have a chat with the girl.

"Hell, you're on vacation," I said winking, "What have you got to lose?"

"You're right. You gonna have a chat with her friend?"

"What? As a distraction?"

"No, man. She's hot too, and what do you have to lose either?"

My dignity, I thought.

But, I was happy to be a wingman, so we sat next to the two girls and spotting my young friend appeared to be a bit stuck for words, I broke the ice by asking about the badges on one of their bags, cracking a couple of jokes, and hoping to hell my friend would join in before I seemed like the sleazy old git in the hostel that people apparently worry about. Luckily he eventually spoke up, and before long the four of us were getting on just fine.

We stuck together as the group of us moved on to the last bar of the night, some outdoors place that was due to shut, but served us a few bottles anyway. It was all going pretty well, and we were sitting with our arms around the girls, until right at the end, when my friend's new found love began to show that she was a little worse for wear, and went a little quiet. Asked if she was OK, she seemed to suddenly perk up, and said,

"Yes. Yes, I'm fine. Sorry, it's just that my boyfriend dumped me just before we came out…"

"Oh.." I said, with a bit of a sinking feeling coming on.

"We'd been together 3 years. 3 years, and he dumped me for another girl a week before I went travelling…"

"Oh.."

"We were supposed to be getting an apartment and everything together when I got back…"

"Oh.."

Well, fuck him. I'm having a great time, and Life is too short to worry, eh?"

"Oh…"

I knew that whatever my friend said next was going to make or break the night. He smiled, and spoke up.

"Well, hey….You've got me now.."

"Oh-oh.."

The girl looked straight at him, and suddenly burst into tears. Quite a lot of tears, in fact.

"I'd better get her back to the hostel," my own new love wisely stated. "If it's alright we'll go back alone. It's only round the corner, and I should talk with Lena."

"Yep." I agreed. "You should."

And they left, Lena still crying.

"let's see if we can get another beer," I suggested.

"Why not. Hey, I thought that went rather well, no?

Yes. Just bloody peachy!

Sadly, due to time restraints on this trip, I'd only allowed myself one full day in Sarajevo, which to be honest I already regretted, as I felt there was so much more to do here. Still, it had been a rather good and fruitful day, so onwards the next day it was to be. I saw one or two of our drinking companions the next morning, looking a bit worse for wear, and hanging into their coffees.

"Seen Hanna and Lena?" I asked. They shook their heads.

"Aren't you feeling bad?", they asked me. "You were the last guy still drinking. You and the Austrian. He's in our dorm, and he puked in his shoes."

"Keep practicing lads, see you again."

With a smile I headed off to the East Bus station, where once again catching a bus would have been no problem, took a comfortable seat, and enjoyed some fantastic mountain scenery all the way to the border of Montenegro, where we stopped for a passport check for a relatively short while, then headed off. First thing I saw as we drove over the border was Hanna and Lena, with their backpacks, their thumbs out, and a sign reading Podgorica. So they were heading the same way as me. I leaned quite rudely over someone on the side of the bus that they were, and stuck my thumb up and grinned. They spotted me and Hanna blew me a kiss.

Heck, I sure liked Sarajevo.

VI

It took about 6 hours or so to get into Podgorica, so it was relatively late when I arrived, and the hostel was a bit of a chore to find. I had noticed a steakhouse on the walk to the hostel, so thought I could go there and get something to eat once I was all booked in. However, as luck would have it, I found myself in a six bed dorm with only two other guests, a very poshly spoken English girl and a very tall Italian guy. I said the usual hallo's, and mentioned that I was going out to get some food.

"Hey, I'm about to cook," The Italian lad said, "and I've got lots of pasta and stuff. Wanna share?"

Well, why not. I offered in return to get a couple of bottles of beer from reception, and the decent young chap who introduced himself as Marco cooked a pretty simple but tasty meal for the three of us. It was a pretty good dorm room, with a couple of chairs and a table rather than just the usual bunks, so we settled in for the night. We got chatting about passports, where Charlotte, she of the public school accent, announced that she had an Irish one, which quite surprised me.

"Really? I don't want to sound all stereotyping, but you really don't sound Irish!"

"I'm not really. But some family were. Daddy suggested I get an Irish one as I could, as it is really the one to have."

Yes. She said Daddy. She was 22.

Growing up, I had heard all the stuff off my parents and school friends about the whole Irish thing, as I have mentioned in some of my earlier shenanigans. And much as I am pretty happy about my Celtic routes, I never saw them as being better or worse than the fact I was born in England. In fact, on leaving school I very much stated I was English as a kind of reaction to my parents and the other teens growing up in the Irish enclave that was County Coundon in Coventry. As the years went by, however, I began to make my own mind up for the right reasons, and not just to piss people off – a favourite hobby of mine – and came to realise that my whole self actually had a good mix of nature and nurture. I was born and grew up to look genetically Irish, and so much of my upbringing, especially as a child, enhanced that in me. But I was also born in England, which is my accent (though with more than a few Irish-isms, which is quite common even now in Coventry), and am to the casual observer quite English. I guess like so many, I'm simply a new generation of Celtic English, and it's about time we edged our way back in. Bloody Saxons and Normans.

Hearing Charlotte mentioning hers being the best passport in the world brought all this back. I remember years after leaving Coundon and moving to the inner city melting pot of Coventry that is called Hillfields, where I still live to this day and at the time lived in one of the tower blocks for a while. I was still with my ex-wife, Eva, and we were sitting in a neighbours flat one night, them being an older couple where she was English and he was Irish. Eva being Swiss, he proceeded to tell her about the wonders of Ireland, and how everything Irish was the best in the world. He was, to be fair, a little drunk, and his wife was getting a bit embarrassed. The night kind of ended when his lovely wife mentioned to Eva that the next time she went back to Switzerland, she should bring some proper Swiss chocolate back, as she knew it was really nice chocolate.

"Chocolate?", her husband interceded. "Chocolate you say? Have you ever tasted Irish chocolate, Eva? Best chocolate in the world."

His wife decided to mention it was getting late, so we agreeably popped back to our own flat, where I racked my brains, but could only remember my mum eating Cadbury Fruit and Nut as her favourite chocolate bar, and never remembering any other products she may have mentioned to outshine the rather fine reputation of Swiss chocolate.

Yes, it is a funny old relationship that the Irish living in the UK have with their children. Like so many of that generation, mine moved over here, found work over here, met, got married, bought houses, and had kids like me who they raised in England, had

226

educated in England, and who naturally spoke with English accents. They chose not to go back the hop over the water to the old country, as they had made good lives for themselves, and usually had lots of family here as well. But deep down, even though they moved here, had us here, and raised us here, they were always a bit angry at us for being English.

Anyway, I mentioned to Charlotte that these days, we all had EU passports, and there probably wasn't a great deal of difference between how powerful- (an expression that means how many countries it will get you into, preferably visa-free) – they were, so all three of us in the room kinda had the same passport. Marco agreed, but Charlotte seemed quite irate with this, and set about looking it up on her phone. Well, I guess she was doing this, as she immediately began plonking away rapidly, then put it down without saying anything and changed the subject. I have no idea where the Irish passport lay that year in world rankings, but as she was basically travelling around the EU and other associated countries, it really was not going to make much difference which European country her passport was from. Still, we had shared a nice pan-European meal, and wasn't going to let a sulky Brit bring the night down over her non British passport, and so began to do what most travellers do, and compared travelling tales, till we somehow got on to sex. Because put a group of people together who get on well enough, and it inevitably will get to that.

Both Marco and Charlotte were leaving the next morning, so we said goodbyes, and I headed off into the city centre, a journey that did not take long. It's not a big place by most European measures, with a population of around 151,000 in the city itself, with the centre being quite walkable. An interesting enough old town, still some signs of an earlier Ottoman influence, mixed with some communist era style buildings – it had been known as Titograd during the Yugoslav era – but I felt it was time to explore a bit further. I'd been looking at towns for quite some time. I found out that there was a place called Lake Skadar, or Shkodra Lake, depending on who you talked to, that you could get to via the local bus, so off out I headed. Expecting something like Lake Bled, I was surprised when the bus driver called out that we had arrived there, and saw more than a few travellers looking at each other, before getting off, and wandering along a path that led to somewhere that clearly did not look anything like Lake bled. Hell, I thought, I've c0me to a duck pond.

But looks can be deceptive, and in fact the lake is the start of a national park area of Montenegro, but just under half of it is in neighbouring Albania, where it is part of a huge nature reserve, and I took a pleasant enough stroll along the edge of it, before heading back to the entrance to the park and looking at a big map on a board with places of interest. Another Italian guy was also looking, and mentioned that he liked the look of a walk that was highlighted into the hills or mountains that we were next to, and I agreed that it looked pretty interesting. We wandered off in the direction at the same time, so I felt obliged to chat. He didn't seem to feel that, to be honest, but heck, I chatted anyway.

It was, as has been on my trip through the Balkans so far, a rather beautiful sunny day, though Montenegro is known to have the wettest weather of the region. There was a little road running up through the mountains which we followed, because after a while my new friend seemed more comfortable, and we were chatting away about the country, the view and such like. We passed by a couple of little stalls along the way selling such stuff as dried fish, or scarfs. I wondered how many scarfs they sold in this heat. My friend asked one lady at a stall if she sold water. She didn't, but it seemed her house was opposite, and she went in and brought him out a glass, which I thought was nice, though I considered that she was missing an opportunity there. We also came across a small, old looking chapel, which was closed unfortunately. As the road turned a corner on a mountain, we witnessed over on the next twist a couple of cars going in opposite directions had stopped in front of each other, and there two women arguing, or so it looked like, about who should back up as they were both stuck. It looked like there was room to pass, maybe, but I guess neither fancied being on the outside. It took us a while to reach that point, and as the road twisted we did not see what happened, but they were gone by the time we got there. We did, however, both take a furtive glance over the side.

Eventually we stumbled across a little village that had a sign saying Café as we entered.

"Do you fancy something to eat? I'm quite hungry", my friend asked.

"No, I'm not, but I could have a drink to be honest. I should have had some water at that stall when you did."

So we walked along the same road till we came to what looked like an ordinary house, but with a sign on the fence with the hand painted word Café and an arrow pointing round the back. We followed the arrow, and found ourselves quite clearly in someone's backyard, but with decking, some tables and chairs, a cooler with beers and soft drinks, and a large wooden barrel with some fresh fish swimming in it. The back door of the house was lying open, so I called in. there was no answer.

We sat down, and waited, but no one came, but as thirst was getting the better of me, I took two bottles of cold Coke from the cooler and we sat back and thoroughly enjoyed them. Shortly after that, a man's face appeared over the fence, and said something to us. My friend began to speak to him, then the neighbour nodded and turned around.

"You speak the local language? What did he say?"

"No, he spoke Italian. A lot of people here do. He says that the café owner is also the local painter, and is decorating someone's house. He has gone off to get him. He said to help ourselves to drinks in the meantime."

We did. We got a couple of bottles of nice cold beer, and continued to feel very chilled and relaxed. After about 10 minutes, a large man in maybe his late sixties wearing overalls and covered in paint came bustling into the back and greeted us in Italian. My friend asked him if he had a menu and told him it was just for one, but the man just smiled and went into his kitchen and began singing.

"I guess he chooses.." I laughed.

In no time, the man came out with a couple of large platters. It looked like I was eating after all. There was cheese, olives, giant slices of tomatoes and fine meats. He went back in and brought some baskets of bread to go with it. There was a lot of food!

"How much do we owe you," my friend asked in Italian, bu again the man just smiled, and then headed back off out of th gate, presumably to his decorating job.

"I don't think he spoke Italian, eh?"

Well, looking at such fine fare, I suddenly had an appetite, so w tucked in. It was absolutely delicious. In all my life I have neve tasted such wonderful tomatoes and olives, the bread was perfec and the meats and cheese a delight. There was ample for both o us, and we finished the lot. We then decided on another bottle o beer each before maybe heading back. We'd been walking a goo few hours before reaching here, and were aware that it would be a dark road if we carried on instead of turning back.

As our host had not returned, we looked at the pricelist he had o a chalkboard, and worked out what we believed we owed him an left the money and a pretty good tip on his table in the kitchen This, I was to later find out, was the done thing.

This little incident, I must say, gave me real food for thought What a fantastic way to live. A beautiful village, where you ca leave your back door open, and if you have visitors to your café just trust that they will pay even if you are not there. Leaving a large fridge full of beer in your open garden, and your neighbou comes and gets you if you have a customer. Coming from the city such a thing just seems incredible. At first I was to think, tha coming from the UK, living like that seemed impossible. But late adventures to come were to show me that there were indeed littl alcoves and corners of home that were not completely dissimilar.

Going downhill, the journey back was much quicker, and we eventually found ourselves at the bus stop with a horde of othe people. The bus arrived, and everyone only just about got on, with people standing everywhere. I got split up from my companion who had already said that he was getting off at a stop earlier, bu he fought his way back, and told me he was meeting some friends and would I like to join them later. Quite a change of tune for a guy who was suspicious of me talking to him at first, which goes to show the wisdom of not being worried about chatting to strangers on these kinds of trips. I told him about the steakhouse near me, and we agreed on a time to meet up later.

They did not show up, however, and I found myself in the steakhouse on my own, which was not a problem as the food was good, and there was a band playing. To be honest, the band played some pretty awful rock covers, but hearing live music was nice, and I'd had two good meals in one day. It was, I considered, a good result, though I did wonder why the place seemed so empty.

I decided on the short walk into town to see if there were any decent bars for a nightcap, and was a little startled when a car drove past me and what sounded like a gunshot came out of it. A bunch of men were cheering as they drove along. This was suddenly followed by the sound of numerous car horns beeping, and sounds of firecrackers going off, with what I was sure was the odd gunshot again. This carried on all the way along the street I was walking down, with flags hanging out of cars and groups of people cheering. I'd clearly missed some major sporting event. Not being sporty, I had no idea what. Had they just won a major soccer tournament? Then I remembered that the Olympics were also on, so maybe they'd cleaned up there? I came across a bar and walked in to find lots of people singing, and hugging. I ordered a bottle of beer.

"What have I missed?" I asked the smiling girl who served me.

"It's a great day," she sighed. "You like Olympics?"

"Er, I've been away," I replied, knowing that saying you don't really care for sports can make you suddenly a leper in some places.

"We have just taken the silver medal. Everyone is happy."

"What in?"

She looked at me momentarily like I had insulted her mother.

"Why, Handball, of course."

"Handball? Well, congratulations"

She got back to smiling and greeted some regulars with a hug and a kiss.

So handball is a sport then?

The next day, I had booked a cheap flight to my next destination, Serbia. This was down to the Kosovo border when I was planning my route. There were two issues I had to take into account, both stemming from the fact that I had a limited amount of time, meaning that for the quickest route I would have to enter Kosovo from Montenegro, rather than Serbia. Due to the time limit, I also would not be passing through Albania. The situation was that there were some notorious roadblocks between Kosovo and Serbia on the Kosovan side, and that Serbia still classed Kosovo as part of its territory, meaning that an entry stamp to Kosovo would not count on the way out, and would cause issues as I would technically be in Serbia without the visa stamp to say I'd entered. I reluctantly figured that I would have to regrettably skip Kosova, and head to Nis in Serbia. The train route was also a long journey it seemed, so I bit the bullet and flew to save time.

I had a bit of time though, so went for a last little exploration of the town centre, which really took very little time, but I was pleasantly surprised when My Italian friend from yesterday popped his head out of a café and called out. I went in to join him and a friend, and ordered a coffee.

"Sorry about yesterday," he said as I sat down. "We were all set to find the steakhouse you mentioned, when Niccolò here got chatting to a couple of nice girls. They wanted to watch the Olympics in a bar near our hostel, and invited us along. Did you know that they won the silver medal at Handball last night?"

"Yep. I heard."

"We thought we'd get there later, but you know, they were nice girls, so that just kinda happened."

"Hey, no problem, I'd have done the same. Local girls?"

"No, Polish. Very pretty."

"Polish? What were their names?"

"Hanna and Lena. They left today for Kosovo though."

Sometimes, you just have to laugh!

VII

It was a short flight to Nis, but already dark when I arrived. I hadn't expected it to be such a small airport either. In fact, it actually shut. As we left, and I was the last guy out, they shut the doors and turned the lights off behind us! There was a bus stop though, but I struggled to read the Serbian alphabet that the notice was in. I did look at the one taxi driver there, who I actually saw rubbing his hands. I waited around for a while as he watched me like a tentative vulture, and was just about to concede that I was going to be in his hands when a bus pulled in. I had the name of the street where my hostel was on a piece of paper, showed it to the woman driving, and she looked puzzled. She said something that I didn't understand, but a young Serbian girl started to translate and said this bus would go to the centre, but I needed another bus, and might miss it. I figured I'd find my way somehow, so paid up.

As we got into a busier part of town, the driver pulled up, and said something to the other passengers, who all nodded.

"She is going to put you on the right bus," the young girl told me.

Sure enough, another bus – and these were ordinary public buses, mind – pulled up a couple of minutes later, and they signalled to me to change. The driver looked at my bit of paper, nodded, and we carried on.

A studenty looking chap spoke to me.

"They told us they had found a lost Englishman, and we swung by to get you."

The other passengers on this bus were all smiling, and clearly found this amusing. I tried to imagine if a bus driver back home told his passengers that they were diverting to pick someone up from off route and just shook my head.

After 10 minutes the driver pulled up at a bus stop, and pointed down the street. I walked down, turned a corner, and there was my hostel. I had to admit, without the help of the locals, I would have been in for a long walk, or a fleecing taxi ride. So I have to say that I was immediately impressed by the local hospitality.

The hostel was quite an old building, with remarkably squeaky floors. There was, however, a snack machine, and as it was late, I decided a bag of crisps would suffice for the night, and I'd just get some kip. My reason for coming to Nis was that I had heard of a place there called the Skull Tower, and it was my plan to see this morbid curiosity the next day. What's not to love about a tower made of skulls? I was in a 4 bunk dorm, and the other 3 people were Japanese students who said hello politely, but talked mainly amongst themselves, while packing their stuff up neatly and precisely, as they were clearly leaving in the morning. Not a problem, I was out cold the minute my head hit the pillow.

There was a computer in the lobby by the reception, so I decided to look up bus times to my next port of call. I found myself stuck behind an older American woman who looked like she was someone's abandoned granny, who clearly struggled to use the PC. She kept turning to the lad at reception and asking him how to do stuff. She was trying to book a hostel somewhere, it seemed. After about 10 minutes I gave up waiting, and huffed a bit too obviously and headed out onto the street. There was a young French lad standing outside smoking, so I asked him if he knew the way to the tower.

"Yes, I am going there too. I will show you."

We walked on chatting about what we knew about the tower. It had been constructed in 1809, during the first Serbian uprising against the Ottoman empire. The commander of a group of rebels, finding himself and his subordinates surrounded in their entrenchments at Cegar Hill, near Nis, was aware that if they were captured they would be impaled. This being a particularly gruesome way to end one's days, he took the decision to detonate a powder magazine, killing himself, his people and many surrounding Ottoman soldiers. The governor of the region ordered that a tower be made of the skulls of the fallen rebels, and so a tower was made with 952 skulls embedded in it. This, in my mind, was a must see building, with the right amount of macabre to make it worth the trip.

Or it would have been, if it hadn't been closed. Not having

ctually seen any pictures of the place, I guess I assumed that I was going to walk up a hill, or something, and this looming tower would begin to appear, the skulls of fallen rebels grinning their eternal smiles, and watching me with long hollow eyes as I approached, like a character in Lord of the rings. I think I also pictured it being dark and stormy too, even though it was maybe only a little overcast with a possible hint of drizzle later.

We did not come to a tower at all. Instead, we came to what seemed to be a chapel, or building of some kind, which had a closed sign on it. I couldn't help but notice that it wasn't really the tallest of buildings, so I figured that there would be no looming. There was an information sign that told us that in 1861, following the Ottoman withdrawal, the structure had actually been dismantled, but in 1878 was partially restored, with many of the original skulls found and re-imbedded in the walls again. Which was probably a bit of an irritation from families who had buried what they believed was the remains of a family member, though many had been removed originally by eager souvenir hunters, possibly due to the lack of a decent snow globe to purchase when visiting the site.

The working theory about it being restored is that its original purpose of installing fear and a warning to the rebels had failed abysmally, and it had in fact been seen as a monument to their courage. Shortly after its restoration, a chapel was built over it, and by 1948 had been declared a place of Serbian Historical interest. Indeed, even now it is the most visited historical site in Serbia, and represents a vital time in the history of the country and people.

This didn't change the fact it was shut, mind you.

The French lad went off to explore somewhere else, and I decided to try out the bar next door to the hostel, as the weather was no great shakes, and which turned out to be the same owners. In fact, it shared a back courtyard with the hostel that had a couple of tables and chairs, and I went out and found the old American woman who had annoyed me earlier sitting there. I sat at the next table, and it wasn't long before she asked me how long I'd been in Serbia.

"Just got here. I'm only really visiting Nis."

"To see the tower, I suppose?"

"You suppose correctly."

I went back to reading my beer bottle label.

"I've been in Serbia nearly a month," She said, after a minute or so. I sighed to myself. We had engaged.

"Are you living here then,?" I asked.

She went on to tell me about how she had come to be out here. She had been an artist, but arthritis and rheumatism had damaged her hands. However, she and her husband had been reasonably successful in life, and had paid off their mortgage, and also bought the house next door with the intent on retiring early, and travelling around America in a camper van.

Unfortunately, as fate can let happen, her husband took ill and passed away shortly after they retired, before they got a chance to do all this. She had grieved for a fairly long time, then woke up one morning after dreaming that her husband had been sitting with her in a café in Paris and had talked to her about the wonderful places in the world and how French pastries were better than American ones.

She knew then it was time to move on, and realised that with the money she had been left, what she had in savings from her own career, and the regular rent from not just next door, but also her own house as well, she could head off on an adventure.

This had been over 5 years ago.

"My children hate it," she told me. "They keep telling me to come back. They say it's for my safety, but I guess they are seeing their inheritance being spent. I'm not losing any sleep over that, they had a good life and a great education. They're both doing just fine. And I've never felt safer than staying amongst young travellers in these places."

So she'd headed out into the world 5 years before, starting in Paris where she found that her husband had been right, and she really enjoyed the pastries. With no real plan, she had carried on travelling alone, through Europe to India and East Asia and back again, with gnarled hands from the arthritis, a very small bag of clothes, and a spirit as free as any I had met before. I'd caught her on her last day in Serbia, and she was heading off to the bus station to explore the next country, safe in the knowledge that she had a hostel booked, even if it had annoyed a certain hypocrite behind her.

I say hypocrite, because I had done exactly what I had been scared of happening to me. I had judged her on her age, and been annoyed at her lack of tech savviness, which is no doubt how younger people saw me on occasions. In fact, after she had left to catch her bus, I thought about this and was indeed quite angry at myself, and quite rightly so. She had told me a fascinating story, and I hadn't even caught her name. But God bless that woman, and all the people just like her. I think I'm a good traveller, with a good story, but I had been well and truly trumped. I like to think that she is still out there somewhere, enjoying the world, and sharing pastries with her husband while she sleeps. And if I meet her again, I will tip my cap to her, and gladly share another beer. It seems then that no matter where we think we are in our lives, there are always older and wiser people waiting to be met, if we are clever enough to take just a tiny bit of our time and talk to them.

I ended up having a couple of beers with the manager of the bar, as I had mentioned while ordering some food that I had been a publican for a while back home, so he picked my brains. It was interesting to chat about his efforts to get the bar going, as he wanted a younger, more international crowd as his main customers. Sounded great, but I noticed that my first visit had been myself and someone even older, but kept this to myself.

I popped back up to my dorm a bit later on to put my phone on charge, and discovered that I had a new roomie, an Aussie woman in her 40's who introduced herself as Debbie. There had been a couple of others in the room who I hadn't met, but their bunks were now empty.

"Do they sell beer here? Debbie asked.

"Hey, they have a whole pub! I'm down there now if you want to join me."

She did, so we enjoyed a bottle of beer, then decided to head out and maybe get a couple of beers around the town. This naturally turned into more than a couple, and we found ourselves getting pretty drunk, and chatting away like we'd known each other for years. She was divorced, it turned out, and had decided to head out to Europe when she had lost her job. She was heading to the UK at some point where she hoped to do a bit of bar work.

"Maybe in a gay bar," She added, laughing.

"Specifically?"

"Nah. But I've been thinking a lot the last couple of years, and I think it's, well, time I got myself to try things with a woman."

"Is that why you got divorced?"

"Nah, not really. Well, maybe. I'd thought about it a bit then. He was a cheating bastard, you know, though?

"Gotcha."

"Yeah, I definitely think I'm ready for a change."

We carried on drinking, and eventually staggered back to the hostel, trying to be quiet on the squeaky floors, but with not much luck. We'd had a great night, talking to some local rock kids, and joking about, so were a bit disappointed that the hostel bar was closed and we couldn't get another beer, but had decided we were going to try the skull tower again before I caught a bus out to my next port of call, Skopje. The bus was in the afternoon, so there was plenty of time.

We got into our respective bunks, still giggling a bit, and decided that whoever got up first should go out and get coffee from the McDonalds just down the road. We chatted a bit, and I felt myself starting to drop off.

"Well, goodnight," I said. "And hey, you're a great laugh. Gonna be a lucky woman who gets you. And good luck with all that, eh.."

She didn't answer, so I figured she had fallen asleep and shut my eyes. The next thing I know, my blanket was pulled back, and Debbie was climbing into my bunk, in just her underwear.

"I said I was ready to try it with a woman, not that I'd gave cock up completely. Now help me get this fucking bra off…."

Suddenly I wasn't tired anymore.

I woke up first, so I pulled on my shorts and a top and headed down to a busy McDonalds and got a couple of very large coffees.

I got back to find Debbie dressed, but lying on her bunk looking a bit worse for wear.

"You alright?"

"Hung over to hell. Let me get this down my neck before we head off."

"No problem. I need this one myself."

"Oh, something we didn't notice, by the way." With that she pointed to the top bunk on the other side of the room, where the form of a body could be seen wrapped in a blanket. Fuck, how long had they been there? Hey, maybe he'd arrived in the early hours of the morning, after our body bumping?

After our coffees, we figured that it was time to head out to the tower, which reception had told us should definitely be open today, and got up to go. As we left, a voice from the wrapped body called out in a cheerful Indian accent,

"Enjoy the Skull Tower, guys."

Hope you enjoyed the bloody show, I thought.

Stopping to get another McDonalds coffee, we walked to the Tower, which was only about half an hour or less from where we were. As we had been told, it was open, and cost only about 150 dinars to get in. Originally 15ft high, it is now less than that, and is down to about 54 skulls, though the insets for the others still told the story of what it would have looked like. The skull of Stevan Sindelic, the leader and igniter of the devastating blast, is kept in a glass container adjacent to the tower, which itself is now surrounded by glass to protect it from more wear and tear and theft of the skulls. There was no scaffold around it though. It seems that the ancient and secret guild of scaffolders were probably hanging out to do the roof of the chapel, always good business, and cause of fundraising everywhere.

Though not the bat infested, vampire housing structure I had expected, It was certainly worth a visit, and easy to imagine in its glory back in the day. I did feel a little tickle of the vibe I get when confronted with places awash with history, mainly when looking at the skull of Sindelic himself. Though there is no 100% certainty that this was definitely his skull – After all, there had been much toing-and-throwing of these wretched bones –

239

Nevertheless, those now empty eyes would still be able to tell quite the tale if they could. But for now it was keeping its story safe behind glass, looking only at its fallen comrades, forever facing out as a reminder of that one fateful day.

The chapel was set in a nice little park, so we had a look around, got a couple of bottles of water, and decided that the visit had been well worth coming to Nis. We wandered back, I got my stuff, and Debbie came with me to the bus station, where we said our goodbyes, and said we'd link up on Facebook but probably didn't. As we sat waiting, a 30-something backpacker girl overheard us talking about the squeaky floor in the hostel, and asked us if we meant the Serb Hostel, and if we knew the way. Debbie told her that she was going back that way and would show her if she hung on for 5 minutes. My bus came, I gave Debbie a quick hug, and the girls left. She did, however, look back at me with a grin, nodded towards the new girl and winked.

I hoped they would remember to check for wrapped up Indian guys later.

VIII

It was a pleasant enough bus ride to Skopje, with the usual pleasant views, especially as we crossed the border into Macedonia. I was looking forward to getting here, and strangely, one of the reasons was that I really liked the flag. Yes, nothing to do with history, geography or politics, I had found myself excited because it has a very interesting flag, which is a colourful yellow sun on a red background. In fact, this flag has only been in use since 1995, replacing another red and yellow flag, the Vergina flag which was a smaller sun on a red background. This had been adopted in 1992, a year after Macedonia's independence from the former Yugoslavia. However, the Greeks then imposed an economic blockade on Macedonia as a result of the flag, claiming they had copyright on the image of the Vergina sun. Hence, the

Macedonians adopted the new, and quite frankly, much better flag that they fly now. I was to discover a lot of tales of disputes between Greece and Macedonia over things that strike me as baffling, but clearly mean a lot to them.

In any case, the bus finally arrived there after 6 or so hours, and I realised that I could not make head nor tail of the instructions on the print out I had on the hostel's whereabouts. With it appearing to not be in the town centre as such and seeming like quite a walk, combined with the street signs being in the Cyrillic alphabet, I decided, against my better judgement, to get a cab, especially as it was already getting dark. Hard to believe now, but my phone did not actually have the ability to direct me, or if it did I had no idea that it could do that. Plus my battery and data at that point would have been an issue.

I asked a taxi driver, a large set man, if he knew the hostel, and how much it would be to get there. He told me an approximate price, and off we went. He asked me if I was going to Greece next, which I was, and suggested he could drive me there. However, I had already stumbled across a snag when planning my trip out here. For reasons I am not sure about, train services were cut in 2011 between the countries. The only bus routes I could find also meant going a very long way through Bulgaria, which was of a length of time I simply didn't have. So, to complete my journey between The Colosseum and The Acropolis, I had booked a cheap flight. So I politely declined my driver's offer, and he chatted about where I had been and such.

Sad to say, the inevitable argument about the fare happened on arrival at the digs, which unusually for a hostel was out in what seemed like a nice little suburb. I realised that we were getting nowhere, so decided to bite the bullet, as the sums involved where not in the ridiculous levels, and quite frankly I was tired, hungry and needed a shower, so I handed him a 2000 Denari note, as that was the only denomination I had after using an ATM at the bus station. As he'd quoted 180 which had now gone up -surprise, surprise – to 1,800, I said keep the change, as naturally "he did not have any". He took the note, seemed to look at it, then showed it to me and told me it was not Macedonian money.

"This is from Serbia" he said, quite politely.

Indeed, he was showing me a 2000 Serbian dinar note. I di
know, in fact, that I had had one of these left over, which wa
possibly not really worth cashing in, if I could at all when I gc
home, so I chucked him a note from the local currency and walke
up the steps to the hostel. A little niggly feeling made me cour
my money, and sure as hell, I was 2,000 short. And there, in m
other pocket, was the bloody 2,000 Serbian note that I knew I ha
had. Yep, the bastard had got me to pay twice!

Have I ever mentioned that I have a strong dislike for airport tax
drivers, even if they are at bus stops? I may well have.

Still, the hostel seemed very nice on first impressions. *
charming young girl was at reception, who turned out to be one o
the co-owners. It was a fairly new place that two seemingly youn;
girls had set up and looked incredibly clean and well attended.
mentioned the taxi driver.

"Pah, yes. So many guests tell us about the taxi drivers. It's a rea
problem."

It was already late, and we were out of the centre, so I askec
about a place to get food. She directed me to head down a littl
dark lane, where I found a shop that did pizza and some kind o
meat sandwiches. A small pizza was ideal, and I headed back to
the hostel and sat in the common room, which had a number o
school aged kids, maybe around 14 or so lounging around, usin;
phones and laptops. There was a film showing in English on the
TV, so I sat back and enjoyed. One of the school party, who
seemed a little older, was looking longingly at my pizza, so
offered him a slice, and we chatted.

It seemed that they were indeed some kind of school exchange
group from Palestine. I decided to hold back on the fact that I hac
been to college in Tel-Aviv many years ago, as I simply did no
want to get into any kind of political debate. The Israel–Palestine
question was not an over-pizza conversation I should be having
with school kids, so I discussed the merits of pineapple on pizza
instead.

The lad headed off at some point, but had actually been a
friendly type who seemed quite knowledgeable for his age. It was

just after he left that a sudden disaster struck the school kids that appeared to be of biblical proportions. The internet went down.

Apparently this could be quite common. However, I suddenly was aware of what seemed to be nothing short of a blind panic as everyone's devices began to fail at the same moment. I have honestly not seen such group distress in a long time. They suddenly began calling out to the teachers, who in turn began approaching the girls on the desk to see what was happening.

"It just goes down sometimes."

"How long will it be?"

"We have no idea. Could be 5 minutes, could be hours."

"But some of them are in the middle of something.."

"Maybe. But the internet is down."

"What are they supposed to do, if they are in the middle of stuff?"

"Tell them the internet is down."

Then the kids began coming up to the desk, showing the girls other Wi-Fi networks.

"Do you know the password to this one?"

"No. We don't know any other passwords."

"What about this one?"

"No, none of them.."

"This one??"

This pretty much went on for the whole hour or so that there was no internet. Even knowing that the internet was down, they frantically tried typing all sorts of combinations into any network they could find, and staring at the internet-less devices the way a child would look at a dead parent. Not one of them wandered over to the fully stocked book exchange shelf, or tried to see what was on TV.

I decided to get a good sleep, then go and explore in the morning. As with the rest of the hostel, the dorms were nice, and comfy bunks too! I was being spoiled, I think. There was one other guy in the room when I went in, one of the teachers from the school. At first he seemed a little grumpy, but then opened up a little. I asked him why they were in Macedonia. He seemed to evade that question, which was a shame. Macedonia had established a diplomatic relationship with Israel in 1995, and the two countries enjoyed a good relationship. In fact, at this point, Macedonia was one of the few countries in the world that had no diplomatic or political relations with Palestine of any kind, which made the visit surprising. The Jewish population of Macedonia had long reported that it was a country where they experienced no antisemitism of any kind.

Israel, when they established relations, initially did so under the UN given name to the country as *The former Yugoslav Republic of Macedonia.* However, shortly after, they decided to recognise the name the country called itself, *Republic of Macedonia.* This conflict about its formal title came from yet another dispute with Greece over the name. So in 1993, when the UN recognised it as an independent state after the break-up of Yugoslavia, it used the provisional name of "The former...". It was not till 2019, a few years after my visit there, that the issue was finally resolved, and Greece and Macedonia agreed that the country should be called *Republic of North Macedonia.* A lot of locals, and indeed nearly all visitors, found all this very behind the scenes, and carried on calling it simply Macedonia, which is much less of a mouthful, and simply enjoy a rather beautiful country that pretty much avoided any of the ravages of the Yugoslav wars, though there had been internal conflict with the large ethnic Albanian population around 2001.

It was the Palestinian teacher in my room that had explained a lot of this to me, but not why they chose to exchange here. Maybe it is simply because these kinds of exchanges are a pretty positive thing, letting young minds meet and talk to people themselves rather than read or hear biased reports of a place in the media. (though these groups tend to visit pre-selected destinations that show good light on a place, as in my own exchange visit to Russia in my 20's. However, sharp young minds will see through this usually, and find a way to see the reality.)

A good night's sleep, uninterrupted by the potential sobbing of a group of youngsters mourning the temporary loss of the internet, and I was up early and ready to head to town. There was breakfast available, the usual hostel fare, so no need to visit the sandwich shop. It seemed that the hostel was only about a 25 minute or so walk from the centre, but would still have been a little tricky to find. I found this out as I was setting off when I bumped straight into Matt, the Australian guy I had met in Bosnia, heading to the same hostel. Though we'd only shared a couple of drinks, we greeted each other like old friends, as travellers tend to do.

"Anyway, good to see you, but where is this bloody hostel?"

"I'll show you. It's only 5 minutes from here."

"Aw, thank heavens. I'm busting for a bloody shite!!"

Arriving back at the hostel, Matt took a long awaited dump, and he told me how he had been going to get a cab, but the driver he talked to was very vague about a price, so he walked. He was trying out a new app with a map, but had struggled reading it in the alphabet. He'd also had a long bus journey, and said he'd got to take a nap, so we decided I'd hang around the hostel then we'd go and explore the centre and get some lunch.

Which is what we did. And I must say, Skopje was indeed a fantastic place to explore. It certainly is a place of much history. Remains of Neolithic settlements have been found going back to at least 4000 BC. By the second century BC it was a city of Paeonia, before being seized and used as a Roman military camp. After the division of the Roman empire, it became Byzantine, ruled from Constantinople, and spent much of the mediaeval period contested between the Byzantine Empire and the Bulgarian Empire, being the capital of the latter for 20 years between 972 and 992AD. In the 13th century it became part of the Serbian Empire, also acting as Capital between 1346 and 1371. Eventually it was conquered by the Ottoman Turks, who ruled for 500 years until 1912 when it was annexed as part of the Kingdom of Serbia during the Balkan Wars, before flitting between Bulgaria (WW1), Kingdom of Yugoslavia, Bulgaria again (WW2), then capital of the federated state of SR Macedonia within Yugoslavia, then independence.

As with anywhere with a rich history, this means a lot of statues. And Skopje sure has those. This includes at least one statue of Mother Teresa of Calcutta. For Skopje is indeed where this great lady was born. Even now, the city sees a divide of ethnicities on both sides of the Vardar river. The south, mainly rebuilt after a

245

devastating earthquake in 1963, is home to mostly ethnic Macedonians, tending to be Orthodox Christian, and was rebuilt including new hi rise areas, whereas the North during its rebuilding was kept low so as to keep the view of the Skopje Fortress, which we visited, and restore the area of the old Bazaar. This side, the poorer side, houses ethnic Turks who are mainly Muslim, Ethnic Albanians, who are mostly Muslim but have a large Catholic community too, which is where Mother Teresa was born into when the country was still part of the Ottoman Empire, and also many Roma.

Most of the statues were very new, due to the country hoping to build up on tourism after an economic crash, but along with several nice parks make for an enjoyable walkabout. We were quite impressed by the Statue of Alexander. We were even more impressed after we had gone to the hostel to get changed, and returned to town for the night. For then we realised that the whole statue lit up, and as it was part of a fountain, this looked fantastic. It is, in fact, the largest statue of Alexander in the world, and now I could feel that I was nearing the end of this journey towards the Greek Capital. Of course, the fact that the Macedonians see Alexander the Great as a famous character from their history could only mean one thing.

The Greeks disagree with them.

This again goes back to the use of the name Macedonia. Whilst there is no doubt that the original empire builder, carving a territory that took in Persia and parts of India, was Macedonian by birth, the fact was he was born in Pella, the capital of Ancient Macedonia, the area of which lies within Greece today. The Greeks see the claiming of Alexander as their own as yet more proof of Macedonian territorial claims on their region. This is pretty ironic, as they are arguing over a bloke who set out to, and indeed claimed a hell of a lot of territory off other people. Possibly the Greeks actually have a point on this one, as the makeup and borders of current Macedonia are so different to back then that it does seem to an outsider to be a bit of a stretch to claim the feller who is, and always will be, seen as the Greek Empire builder.

246

But history aside, myself and Matt had some drinking to do. We found a decent street off Macedonia Square that seemed to consist mainly of bars and restaurants, and bedded ourselves in, chatting to numerous other travellers from all over during the night, before linking our last couple of glasses and heading back to the hostel. I actually only had a couple of hours to get a bit of sleep, as I needed to be at the airport for 4.00am, but the girls who ran the place had sorted me a reputable taxi they knew to pick me up. As we arrived back, the girl behind reception was looking a bit flustered, but reminded me that the taxi was all booked and would be here on time. The flustered look was because the internet had gone down again, and they had a gaggle of young backpackers asking them if they knew the passwords to other networks they could see. Technology, eh?

IX

The trip to the airport was relaxed, I had a bit of breakfast – or was it supper? – at the Airport, and waited for the hour and a half flight to get me into Athens. There is a 24 hour bus service into the centre every half hour or so, and my hostel was only about a 20 minute walk from the bus station. Hence, I arrived way too early to check in, so put my bag in the luggage room and took a stroll.

First impression was not great, to be honest. Maybe it was just the area I was staying, but I walked out around a very shabby area, with some rough edged hookers standing around, and was offered plenty of drugs from the cliché looking dealers. The area had a very depressed kind of look to it. However, when I eventually booked in, and before grabbing a nap to catch up with a more or less lost night's sleep, another lad in the dorm told me that apart from the tourist areas, that pretty much summed up the city. It really wasn't what I had in mind. On waking up, by this time in the early evening, I joined the same lad looking out of a balcony we had at the hookers picking people up, and disappearing into the hotel opposite us. We'd guess what room they would appear, an shut the curtains in. It seemed to be the same 5 or so rooms w eventually noticed, and I wondered why they bothered opening th curtains after each punt.

I decided to go and get some food and beer, and asked the lad he fancied coming, but he declined. In fact, the whole time I wa there, he did not seem to leave the room, but instead kep watching the hookers, long after my own amusement had bee satiated.

I wandered along a sort of main road till I found a little block o shops and cheap food places, and there was a good old Rock ba called Doctor Feelgood. This will do, I thought, and found mysel inside every rock bar in the world. As I have observed before, m theory is that there is a large warehouse in the centre of Europ somewhere that provides second hand pub furniture, none o which – not one single table or chair – matches. Nor do any o them not wobble. This is where every rock or indie bar goes t furnish themselves. They also provide piss coloured paint for th toilets, a slightly brown coloured solution to take the sparkle of any beer glasses, and a special spray that goes on the carpet or any flooring to make them sticky even when the pub has just opened.

Doctor Feelgood did not let me down. I have no idea how th fantastic R&B band of the same name feel about the pub havin their name, but I suspect they would find it amusing, havin probably drank in many such places in their day. Of course, could be wrong, and the lads drank in posh cocktai establishments and wine lodges their whole career. Yeah, right. I any case, it was early, and there were only a couple of othe people in there. At one table were a couple whose age was kind o hard to guess as they looked like they'd consumed half of Athens drugs themselves over the years. The other customer was the guy fully expected to be in such a bar. The fat old rock guy with wispy long hair, a faded tee shirt with the name of some ancient band – in this case it was Deep Purple. It often is – and a pair of shapeless jeans held up with a studded belt. These guys are a solitary kind o creature, who tend to stand on the left hand side of a bar all the time they are there, and drink either Guinness, or the cheapest beer in the place. They don't really engage in much conversation.

248

and look to the door every time it opens, possibly hoping that one of the lads they drank with 20 odd years ago was going to walk in, so they could stand in silence together, after comparing notes on which ones of the old crowd were dead now.

I had a couple of beers, then ventured to the toilet. It pretty much lived up to my expectations. I left, and got what turned out to be a pretty good kebab from a place on the way back, saving it to eat back at the hostel. My roomie was still sitting out on the balcony when I got up to the dorm, and I mentioned the rock bar, as he had a bit of a metal vibe going on.

"I heard about it." He said, with no real enthusiasm.

"It was a bit sleazy, but the beer was OK."

"I heard that too."

"And cheap. Pretty cheap, really."

"Yes, I heard that."

I wondered if the hookers had been shouting information up to him.

Well, the next morning was the day I'd been looking forward to. Today was the day I was heading to The Acropolis. Or more correctly, the Acropolis of Athens, as Acropolis is a generic term that also applies to a number of other sites throughout Greece. I had begun this trip in Rome, and visited the mighty Colosseum, before heading through Italy to Venice, then crossing into the Balkan countries, and ending up here in Athens. I was slightly surprised that at the colosseum, I had not felt my expected empathy with the ancients, a strange tingly feeling of oneness that I have experienced at other constructed sites and natural places from the old world. So I found myself wondering what this site would bring. Would I get that exciting feeling or not? Either way, today was still the last stop on this particular trip, and I would be heading home tomorrow, after seeing some amazing things, and meeting some incredible people. I had some breakfast at the hostel, which was a couple of bread rolls and some kind of jam, plus some actually rather good coffee, then headed out to see what today would bring.

I walked there, and realised how gloomy this part of Athens looked, even in the bright hot sun. Greece was at this time going through a shocking financial crisis, and it showed. This air of despondency seemed to suddenly end as I neared the monument and it began to turn into a more tourist orientated area, with better looking shops, and plenty of stalls selling the usual tourist fare. I had gotten to the walls of the Acropolis, and had no idea how to get in, so I just kept walking in the direction that most of the tourists and sight seers seemed to be heading.

I'd always thought of the Acropolis as only being the most famous building in there, The Parthenon, but I had of course been wrong. The Parthenon is the most famous of a number of temples and buildings within, whereas The Acropolis is in fact the term for the ancient citadel on the limestone hill that sits above Athens. The main monuments there were built around the fifth century BC, when Athens was at a particularly flourishing period of its rich history. Even walking along the street looking at the outside walls felt exciting.

I finally came across the main entrance, and was glad that I had come really early, as already it was turning into a blazer of a day, heat wise. Never having been particularly good with the heat, this turned out to be a godsend, as I hadn't realised at this point that I would be walking a fair bit uphill, another thing I am never too keen on. The entrance fee was pretty reasonable, and allowed you access for as long as you wanted.

There were, of course, plenty of other tourists around, but not too rammed to start with. I took the time to wander round the different buildings. Some of the highlights were, and in no particular order, buildings such as the Temple of Athena Nike, dedicated to the two goddesses of the same names. Built around 420 BC, it holds a prominent position in the south-west corner of the complex, and as with all the buildings held a history of being ruined and restored. In fact, It had been completely demolished by the Ottomans to use the stones for their defences in 1686, and not rebuilt till 1834 after the independence of Greece. It was closed due to work being done, but still looked pretty impressive from the outside.

I also enjoyed seeing the Theatre of Dionysus, which as its name suggests is an ancient Greek theatre on the south slope. It's believed that the first orchestra terrace there was built around the

4th and 5th Century BC, and was home to the city Dionysia, a huge festival dedicated to The God Dionysus. One thing you had to say about the ancient Greeks is that they sure seemed to know how to party. They had a whole pantheon of gods – yes, there is a collective name – and held festivals for just about all of them. It reminds me of the time that myself and a group of the lads decided that St Patricks and St Georges day were all very well (Because us Anglo-celts are quite happy to celebrate both) but what about the other nights out? Well, there were plenty of saints' days, it turned out. I think we'd been drunk for nearly 2 weeks, when we realised whilst celebrating the patron saint of Haiti's day, who incidentally is Our Lady of Perpetual Help, that we really needed to go back to work as we had all thrown sickies. So we decided to celebrate one last day, and noticed that there were a number of patron saints for the sick, the dying, healing the sick, etc. We finally agreed on St. Joseph, got pissed on his day, then went back to work telling our bosses that we were now all well and good again, and this was down to the intervention of St Joseph himself, so we should be good for a while.

The Odeon of Herodes Atticus is another theatre, but this time built by the Romans in AD 161, by the feller with that name, in memory of his wife. Originally it held 5,000 people, most of whom I would imagine did not really know his wife. Well, maybe not. I did have a girlfriend back in the 80's who, if she kept up the track record she had while we were dating, probably has "known" at least 5,000 people by now. I should have guessed about her early on when we had a threesome with her friend once, and when I asked her if she enjoyed it she muttered that she couldn't believe she was down to just three. Still, you like to give the benefit of the doubt, eh?

The Erechtheion was another old temple that was great to see. Over on the North side, it was another temple dedicated to Athena. I guess this being Athens, she was bound to crop up a lot. She was strongly associated with, amongst other things, wisdom, warfare and handicraft. That is quite a mix really, and one can only imagine a bunch of ancient Greek warriors, maybe led by Alexander the Great himself, taking a break from wondering where the hell Macedonia really was, charging into battle wearing beautifully crocheted armour, and helmets knitted from ethically sourced wool. Any of them questioning the wisdom of this would be pointed in the direction of Athena, and told that if it was good enough for her, it was good enough for them.

After visiting buildings, and the sites of former buildings that helpfully displayed pictures of artists' impressions of what they would have probably looked like, I headed up to the final stop on this exploration, the Parthenon itself.

Now here was history. Building commenced in 447 BC, and was completed in 438 BC, though the decoration continued till 432. In fact, the decorative structures are considered some of the high points of Greek art, which is quite something. As with most Greek temples, it also served as a treasury, including its time during which the original constructors, The Delian League, had become the Athenian Empire.

Time went by, and eventually during the 6th century AD, it was converted to a Christian church, dedicated to the Virgin Mary. This lasted until the 15th century when The Ottoman invasion resulted in it becoming a Mosque. More drama happened in 1687, when a Venetian bomb caused much damage during a siege there in the Morean War, when it was being used by the Ottomans as a munitions dump.

Controversy was to follow when in 1800 – 1803, some of the surviving sculptures, amongst other relics from the Acropolis, were taken by the 7th Earl of Elgin to Britain, where they sit to this day in The British Museum. The Earl's claim that he was granted permission by the Ottoman government is hotly disputed by Greece, who believe that if nothing else, it is morally wrong to refuse to return them. Known as the Elgin Marbles, this is no doubt going to be a stickier subject than a rock bar floor for a long time to come. And if truth be told, they do seem to have a point.

The closer I got to this mighty temple, the noisier and busier the tourists became. This was the highlight, and everyone knew it. The last couple of hours had been relatively relaxed, with reasonable or even small numbers looking at the other sites, but this was absolutely packed. It was not possible to go right up. In act, it seemed, as one would expect, that The Ancient Guild of scaffolders, who no doubt helped its construction, were there now as well. Of course. Much as this can seem annoying, it has to be remembered that this is a completely necessary operation to preserve the building, unlike the work done by the British ancient guild of road-coners, who place their conical icons in spots where no work seems to get done for months before taking them back.

A little area had been cordoned, and a sign erected to let people know that this was the best spot for a photo. Sure as hell, the numbers there jostled and pushed, and frantically stuck phones and cameras over each other's heads to get the shot. The one they would rarely look at. I did wander over there, then spotted not 20 yards away what looked like a marble bench with no one on it. I went over to it and sat down. Here I was, at the pinnacle of my journey from Rome to Athens, and I wanted to savour the moment. I breathed a deep breath, and looked at the monument in front of me. And within no time, the noise from the crowd, the atmosphere of the jostling, and even the work of the scaffolders was gone.

There it was. The feeling I hadn't had in Rome. The connection I often felt with the Ancients. Suddenly, I was there. My mind's eye projected the people who had come before into the scene, and for a brief, beautiful, timeless moment I sat on that bench and felt everything.

And I smiled. I sat and I smiled.

X

I managed to pick up an Athens patch for my collection from the endless knick -knack stalls along the streets outside after I left. My mind had, of course, came back, and the sound of the snappers made me smile again, but for different reasons. I hoped at least some of them would leave the mass and sit on the bench, even if just for a little while. I know some of the people I had met, The

Timetable Man, Babyface, The American Artist, and many of the others all would.

I spotted some catapults on the way as well, so I picked a couple up for my daughters. I could imagine the fun they would have with them. I spent one last evening in Doctor Feelgood's, then returned to find my roomie still watching hookers. I guessed he wouldn't sit on the bench. Pleasant enough feller though.

Security at the Airport unfortunately confiscated my catapults. As always, I did not have any hold luggage, just my usual bag that I could take in the cabin. I was going through a phase of using the old fashioned safety razor blades – a wrong description if ever there was one – and they confiscated those as well. In fairness they did look apologetic about it. I imagine that they absolutely knew that I was unlikely to initiate an airborne act of terror by catapulting my six razorblades around the plane, but I guess the rules are the rules. Even daft ones. It's a good job Alexander and co travelled by land, I guess. And the Trojans might not have been so smug if Wooden Horse Transit Ltd. had made them leave their weapons back at camp.

It was straight behind the DJ booth that night when I got back, so it was during the week I was able to reflect on that, along with my other two recent journeys around Europe, and compare my thoughts with Shenanigans of the past. Sure I was older now, but how much difference did it make? Technology had moved on, as had my years, and a new tech savvy generation of backpackers had appeared.

I didn't realise it at that moment, but I was on the verge of changing some of the things about the way I travelled. I hadn't quite finished with Europe yet either, and there was a bit more to come, it turned out, before I was to find myself vagabound, but the travel bug was as strong as ever, and it was going to be a stopover during one of two visits to Ireland starting later that month, the very country that had been such a strong influence on me growing up, but I had never been to, that was to throw up a moment that I never thought I'd see. However, at this particular moment, I was content, happy, and feeling on top of the world.

254

Afterthought
The Irish Question

I did actually once question if it was time to give up travelling. Once.

For the bulk of my adventures I had usually headed out alone, apart from short trips and the odd holiday or so. The majority of serious travellers will usually tell you that this is the best way to do it, or at least until you get a great partner. Of course, you are never really alone. You head out on your own, sure, but you meet so many fellow wanderers and like-minded travellers along the way that perhaps solo travel is a bit of a misdemeanour. But compared to the shenanigans of my youth, hitching and squatting round Europe, backpacking around Asia and Australia, overlanding across Africa, and driving across the states, the later adventures had seen a gap beforehand where I'd become shockingly adult, which is in fact quite a rotten state of development that should not be recommended.

Adulthood brings with it a number of horrible and soul destroying conditions, one of them being responsibility. That one kind of creeps up on you. Having kids certainly is a symptom of that, if not the cause, and you find all your old attitudes of "Fuck it, just do it" don't really apply anymore, and so you become this kind of subservient housekeeper and financial provider to these little people that seem to love you unconditionally at first, but by teenagehood are showing their true colours and resent most of what you do, and believe that their complete lack of experience in the world means that they know more about everything than yourself.

I should really say that my own were nothing like that, of course. I should say it, but as the chances of them reading anything I write are pretty slim, I might as well stick with the facts. In any case, you love them, and give up things for them, and they find you annoying, till one day they are big enough that you can actually leave them for a while. Which is how my last couple of adventures had been able to happen.

But that gap showed me that I, as does everyone, had aged, and though it wasn't a complete handicap, it does change some of the perspectives, both in the way others see you, and how you see them, as well as how you see yourself. Nightclubs are a good example. I might still end up in them, but maybe as I worked in so many of them as a DJ for so many years, I had long reached a point where I couldn't care less if I never saw the inside of one again. That didn't exactly stop me trailing along to them sometimes, but I would rather be in a good pub.

The first trip to Cork was a direct flight to and from, which is surprisingly cheap from Birmingham airport if you go on anti-social hours. I went out there with my friend, Wee Keith, primarily to see the Boomtown Rats, the original punk band with Bob Geldof, a man who invested a lot of his life raising money for starving people and in doing so made himself unpopular with the less hungry folk, especially the old punk crowds who due to his giving up a musical career to save the lives of millions, decided that this made him a sell out and generally called him a wanker. Personally, I loved the Boomtown Rats, and thoroughly enjoyed the show, including the bit where he announced a thank you to all the English kids who had come over to see them, and as me and Keith cheered and jumped up and down, we realised that it was just us two then.

That trip had indeed been quite fun. The highlight though, had not so much been the band, but our trip during the day to see the

Cork City Gaol, which is now a museum showing the conditions of such a place in the 19th century with the use of groaning sound effects, and brutal looking waxworks.

"Would you like a ticket to the Radio Museum as well?," the charming young Polish girl at the ticket table on the way in had asked us.

"Where's that?"

"It's here as well. Just costs two Euro's more to see both."

"Ok, why not."

And with our two tickets, we wandered around the gaol which was actually a pretty good way to spend the afternoon, and found the whole experience pretty interesting, though maybe a bit cold. Which is probably how the prisoners had felt. Cold that is, not it being pretty interesting. There were lots of realistic waxworks in cells showing the hardships of prisoners, including some famous names if you are up in the history of Irish nationalism. Finally, we considered we had seen everything we could, and popped back out to the front to find the other part of the trip. Another charming young Polish girl had taken over, so as we couldn't see any signs, we wandered over to her.

"Hi. Where is the entrance to the Radio Museum?"

"The what?"

"The Radio Museum. Here, look, we have tickets for it."

She looked blankly at the stubs in my hand.

"Is it here?" she asked.

"What? Yes. Well, I think so. Your friend told us it was."

"Who is my friend?"

"The other girl, here earlier. She sold us tickets to a Radio Museum."

I was now beginning to wonder exactly why I had bought a ticket for a radio museum anyway, and was about to say don't worry about it, when a bloke who sort of looked in charge came over."

"These guys have tickets for a Radio Museum."

"Yer's do?" he said, looking surprised. "It's just down that corridor there. You just follow the sign."

"There isn't a sign…"

"No, it fell off. I'm meaning to fix it, sure. Enjoy it now."

We headed down the corridor, and eventually found the Radio Museum. Now this wasn't what we expected at all. I had kind of imagined lots of radios and stuff, But this wasn't the case. In fact, the whole room was a recreation of the Cork Radio Station as it was on the 28th of June, 1963. The day J.F. Kennedy landed at Cork airport. And there was, in the centre of this, the seemingly one item on display. It was, as the sign proudly said, the very microphone that the President had used to address the jubilant crowds that greeted him when he arrived by helicopter in an originally unplanned visit during his 4 day tour of Ireland.

A bloody microphone.

Meanwhile, as I looked at the world famous microphone, Wee Keith had noticed another room, and called me over. It was dark, so he flicked on an old switch, presuming it was for the lights, and suddenly some strange noises happened, and a screen lit up showing newsreels of the visit. To be honest, it scared the crap out of us, as the loud creaking noise it made had us thinking that we'd set some kind of alarm off.

"I don't think many people actually come here, you know." I remarked.

"Why?"

"Well, look at that."

And here was the true highlight of the trip. Obviously, some of the waxworks from the Gaol Museum must get broken sometimes, or replaced. These were quite realistic, depicting the poor bloodied, beaten and half-starved prisoners of old, and probably quite expensive. So where would you store the old ones?

Apparently, you would take them into the little used Radio museum and kind of chuck them in. This, I'm sure, quite unwitting act of sloppiness, gave the impression that on this day in 1963, there had been in fact some kind of terror attack on the staff of the Radio station, who had been mowed down, some decapitated, others with limbs missing, all covered in blood and looking hungry enough to have Bob Geldof come rushing to their aid and here they were lying all over the place in front of the very microphone that none other than J.F. Kennedy had addressed the cheering crowds with. This highly inaccurate historical diorama may only have happened the day we visited, maybe as part of a

258

lear out or spring clean, but it made it the greatest museum visit I have ever had, and until my dying day I will never forget the nage of the worst Radio Station Massacre that never happened.

The show, as I said, had been great, and after an argument with a ixi driver on the way back from the venue, (a whopping great big ent called, appropriately enough, The Marquee), we hit the town, vhere much to the real ale loving and CAMRA card holding Keith's annoyance we drank lager and listened to chart DJ's. I ound I enjoyed it all the more knowing that he really wasn't.

So I was looking forward to returning there for another gig in the Marquee the next year, via Portugal and Dublin. I spent a pleasant nough couple of days exploring Lisbon, but did manage to get a pretty bad sunburn on my head by going for an early walk without a hat and not realising how hot it would get so quickly. But though enjoyed walking around exploring, on this occasion I didn't get o connect with anyone else in the backpackers I was staying in. They all seemed incredibly young to me, and it wasn't so much hat I would have to make more of an effort to join in with them, t's that I realised that on this occasion that I didn't really want to. They were fine, no doubt, I just didn't feel I had anything in common with them. So for a few days, other that barmen and café owners, I didn't really speak to anyone.

I flew into Dublin, and found myself in another hostel where I didn't really meet anyone, but nevertheless enjoyed exploring, hough found myself in the evenings drinking around the famous, and hence shockingly expensive Temple Bar area, sitting drinking on my own and pondering that something seemed to be missing.

So it was that I found I was looking forward to arriving in Cork and catching up with Wee Keith, though he was a man of few words himself.

I had also arranged to meet up with an old friend of mine, Marie, who I had known in Coventry, and even been on a couple of dates with, but had since gotten married and moved out to Cork and thoroughly enjoyed it out here. Unlike the first visit, where we stayed in a specific backpackers, this time we had found a hostel above a pub, which is always a good idea.

I took the bus down to Cork, which took about 3 ½ hours, and found our pub. It seems Wee Keith had already booked in, and left a message he would be in a bar down the road. I dumped my stuff in my dorm, and went down to meet him. I knew the place as we'd been here on the first trip too. It was another craft beer bar, this time for real. On that first occasion we had been in, it had been busy and bustling, with just one Hungarian barmaid serving, and not missing a customer. She chatted to everyone, and even told us that they served the world's strongest bottled beer, which we were sceptical of, but a quick google proved her correct. The product aptly named Armageddon, is apparently brewed by freezing the beer then removing the water somehow. This meant a rather potent 65% proof bock beer, basically a strong German dark lager. Though at a price of 60 euros a bottle, we took her up on her offer of 15 euros for a shot. Yes, we actually had a shot of beer. I expected some disgusting strong syrupy type thing, but in fact it did indeed come across as a beer. Though I definitely would not be drinking a bottle of it.

However, finding my friend in the bar, I was a little disappointed to discover that the place seemed to have waned in popularity somewhat. The pub was barely quarter full, yet the two eejits behind the bar seemed to struggle to serve everyone. Unlike the Hungarian girl who served a busy pub, took meals out, chatted to everyone, recommended products, managed to tell us her life story, kept the tables emptied and wiped, possibly was running a small boutique in between orders and no doubt had a quiche in the oven for later. The beer range seemed to have diminished as well.

Apart from that bar, we returned to another couple of craft beer bars we'd found on our first visit, including the Franciscan Well Microbrewery, home to one of my all-time favourite beers, Rebel Red, which is pretty hard to find in the UK. We did not pop into though, the very first pub we had gone into on the first visit which advertised itself as a craft beer bar. We had seen the blackboard outside and walked in to check out the exciting range of ales we would no doubt find. Hence, we were surprised to see a very small bar with possibly the grumpiest pub owner in the world stood behind it. The pub was not much bigger than my living room, and the few customers in there all looked incredibly grumpy too.

"Er, Hi. You do craft beers?"

"That's what the sign says."

"What do you have?"

"Beamish or Murphy's."

So. Two of the largest breweries in Ireland, which were in fact both in Cork. These were actually quite big selling beers, and apart from being brewed locally could under no circumstances be called craft beers. Ah, what the hell, we thought, and ordered two pints of Beamish. In fairness, it wasn't a bad pint, but a clean glass would have been nice.

I took out my phone in one of these pubs to call Marie, the former Coventry girl I would be meeting, and Wee Keith managed to promptly spill his pint all over it, and I watched it fizzle. A guy at the next table immediately jumped up, asked the barman for some rice, and plunged my phone into it, whether I wanted him to or not. We sat and looked at it, and wondered how the hell I was going to get in touch with my friend.

"How's your phone?" The barman asked when we ordered another beer.

"Not sure. Probably fucked. Still, worth a shot, trying to dry it, just in case."

"Yes, you never know. I hope it's OK. Are you here for that gig tomorrow?"

"Dropkick Murphys? We are indeed. No photos for me though, eh?"

"Hah. Sure, it'll be grand. Anyway, that's 12 euros please."

"I thought the drinks were 5 each?"

"They are. And 2 euros for the rice."

Luckily, My friend had a public profile on Facebook, so we were able to message her on Keith's phone. She met us the next day, and we sat outside the pub we were staying in for a great afternoon catching up. Many jokes were made about Keith drowning my phone.

"Last time we were here, we went to the Radio museum. That was something else!" I told her.

"There's a lot of odd stuff like that. If you really want an experience, you should try the butter museum."

We didn't.

As we sat, we started to see the street and bars filling up with others here for the gig. Dropkick Murphys and Stiff Little Fingers T-shirts galore. And, like myself, the old flat cap. Mine I wore with jeans, braces, and a collarless shirt. Hell, I looked more Irish than the Irish. Though in fairness I had been dressing like this for some time now. Something to eat, and we headed off, taking in a couple of pubs on the way. I'm glad to say that the Murphys did not let us down, and after the last few quiet days, I was happy to let my admittedly metaphoric hair down and I was enjoying the fact I'd had good company between Keith and Marie.

We decided to walk back, which was quite a hike after a gig and beers, and I was delighted to spot the first pub as we hit town.

"Get a drink?"

"Nah. Plane."

Keith was going the opposite way to me. We'd met up in cork, but he was heading out to a couple of stops in Europe for a couple of psychobilly festivals he knew of, and had an early flight to catch. Undeterred, I stopped at the bar and grabbed a beer. Here it occurred to me that this was the third city in a few days that I was sitting alone at night drinking in. I only had the one, and then headed back, to discover that the pub we were staying in closed at midnight, but then the side door opened for guests in the hostel. It looked pretty lively, so I grabbed a beer, and sat at the bar. I noticed a group of young English lads at a table in kind of EMO t-shirts, and asked if I could join them.

"No problem. More the merrier."

It turned out that they were a bunch of young gay lads, and they were sharing stories of who they had, or wanted to bang, then how they had snorted coke off some old fellers cock as it was free coke, and then, bizarrely, a long dialogue about socks, and how they should look in shoes. Much as the coke story amused me, I really didn't feel part of this group at all, and mooched back over to the bar, again by myself, but by this time worrying that my socks may have made a bad impression.

So, as I sat at the bar, looking into my glass, I began to reflect on my many adventures in the past, especially when I was younger. All those places. All those people. Hell, I'd often as not been the life and soul of the groups. Now, I thought, look at me. Sitting in backpackers hostels, on the outside looking in. The old geezer that I'm sure some of them thought should be wearing a faded band t-shirt, and standing at the bar in some run down rock bar, or worse, they simply didn't think of me at all.

For the first time ever, thoughts began to enter my head about the wisdom of all this. Did I really want to do it? Was I kidding myself when I told people I love travelling that way, in cheap hostels, and was happy to travel alone. Sure, I still wanted to see the world, but was it time to do it more gracefully? Maybe find someone to share these adventures, and be like the gleaming toothed couples in the saga or cruise ads that would pop up while I was booking stuff? Basically, I pondered, who am I now? What am I now? Is it time, in fact, to maybe give this up and settle down a bit?

I was just coming to the decision that it was no doubt time for a rethink when suddenly one of those life changing moments happened. And it happened in the form of a drunk American girl barging in through the side door.

Clearly a guest in the hostel, and clearly pissed out of her head, she seemed to stare right at me as she burst in. I actually looked round to see who she was looking at, but it was indeed me. She then, drunkenly but determinedly, marched right over, still staring, till she stood in front of me at the bar.

"You!" She declared. "You're staying in this hostel!"

"Er, yes, I am."

"And you were at the Dropkick Murphys."

"I was…"

"And you were drinking here today. And then you went to a couple of pubs on the way to the gig!"

Who the hell was this girl?

"And you have a friend. And he's quite little."

"Yep, Keith. He's from the…"

"And My friend is quite little too. So they'd like each other…"

263

"Er…"

With that, she sat at the bar on a stool next to me and began talking about the gig. Or her hair. It was hard to tell.

"I'm going to buy you a drink. Let's get shots. Barman, two Jamesons please…"

"No, not for me, but thanks. I don't do spirits."

"Oh. Nor me," She said, then downed the Jamesons when it arrived.

Then, she actually began to sidle up close, and put her hand on my leg.

"Let's get selfies" she slurred, and took a couple. Her hand wandered up my leg. I pushed it down. I'm no angel, God knows, but an inebriated girl in her early 20's was off limits by my reckoning.

And other peoples too, it seemed. A couple of other American girls, who were not with her apparently, saw this scenario playing out, and came to the rescue. Though it was quite clear that they did in fact think I was a dirty old man trying to ply a young girl with drink, I was quite relieved that they came and took her, and got her up to her room. I really did not know quite what to do, and the barman was no help as he kept winking at me.

As the girls walked her out, I found myself smiling. Yep, that was the sort of shit which is why I do this. And I'm worrying? Sure, she might have been drunk by the time she bee-lined over to me, but bee-line she had. Hell, I'll take that one!! Then the gay lads got up to leave, and popped over to say goodbye. This left me sitting with an obvious couple at the bar.

"By the way," The lad, an Asian American, said, "I must apologise for my countrywoman there. Not all Americans get as wasted as that."

"Hey, I know. I'm a huge fan of your country. I was out there a few years ago, done the whole route 66 thing. Great people."

We ended up chatting, myself, him, and his English girlfriend. We sat up till the bar closed, then hit the sack. Keith had gone by the time I got up, so I got my bag and left the hostel to go to the airport bus stop, and bumped straight into that couple again.

"Hey, Rich, how are you?"

"Great. Yourselves?

264

"Oh fine, we heard your girlfriend being sick last night. She was in a bad way, eh?"

"Yes, nice girl though."

"Anyway, we are heading off to a couple of bars. Do you want to come with us?"

And there it was. Sadly, time was against me so I didn't go, but finally at the end of this trip, a bizarre moment had happened, and a connection with other travellers had been made. I knew, right here, when they called me on that street to go for a beer that I may well have had a point about looking at what I want but maybe I was just feeling a bit sorry for myself. Or at least I was till an attractive young drunk called Aime had staggered into my shenanigans!

I have no idea if the girl would have remembered that she had been talking to me or not when she woke up. My best guess is that it wasn't till she looked through her photos of the night before that she stumbled across the selfie of me and her at the bar and thought, "What the....When the hell did I get talking to that bloke? And what the hell happened?" Truth is, if that's the case, she'll never know. Boy, I know that feeling!

She'll also never know that by drunkenly stumbling into the pub and sharing a single drink with me, she helped me see sense while having a reflective moment. She'll never know that she was a part of the jigsaw of thought that led to the next steps in my adventures. She'll also never know that I was probably judged to be some dirty old geezer the same night, and that she brought a bit of a smile to some daft eejit's face, and totally reminded him of why in fact he heads out there.

No, she'll never know that. She'll have looked puzzledly at the photo on her phone, taken a couple of aspirin for her headache, and continued her own adventures, briefly crossing lives from time to time with people that would influence her either wittingly or unwittingly. Which is pretty much how we go through our lives anyway, just with more familiar background scenery.

Nevertheless, that little moment of questioning myself did give me some clarity on who I actually was, and what I wanted to do. Until I had headed off on the road to L, I considered that I was still the boy from County Coundon, the young Punk Rocker bumming around the world, though I reluctantly admitted I was somewhat plumper and had a more, ahem, lived in face. Oh, and a bit stiffer.

And in fact, this was partly true. In my mind, I was, and still am, the same person. The very essence of me hasn't really changed, but there have been add-ons, so to speak. Things annoy me that really wouldn't have done before, such as people stopping in mid conversation to look and reply to a text, something they wouldn't do if the person had just come up and interrupted during the conversation. I couldn't really care less about nightclubs as I have done them to death either going to them or working in them. I appreciate beer for its taste, and not just the fantastic liquid that led me into chaos and bliss in the past.

So the young Mulligan, much like Kafka's Gregor Samsa, is still very much ticking away nicely, but on the outside seems very different to the casual observer. Maybe coming across as a bit grumpier, certainly more cynical (The one absolute certainty of the ageing process) and wearing the type of clothes more likely to blend into the background than ever before. That hostel in Cork was the morning I suddenly mentally metamorphosed into another Mulligan. I had become, I was both shocked and proud to realise, a bit of an old bugger compared to the average backpacker these days. Or any days, in fact.

However, old bugger now or not, as soon as I was back I was already planning on where to go next. It was time for new shenanigans, and I was, it turned out, to become very aware that there was somewhere that I had overlooked on my travels around the globe. Somewhere that needed exploring and would bring new adventures and stories. Because it's always about the story.

Interestingly, at the airport on the way back from Cork, I actually bought an item of clothing. I had always wondered how airport shops kept going, for I could see no reason for anyone to want to buy overpriced clothes on their way out or in from a journey. A sure sign of my metamorphosis had been that I had taken to wearing a flat cap, which though popular amongst the Hipsters had actually made me look even more Irish somehow than even my pale freckly skin managed to do. And there in an airport shop was a pretty snazzy blue one, which I thought looked better than my current grey, so I purchased it and was now the sort of bloke who had a choice of which cap to wear.

My leather biker jacket, and the leather jeans I had purchased in Portland were a long time behind me. I was in shirts, waistcoats and caps now. And that flatcap, if nothing else, defined the current me, the one about to explore these new lands. I was officially an old bugger now, and even had a whole bunch of embroidered backpack patches since my 50th birthday to prove it. But not just any old bugger. I was a Bonafede Travel Bugger. Yes, the road was still calling, and my bags were packed, so the world should get itself ready to say hello to this old feller from County Coundon. Because the Travel Bugger was ready to get onboard anything going anywhere…..

…So long as it has a comfy seat and easy access to a toilet.

Printed in Great Britain
by Amazon